SERIAL BIBLIOGRAPHIES AND ABSTRACTS IN HISTORY

**Contributions in
Bibliographies and Indexes in World History**

Iran Media Index
Hamid Naficy, Compiler

SERIAL BIBLIOGRAPHIES AND ABSTRACTS IN HISTORY

AN ANNOTATED GUIDE

Compiled by David Henige

Bibliographies and Indexes in World History, Number 2

Greenwood Press
Westport, Connecticut • London, England

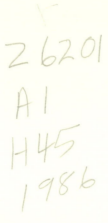

Library of Congress Cataloging-in-Publication Data

Henige, David P.
  Serial bibliographies and abstracts in history.

  (Bibliographies and indexes in world history,
ISSN 0742-6852 ; no. 2)
  Bibliography: p.
  Includes index.
    1. Bibliography—Bibliography—History. 2. History—
Bibliography—Periodicals—Bibliography. 3. History—
Abstracts—Periodicals—Bibliography. I. Title.
II. Series.
Z6201.A1H45 1986 [D20]   016.9   85-27178
ISBN 0-313-25070-7 (lib. bdg. : alk. paper)

Library of Congress Catalog Card Number: 85-27178
ISBN: 0-313-25070-7
ISSN: 0742-6852

First published in 1986

Greenwood Press
A division of Congressional Information Service, Inc.
88 Post Road West
Westport, Connecticut 06881

Printed in the United States of America

The paper used in this book complies with the
Permanent Paper Standard issued by the National
Information Standards Organization (Z39.48-1984).

10 9 8 7 6 5 4 3 2 1

CONTENTS

PREFACE

It is odd and a little perplexing that historians, who above all other scholars are both legatees and creators of a vast corpus of written work, should on the whole be indifferent to the fruits of systematic bibliographical production. That this is so, nevertheless, is clearly and confessedly indicated in a recent article in which some historians admitted that systematically availing themselves of bibliographical tools was not one of the chief means by which they become aware of recently published work in their field.[1] At first this hardly seemed possible to me and I assumed that the view did not represent the field at large, but was idiosyncratic. In one way or another, though, I have since become disabused of my initial reaction.

In any case, the nonchalance of many historians is exhibited further by the absence of a guide to serial bibliographies covering the domain of history in its entirety. This nonchalance contrasts with the recent publication of excellent guides to serial bibliographies in both religious studies and modern literature.[2] Certainly specialized and retrospective bibliographies in history abound, to the point where bibliographies of such bibliographies have already begun to be produced. Yet, it is no exaggeration to say that serial or otherwise recurring bibliographies provide the cutting edge in any field, since they are reasonably up to date and carry the promise of continuing currency, even as time passes.

The present guide is an attempt to provide coverage of such works in history, broadly defined, as they exist in mid-1985. Approximately 875 titles are listed. Materials included were gathered over a period of three years, while the information in the entries themselves was accumulated primarily during a six-month period beginning in December of 1984. During this latter period all entries were written (and occasionally rewritten). The surprisingly large number of items included here is in part the result of the encompassing definition of 'history' which I have adopted, and in part testimony to the diligence and commitment of many historians, bibliographers, and other scholars in undertaking the often thankless work of compiling relevant bibliographies. The purpose of this guide is to enhance the opportunity to exploit their work.

A note of caution should be sounded with respect to some of the materials listed here. Serial bibliographies usually begin and cease without fanfare, a point that can be seen in the incipient outdating of even such very recent guides as those of Walsh and Wortman. In this sense, there is an inescapably built-in obsolescence, and it may be that by the time of publication, some of the titles included here will no longer be compiled and published. Just as certainly, others will have sprung into existence. With the field constantly in a state of flux, I hope that at appropriate intervals I will find it possible to introduce new works in order to maintain the value of this guide. With this possibility in mind, I would be grateful if users would call my attention to missing titles which should be included according to the criteria which follow.

Scope of This Work

To explain the scope of this guide, it is easiest to address the ways in which each of the title's main terms--"serial," "bibliography," and "history,"--as well as others, have been defined. As they stand now, the definitions are in some ways rather different from the original conception. When I began, I tended to identify a serial bibliography as one which appeared no less often than every two years and, by and large, I have held to that definition. With experience, though, came a realization that many useful and irreplaceable bibliographies appear less frequently and should not be excluded simply by applying a formula too rigidly. As a result, many titles are included which appear less often but are valuable nonetheless.

A similar change of view came, even more inexorably, with my working definition of "current." Initially I assumed that materials would appear in bibliographies no longer than two or three years after their publication, but I came to recognize that, while reasonable, this was not entirely justified. For better or worse, many very useful serial bibliographies appear later than one might wish. To exclude them would have made nonsense of the entire enterprise. As a result, some tools that are as much as a decade or more in arrears have been listed because no more current bibliographies covering the same fields as thoroughly are available. Conceivably, too, these tardy titles may eventually achieve greater currency (as was the case with [655]).

Somewhat idiosyncratically, perhaps, I have, with a few advertent exceptions, excluded bibliographies (such as national bibliographies) which list only books because books no longer exclusively convey the results of recent scholarly work in any field. While the preponderance of article literature in the humanities and social sciences is not as overwhelming as it is in the natural and physical sciences, it remains the case that even in the two former fields, far more research appears as an article than as a book. Ideally, of course, a bibliography indicates relevant literature in many formats and this is true in the majority of the bibliographies listed here.

Finally, something must be said about how I have defined "history" for this occasion. Perhaps the most significant trend in modern historiography has been its determination to describe the past more broadly, and consequently to study more of its aspects than has traditionally been thought fit or possible. Coupled with this has been the explosion of knowledge in many fields with some relationship to history. Partly owing to such technological advances as archeological dating techniques and content analysis, historians have been challenged to become and remain aware of developments in a growing and bewildering galaxy of disciplines. With this in mind, I have tried to define history as broadly as possible without losing touch with its main purpose, with the hope both of intriguing users and of satisfying their need to be alert to advances in such seemingly remote fields as glaciology.[3] My hope then is to have included all bibliographies which address in whole or part *any* aspect of the past. It is probably not too much to say that, if the once-conventional and restricted conception of history had been adopted, the number of entries would have fallen by fully one-half.

My canvass of serial bibliographies in history (including many hundreds which did not fit the present scheme for one reason or another) covers volumes ranging in format from the monster *MLA International Bibliography* ([513]), a paragon of completeness, organization, and currency; through comprehensive but more restricted listings; through selected abstracts; to very brief and specialized bibliographies.

After some hesitation I decided to include the "current contents" literature, a recent phenomenon in the field of providing current bibliographical information. These are not really bibliographies in the accepted sense of the term, but they have several important advantages, not least of which is their outstanding currency. Though a few of these are indexed or arranged thematically in traditional fashion, most require more effort to canvass them thoroughly, but this can itself be advantageous since it introduces the opportunity to reap the rewards of serendipity.

There are good reasons for including miniscule bibliographies on miniscule subjects here, even when there are omnibus bibliographies available in the same sub-fields. The smaller bibliographies generally appear much more quickly and are easier to use. *Eventually*, most of the items in them will reach one or more larger bibliography, but it is questionable whether those interested in recent work should be satisfied with the prospect of "eventually."

In preparing a guide of this nature, the uneven quality of the bibliographical structure of history, as measured by serial bibliographies, is readily apparent. For instance, far more bibliographies are devoted to William Shakespeare than to all of South and Southeast Asia; the southern United States is much better served than any other region of the country; writings about the past of eastern Europe (particularly that of Poland) is more thoroughly indexed than any other area of the world; and so on. Disclosing these gaps may encourage others to fill them.

I have included bibliographies in literature, including some on individual authors. All those which deal with living authors I have excluded categorically, but many authors of the past are themselves historical figures because they mirrored their own times so completely, or because bibliographies which deal with them go beyond "the man and his work" to encompass "the man and his times." Others, such as David Hume, have been included because they counted the writing of history among their accomplishments. In other cases I made the choice on the basis of the quality of the bibliography rather than on the importance of the author.

Organization

    Both separately-published bibliographies and those which appear reg-
ularly in journals are listed in a single integrated alphabetical arrangement, supplemented by extensive cross-referencing and a detailed index.
The individual entries include a core of basic information, which is il-
lustrated by the following sample entry.

[376] *Hémecht*[1] ("Bibliographie d'histoire luxembourgeoise")[2]

    Prepared by the Bibliothèque Nationale, this is essentially the
    historical items from [170][3] abstracted and published separately.
    In 1983 647 items, mainly from 1982, were listed and divided into:
    bibliographies; auxiliary sciences; general history; and cultural
    history. Religious and monastic history were particularly well
    represented. There is an author index but no list of journals.

    [4]0018-0270/2412470[5]   170/424/582[6]

[1]main entry for title of book or journal as it appears in library printed
card catalogs or in bibliographic databases; where a publication is published by a corporate body, the listing is by that body

[2]specific title of bibliography appearing as part of a journal

[3]references to other entries likely to be of interest

[4]ISSN (or occasionally ISBN) number

[5]the number given to this title in the OCLC database; where more than
one number has been assigned, that with the most holdings is listed

[6]references to other items in this guide which may be of interest to
those consulting this entry

    In this arrangement I would emphasize that the format of each entry
is determined by the standard library practice regarding "main entries."
Thus, when a journal is published by an organization of some kind, the
"corporate entry," and not the title of the journal, is considered to be
the form under which it is cataloged. In a concordance at the end of
this preface I have tried to list those few truly distinctive titles
which are listed here by corporate entry. Most, however, simply have
such titles as "Yearbook" or "Bulletin" and listing these would serve no
purpose.

Minimally, the body of each entry includes information on the size, scope, organization, periodicity, and currency of each bibliography, as well as details on the extent of indexing and journal listing. ISSN numbers and OCLC numbers provide unique identification of specific items and should be of help in distinguishing the many similar titles. As importantly, the OCLC number should facilitate access both to holdings and to additional bibliographical information as provided by that database, which includes records from more than 6000 libraries. Where no consolidated record exists in OCLC, I have provided either the number of the record that was established by the Library of Congress or (if different) that which includes the largest number of holdings.

Finally, each entry includes a varying number of cross-references to other entries of related or complementary interest. This provides an internal and logically-dispersed indexing mechanism supplementing the index at the end of the guide.

The Future of Serial Bibliographies in History

It is frequently heard these days that the information networks of the future will obviate the need for plowing laboriously through printed bibliographies by permitting scholars to search electronic databases by keywords, or even concepts, thereby rendering instant and painless gratification. Some may be beguiled by this prospect, but on several grounds it must be considered illusory. Humanists are not likely ever to be well served by such databases, particularly those whose interests require an awareness of foreign-language materials.[4] More importantly, the keyword concept is too devoid of context for truly successful searching. Titles too seldom describe the contents of a piece of writing and any system would require content analytical capabilities well beyond practical limits (as they stand today) in order to be effective. Moreover, losing contextuality of wording involves losing the context of listing since there are no longer any potentially useful neighboring items. Good fortune then, always a consequential ally in bibliographical hunts, is seldom allowed to play a role. On these grounds (and others could be advanced), the loss of any well-conceived printed bibliography would be unfortunate. Even more unfortunate would be the loss sustained by historical scholarship were historians to become converts to the notion that electronic database searching is an adequate, or even a superior, substitute to scouring available printed bibliographies "manually." It is with this in mind that the present guide has been prepared.

Notes

1. Margaret F. Stieg, "The Information of Needs of Historians," *College and Research Libraries*, 42 (1981), 549-60.
2. Michael J. Walsh, *Religious Bibliographies in Serial Literature: A Guide* (Westport, CT: Greenwood Press, 1981); William A. Wortman, *A Guide to Serial Bibliographies for Modern Literatures* (New York: Modern Language Association of America, 1982).
3. Recent ice-core evidence from Greenland can actually provide closer dating evidence than any ancient records for such events in antiquity as the Thera eruption. See C.U. Hammer, H.B. Clausen, and W. Dansgaard, "Greenland Ice Sheet Evidence of Post-Glacial Volcanism and Its

Climatic Impact," *Nature*, 285 (20 November 1980), 230-35.
4. In this argument I differ from the view of Joyce D. Falk, "In Search of History: The Bibliographic Databases," *History Teacher*, 15 (1981/82), 523-44.

ACKNOWLEDGMENTS

Principal thanks obviously belong to the hundreds of bibliographers who, convinced of the value of their work, have compiled and continue to compile the works cited here. Without their dedication, usually unrewarded in practical terms, the effective pursuit of knowledge about the past would be impossibly difficult.

During the course of my work on this guide I found it necessary to visit several other libraries, including the Library of Congress and the libraries of the University of Chicago, the University of Illinois, the University of Michigan, the University of Minnesota, the University of Wisconsin at Milwaukee, Marquette University and Northwestern University. For access to their materials, I am grateful to their respective librarians, as I am to James Danky of the State Historical Society of Wisconsin.

Even so, some materials escaped my personal grasp, but I was able to rely on friends and colleagues for assistance. I am especially grateful to Joseph Lauer and Pamela Willoughby of the University of California at Los Angeles, Joseph Miller of the University of Virginia, and Moore Crossey of Yale University.

As the project neared completion and some materials continued to elude me, the Interlibrary Loan Department of Memorial Library at the University of Wisconsin-Madison relaxed its already generous borrowing policies and undertook to track down for me numerous requests, many of them of a nearly impossible nature. I am, as always, grateful to Judy Tuohy and Priscilla Neill for all their help. Jill Rosenshield was also kind enough to help me through the large number of tools in Slavic languages which are included here.

I cannot forget my typist (and wife) Janice Behn for her willingness to spend a good deal of her personal time, very early on most mornings, in preparation of the camera-ready manuscript. I am sure that users will judge her work to be exemplary.

Finally, in dedicating this work to the staff of the Serials Acqui-

sitions Department of Memorial Library, I am thanking them for more than
their help on this particular project. Without early and easy access to
their daily intake, I would never have become aware of many of the titles.
It is equally true that during the past several years, such access has
brought countless other rewards. It is a perquisite of the job that I
value beyond all others.

TABLE OF
ABBREVIATIONS

Since several entries are alphabetized by acronym or corporate entry when there is also a distinct title, the following concordance keyed to entry number, may be useful:

SERIAL BIBLIOGRAPHIES AND ABSTRACTS IN HISTORY

SERIAL BIBLIOGRAPHIES
AND ABSTRACTS

[1] *ABC Pol Sci*

This is published five times yearly with articles grouped under
journal title and journals arranged alphabetically in each issue.
Articles are numbered and in 1984 about 10,000 were listed, many of
them from journals directly or indirectly in the field of history.
Each issue has subject and author indexes and these are cumulated
annually into a sixth issue along with a list of all journal issues
canvassed and publication details on the 275 to 300 journals regularly analyzed (and this feature appears in each issue as well).
As is the wont with current contents formats, listings are very
current and, as is not always the case, access is quite good.

0001-0456/809405   209/298/431

[2] *ABHB. Annual Bibliography of the History of the Printed Book and
Libraries.*

The volume for 1982 was published in 1984 and includes 3343 items.
Coverage is international and encompasses about 1800 journals,
which are listed, as well as books and collective works. *ABHB* is
based on materials compiled by national committees in 25 countries.
The entries are arranged into 12 categories each of which is further subdivided and within which the arrangement is largely geographical. Technical, social, economic, and intellectual aspects
of the history of the book, as well as library history from the
fifteenth century to the present are covered, though there is relatively little attention paid to contemporary issues. *ABHB* should
be compared with [156], which has more entries from fewer sources.
There are author/anonymous work and geographical/personal name indexes.

0303-5964/1791729   156/833

[3] *ABSEES: American Bibliography of Slavic and East European Studies*

Prepared by the European Division of the Library of Congress, cover-

age for 1981 was published in 1984 and included 4206 references
and notices of 747 reivews. The eastern European countries as well
as Greece, Cyprus, and emigrés in North America are included. The
major categories (each in turn subdivided) are: General; Anthropology, Archeology and Folklife; Culture and the Arts; Economics; Education; Geography and Demography; Government, Law, and Politics;
History; International Relations; Language and Linguistics; Literature; Military Affairs; Philosophy, Political Theory, and Ideology; Psychology; Religion; Science; and Sociology, with the reviews
being listed separately. In addition there is a list of more than
500 journals and an author/reviewer index. The print is both too
small and too light for easy consultation.

0094-3770/1783626   237/323/674

[4]   *Abstracta Iranica*

Published annually as a supplement to *Studia Iranica* by the Institut Francais d'Iranologie in Teheran and covering "the Irano-Aryan
domain." The 1984 volume included 919 items, most of which were
annotated in French, sometimes quite extensively, and which were
arranged in 17 categories. Coverage is from the Ancient Near East
to the present (but with skimpy coverage of the former) and embra-
ces present-day Iran, Afghanistan, and the Kurdish areas. There is
an author/translator index and a list of more than 75 journals consulted.

---- ----/6644394   422/528/529/621

[5]   *Abstracta Islamica*

Issued as a separately-paged supplement to *Revues des études Isla-
miques*, AI is similar to, but slower than, [621] with coverage for
1979 appearing only in 1983. Each year about 1000 items are divided into: Histoire et Géographie; Islamologie; Langues et Littérature; Art, Archéologie et Techniques; Islam Contemporain; Bibliographie et Documentation, with each of these being subdivided further. Most items are annotated in French in varying degrees with
some annotations approaching the status of reviews. Books, articles, and collective works are covered and there is a list of journals (about 100) as well as an author index.

0336-156X/1641951   226/330/447/528/529/542/621

[6]   *Abstracts: European Muslims and Christian-Muslim Relations*

This is published twice yearly by the Centre for the Study of Islam
and Christian-Muslim Relations, Selly Oak College, Birmingham, United Kingdom. Each number features from 100 to 150 brief abstracts
on present (the majority) and past relations between Christianity
and Islam. The coverage is global and materials are arranged geographically. About 100 journals, many ephemeral, are canvassed and
listed, but there are no other indexes.

0143-9715/8089688   218

[7] *Abstracts in Anthropology*

Published quarterly, in 1984 each issue included 1000 abstracts of
50 to 200 words. Only English—language materials are included.
Broad categories are Archeology; Physical Anthropology; Linguistics; and Cultural Anthropology, with sub-divisions within each.
Each number includes an author index and a subject/geographical index as well as a list of the journals (with publishing information)
abstracted in that issue, usually numbering from 75 to 150.

0001-3455/1460581   60/61/62/429

[8] *Abstracts in German Anthropology*

Published twice a year (though the latest is Winter 1983), this includes abstracts of books, articles, and films in German compiled
by the Arbeitskreis für internationale Wissenschaftskommunikation
in Göttingen. The abstracts (which are in English) usually run
from 100 to 200 words. "Anthropology" is interpreted generously
and numerous historical items are included in each issue. Between
400 and 500 abstracts are published each year. In addition each
number includes a list of journals abstracted for that issue (about
60 in the most recent) and author and subject indexes.

0178-2986/7562980

[9] *Abstracts of English Studies*

Published quarterly and in 1984 included more than 3000 items arranged by General; Britain; United States; World Literature in
English and Related Languages (e.g., Creoles), each of which is
further divided, generally by authors studied. There is an authors
studied index in each issue which is cumulated in the fourth issue
of each year and a yearly author index in the fourth number, which
also includes a list of journals (125-150 in 1984). *AES* is not
particularly current and would not ordinarily be a first choice
with so many excellent bibliographies available in the field of
language and literature.

0001-3560/1460584   49/513/841

[10] *Abstracts on Tropical Agriculture*

This is published each month by the Koninklijk Instituut voor de
Tropen in Amsterdam. Each issue contains about 300 brief (75 to
200 words) abstracts arranged in 17 categories, largely by crop
type. The historical component is fairly small and not easy to locate through the indexes, but such as there is is not likely to be
included in other, less specialized, bibliographies. Each number
contains subject, geographical, taxonomic, and author indexes, the
first two of which are cumulated annually. Apparently there is no
master list of journals consulted.

0304-5951/2241004   143/835

[11]   *Acadiensis* ("Recent Publications Relating to the History of the
       Atlantic Region")

       This bibliography deals with the Maritime Provinces of Canada (New-
       foundland, Prince Edward Island, Nova Scotia, and New Brunswick).
       The most recent, which appeared in the Spring 1984 number, includ-
       ed 275 to 300 items arranged by author under five geographical di-
       visions. There are no indexes or list of journals consulted.

       0044-5851/1670823   235/657

[12]   *Das Achtzehnte Jahrhundert* [Wolfenbüttel] ("Germanistische Arbei-
       ten zum 18. Jahrhundert")

       The 1984 bibliography largely dealt with items published during
       1981 and included 556 items arranged in a general category (one-
       third) and individually by eighteenth-century author (two-thirds)
       except Goethe and Schiller, who are not included. Special bibli-
       ographies also appear from time to time; for instance, "Biblio-
       graphie zur protestantischen Kirchen- und Theologiegeschichte
       Deutschlands in 18. Jahrhundert, 1980-1983," a listing of 386
       items which appeared in 1984. There are no indexes or a list of
       journals consulted.

       ---- ----/5717213   290/355/436/484/832

[13]   *Acta Historiae Neerlandica* ("Survey of Recent Historical Work on
       Belgium and the Netherlands Published in Dutch")

       Essentially a bibliographical essay in English, covering books
       and articles on all aspects of Low Countries history since the
       Middle Ages. The arrangement is in roughly chronological order
       and full citations (including ISBNs) are invariably given. The
       most recent issue, that for 1982, included about 100 items, mostly
       published in 1981.

       0065-129X/5340235   640/797

[14]   *Acta Historica* [Budapest] ("Bibliographie choisie d'ouvrages
       publiés en Hongrie en 19--")

       The 1983 bibliography included some 350 books and articles pub-
       lished in Hungary, largely in 1981. There are ten categories,
       nine on Hungarian history, the tenth on the rest of the world.
       Titles in Hungarian are translated into French. There are no in-
       dexes, nor a list of journals consulted.

       0001-5849/1460901   72/112/363/518/783

[15]   *Aegyptus* ("Bibliografia metodica degli studi di egittologia e
       papirologia")

       The bibliography for 1982, appearing in 1983, included nearly 900 items arranged into: General; History and Geography; Literature, Philosophy, and Science (including much on fragments of Greek and Latin authors); Linguistics, Poetry, Music; Palaeography and Bibliology; Law and Administration, each further subdivided. Pharaonic and Ptolemaic Egypt are included, but the emphasis is on materials from or dealing with Roman and Byzantine Egypt. There is an author/reviewer index but no list of journals consulted.

0001-9046/1461304   83/309/310

[16] *Africa* [Rome] ("Bollettino bibliografico africano")

This is appearing less and less frequently, but when it appears it is useful for recent monographic and periodical literature in Italian, most particularly that which deals with the recent period. Material is included haphazardly and is arranged by journal in a modified current contents format. There are no indexes.

0001-9747/1779989   136

[17] *Africa Bibliography*

This is to begin in 1985 as a separate issue of *Africa*, published by the International African Institute in London. In each annual issue some 3000 books and articles on Africa will be included, covering all subjects and arranged geographically and thematically. It is expected that each issue will cover the preceding year's materials. It is not clear whether this new publication is intended to replace, complement, or cumulate [426].

0266-6731/-------   18/154/297/426/631

[18] *Africa Index to Continental Periodical Literature*

Published by the Centro de Estudos Africanos of the Universidade Eduardo Mondlane in Maputo, this is becoming one of the most important bibliographical tools for African studies, though not yet sufficiently current (1979/1980 published in 1983). It includes scholarly and semi-scholarly materials published in Africa (except South Africa), including some material not related to Africa, all arranged into 31 categories. 3445 items drawn from 158 journals were included in the 1979/80 volume. Titles in vernacular languages are translated. The geographical arrangement is unnecessarily recondite (being based on ALPHA-2 and ALPHA-3 geographical codes) but not impenetrable. There are author and subject indexes as well as publishing information on the journals canvassed.

0378-4797/5156946   17/154/297/426/631

[19] *African Affairs* ("Select List of Articles on Africa Appearing in Non-Africanist Journals")

Indexes more than 150 journals but does not attempt to do so com-

prehensively. Each quarterly issue has fewer than 50 entries but
it remains useful for odd journals of recent vintage which are not
canvassed by other Africanist bibliographies. The emphasis is on
economics and contemporary history.

0001-9909/5330671   270/644

[20] *Agricultural History Review* ("Annual List and Brief Review of Articles on Agrarian History")

Materials published in 1983 appeared in the 1985/1 number. Here
some 250 items were listed by author, preceded by a short bibliographical essay discussing the most important of them. Coverage
is limited to materials wholly or partly concerned with the British
Isles, although "agrarian" is defined generously. There are no indexes or a list of journals.

0002-1490/1478540   143/443/708

[21] *Air University Library Index to Military Periodicals*

Prepared at the Air University, Maxwell AFB, Alabama, the *Index* is
published quarterly and cumulated annually. Presently it canvasses
77 English-language periodicals (which are listed with full bibliographical details). All articles, news items, and editorials are
indexed. The arrangement is alphabeticaly by subject, with extensive cross-referencing. It is difficult to estimate the number of
citations but certainly not fewer than 10,000 annually (not allow-
ing for duplication). There is relatively little historical matter
included and most of that modern or contemporary. There are no indexes.

0002-2586/2500050   165/530/531/818

[22] *Akkadica* ("Bibliographie 19--")

Eighty-one items, briefly annotated in French and listed by author,
appeared in 1982 and 1983 numbers, but none since. The focus is in
Mesopotamia, Western Iran, and Anatolia in the third and second
millennia B.C. No indexes have appeared. Compared to [82] and
[584] this is very small potatoes but in some regards it may be
more current.

---- ----/3295049   82/584

[23] *L'Alighieri* ("Repertorio bibliografico dantesco")

One of several bibliographies devoted to Dante, more than 50 items
were listed in the 1984/2 number (largely from 1982). There were
no indexes. Given the bibliographical attention to Dante and his
times, it is unlikely that this bibliography would well repay consulting it.

0516-6551/2029489   286/684/764

[24] *Amerasia Journal* ("Selected Annual Bibliography")

The Fall-Winter 1983 number included 350 to 375 items, largely published in 1983. It was arranged by Asian ethnic group in this
country and covers all fields. There are no indexes, but a list
of about 160 journals, useful in itself, was included.

0044-7471/1666962   402

[25] *America: History and Life*

This North American counterpart to [383] is organized as follows:
Part A: Article Abstracts and Citations (three times a year and
totalling about 8500 50- to 150-word abstracts in 1984); Part B:
Index to Book Reviews (twice a year and totalling about 4000 reviews in 1984); Part C: American History Bibliography (includes
bibliographical details for items in A and B, plus dissertations
and is published annually); Part D: Annual Index: subject and auth-
or indexes to A, B, and C; reviewers' and title indexes for B; and
a listing of several hundred periodicals analyzed. Each issue of
Part A is divided into: North America; Canada; United States to
1945; United States since 1945; Regional, State, and Local History;
History, Humanities and Social Sciences. In addition to the annual
index, each issue of Parts A and B carries its own relevant indexes. Coverages is quite prompt and this is a much more comprehensive and current tool than [383].

0002-7065/1328815   464/631/837

[26] *American Jewish History* ("Judaica Americana")

Prepared by the American Jewish Historical Society, the most recent
(June 1984) bibliography included about 250 items (many briefly annotated) on the Jewish experience in the United States. There are
no indexes but the material is divided into general and special
studies, most of which are sub-divided.

0164-0178/4304304   402

[27] *American Literature* ("A Select Annotated List of Current Articles
on American Literature")

An annotated checklist appears in most issues, arranged by author
and usually encompassing no more than 20 to 30 items. Its use is
restricted since its only value is its currency.

0002-9831/1480320   826

[28] *Analecta Bollandiana* ("Bulletin des publications hagiographiques")

Appearing in each semi-annual issue, this purports to be a comprehensive presentation of recent books, articles, and collective works

on hagiography. These take the form of extensively annotated abstracts arranged in no particular order and without any indexes,
rendering access problematical. In addition, there is a section
entitled "Ouvrages envoyés à la rédaction," arranged in alphabetical order by author, which, despite its name, includes articles as
well as books, but without annotations.

0003-2468/1481044

[29] *Analecta Linguistica*

Published twice yearly by the Akademaia Kiadó in Budapest, this is
a current contents approach to linguistic material, largely that
published in the Soviet Union and eastern Europe. No indexes, as
usual with this format, but also as usual, very current.

0044-8176/1711036   481/504/551

[30] *Analecta Praemonstratensia* ("Chronicon")

Prepared by the Commissio Historica Ordinis Praemonstratensis at the
Abbey of Averbode in Belgium. In each semi-annual number appear
about 100 briefly annotated citations to books and articles in no
apparent order. Materials in all languages are included but the
annotations are in Flemish. There are no indexes.

---- ----/2029694

[31] *Anales Cervantinos* ("Bibliografía Cervantina")

Most numbers contain from 75 to 100 items, which are often annotated so extensively as effectively to be book reviews, although both
books and articles are included. The materials are arranged by:
Repertorios Bibliográficos; Estudios Generales; Biografía de Cervan-
tes; *Don Quijote*; *La Galatea*; Novelas Ejemplares; Teatro; Poesía;
Miscelanea. Not a truly comprehensive listing of material on Cer-
vantes but important because of the critical analyses that are included. There are no indexes.

0569-9878/1695318   217/246

[32] *Anglo-Saxon England* ("Bibliography")

Appears in each annual volume; the latest--for 1983--appeared in
the 1984 volume and included about 800 items and 200 reviews arranged by author in nine categories. There are no indexes but a
list of about 70 journals was included. The bibliography covers
the British Isles and surrounding areas from the fifth to the
twelfth centuries and is especially strong in literature, history,
and the auxiliary historical sciences.

0263-6751/1716466   198/577

[33] *Annales de Bourgogne* ("Bibliographie Bourguignonne")

Issued as an annual spearately-paged supplement, the bibliography
for 1982 was published as part of the 1983 volume. It included
nearly 900 items arranged in 6 chronological and 6 topical categories covering various aspects of the history of the Burgundian region from prehistory to the present, each of them in turn subdivided. Entries were occasionally briefly annotated and there was an
author index as well as a list of about 100 journals analyzed.

0003-3901/2026698   663/740

[34] *Annales de l'Est* ("Bibliographie Lorraine")

Published as a separately-paged supplement to *Annales de l'Est* by
the Académie Nationale de Metz, Foundation Chabot-Didon. The bibliography for 1981, which was published in 1983, included 985 items
arranged in 10 thematic and chronological categories, each further
subdivided. Books, articles, collective works, and maps are covered. There is a combined author/historical personage/place index
but no list of journals.

0365-2017/7185519   148/656

[35] *Annales de Normandie* ("Bibliographie normande")

Published as a separately-paged annual supplement, the latest, published in 1984, includes 866 books, articles, and parts of collective works divided into: général, histoire politique; institutions;
histoire économique; histoire sociale; histoire réligieuse; his-
toire littéraire et histoire des idées; histoire de l'art et archéologie; biographies et généalogies; histoire locale. Some attention is also paid to the Normans abroad. There are personal name,
geographical, and author indexes but no list of journals.

0003-4134/1481276

[36] *Annales du Midi* ("Bibliographie de la France méridionale")

The most recent "Bibliographie," covering 1981, appeared in 1982.
This included 2074 items in 7 general categories (civilisations de
la France méridionale; instruments du travail; bases géographiques
et humaines; économies et sociétés; industries, commerce, et villes;
vie réligieuse et clergé; vie de l'esprit), each subdivided, and
another 365 items in six chronological categories. Coverage of the
many local French historical journals is particularly strong, but
there is no list of these or any indexes.

0003-4398/1481318

[37]   *Annals of Iowa* ("Bibliography of Iowa History")

This appears each year, the latest being in the Winter 1984 number, where 250 to 300 items are arranged in more than 20 categories. There are no indexes.

0003-4827/1481386

[38]   *L'Année Epigraphique*

This is a major tool for epigraphy in Classical Antiquity. The volume for 1981 includes 999 briefly annotated references to inscriptions from the Roman world arranged in several geographical classifications. There is a list of over 100 journals and collective works and several indexes, including provenance, personal name, and geographical indexes. Finally there is a corcordance with entries in earlier volumes of *L'Annee Epigraphique*.

0066-2348/1196530   73/354/673/859

[39]   *L'Année Philologique*

The major tool for classical philology and history, covering the Mediterranean area (but not the Ancient Near East) from prehistory to 800 A.D. The volume for 1983 (published in 1985) includes 14,807 books, articles, reviews, dissertations, and parts of collective works in nine broad categories. By far the largest of these (5238 entries) is "Auteurs et textes," an alphabetical arrangement by author studied of works emanating from Classical and Late Antiquity. A list of about 1100 journals is included and there are indexes of collective titles (important in the field), ancient names, place names, humanists, and authors. Many items include brief annotations, mainly in French.

---- ----/2702219   73/809

[40]   *Annuaire d'histoire liégeoise* ("Bulletin bibliographique d'histoire liegeoise")

Published by the Commission communale de l'histoire de l'ancien pays de Liège, the latest "Bibliographie" seen covering the years 1976 to 1978 was published in 1981 as a supplement to the 1978 *Annuaire*. In it 2127 items are listed alphabetically by author or anonymous title and, while there is a brief subject index, access must be rated as poor. There is no list of journals consulted.

---- ----/2313551   654/676

[41]   *Annuaire de l'Afrique du Nord* ("Bibliographie systématique: langue arabe")

AAN is published as an annual supplement to *Jeune Afrique*. Included

in the latest (1981) bibliography are 349 items in Arabic (for
which French translations are provided) which were published in
the Maghreb countries (Morocco, Algeria, Tunisia, and Libya).
These are classified into Documents Généraux; Histoire; Politique
Intérieur; Défense Nationale; Politique Extérieur; Economie; En-
seignment, Cultures, Réligion; Questions de Société, Espace; Emi-
gration. An author index is included but no list of journals used.

0066-2607/1481450   42/519

[42] *Annuaire de l'Afrique du Nord* ("Bibliographie systématique: langues
européennes")

A companion bibliography to [41], in 1981 this included 1529 items
(and a short addendum) classified in the same way as [41] but with
more numerous subdivisions. This is particularly good on such
ephemeral materials as government publications, pamphlets, and articles in newspapers and weeklies. There is some cross-referencing
and an author index, though no list of journals consulted.

0066-2607/1481450   41/519

[43] *Annuaire des pays de l'Océan Indien* ("Informations bibliographiques")

Published by the Faculté de Droit et de Science Politique, Université d'Aix-Marseille and the Groupement de Recherches Coordonnées
Océan Indien of the Centre National de la Recherche Scientifique.
The volume for 1981 (published in 1984) includes from 600 to 700
items arranged geographically and then by format (theses and mémoires; books; articles; studies and reports; colloquia). There are
no indexes or list of journals, but there is good overage of elusive materials. Occasionally a specialized bibliography is included; for instance, in 1981 one on tourism.

0247-400X/4511432

[44] *Annuaire du Tiers Monde* ("Bibliographie")

Published by the Association pour l'étude du Tiers Monde in Paris.
The volume for 1981, which covers 1979 and 1980, includes about
1500 items classified into: Biographies; Etudes Générales; Problèmes Intérieurs; Problèmes Internationaux, each but the first
further subdivided. There are author as well as subject/geographi-
cal indexes and a list of about 650 journals canvassed. The 1981
volume also includes a special bibliography on the PLO.

0396-2156/2754107   433

[45] *Annuaire français de droit international* ("Bibliographie systématique des ouvrages et articles relatifs au droit international public publiés en langue française")

In 1983 this included more than 2000 items arranged in 13 categories,

including regional and international organizations and the law of
war. There were no indexes. This was preceded by a section entitled "Revue des revues" which included about 250 items in 10
categories drawn from more than 50 listed journals in languages
other than French.

0066-3085/1481462   185/548

[46] *Annuaire Suisse de Science Politique/Schweizerisches Jahrbuch für
      politische Wissenschaft* ("Bibliographie suisse de science politique")

The 1984 volume carried a bibliography of 458 items divided into
six classifications including some historical matter, e.g., the
history of political thought. Not surprisingly, emphasis is on
material relating to Switzerland. There are no indexes or lists
of journals.

0066-3727/3352065   159

[47] *Annual Bibliography of British and Irish History*

Published by the Royal Historical Society, the aim of the *Annual
Bibliography* is to "subordinate absolutely total coverage and refinement of arrangement to speed of production." The volume for
1982 managed to include more than 2700 items divided into two general and several more chronological and/or regional classifications,
each of which is in turn subdivided with apparently random listings
by author. The British Isles are covered from the Iron Age to the
present but not British colonies. There is no list of journals
consulted (though they certainly number in the hundreds) but author
and subject indexes are included.

0308-4558/2813271   568/710/752/820/838/839

[48] *Annual Bibliography of Christianity in India*

Published by the Heras Institute of Indian History and Culture, St.
Xavier's College, Bombay. The most recent volume, covering 1983,
includes over 500 items arranged into 10 classifications, the largest of which are: Generalia; Philosophy and Theology; and Studies
of Christianity in India. There are author and subject indexes as
well as a list of over 100 journals consulted. There is good coverage of local Indian materials, which in all likelihood escape the
net of the European and American religious bibliographies discussed
elsewhere.

---- ----/10810852

[49] *Annual Bibliography of English Language and Literature*

Published under the aegis of the Modern Humanities Research Association, the volume covering 1981 was published in 1984 and includes

13723 items classified as follows: General; Festschriften and Other Collections; Scholarly Method; Language, Literature and the Computer; Newspapers and Other Periodicals; The English Language; Folklore and Folklife; and English Literature. The last comprises fully 70% of the total and consists largely of an 'author studied' arrangement. The scope is from Anglo-Saxon times to the present and is worldwide. There is a list of 1100+ journals consulted as well as author as subject and scholar (i.e., author) indexes.

0066-3786/1758457   9/513/841

[50] *Annual Bibliography of Indian Archaeology*

This bibliography is unconscionably in arrears; the volume covering 1970 to 1972 was published in 1984. Yet it covers a field not otherwise covered by any serial bibliography and one can only wish that it can become more current. The latest volume includes 2788 items classified into: General; India and Regions Within Its Cultural Influence; Indian Subcontinent; Regions Within Sphere of Indian Cultural Influence, each in turn subdivided. The coverage of epigraphical data is particularly strong but fields like the fine arts in ancient times and economic history are also selectively covered. There is an author/reviewer index and a list of about 250 journals consulted.

90 277 1642 0/1753304   361/405

[51] *Annual Bibliography of Ontario History*

Published by the Ontario Historical Society, this formerly appeared in *Ontario History* but in 1980 began to be published separately, though there appear to have been none since. Some 350 to 400 books and pamphlets and about 200 articles were included. There were no indexes.

0227-6623/10582703   235

[52] *Annual Bibliography of Scottish Literature*

Published as a supplement to *Bibliotheck* by the National Library of Scotland. The bibliography for 1982 was published in 1984 and included about 800 items under General Bibliography and Reference Material; General Literary Criticism; Individual Authors (over half the total); and Ballads and Folk Literature. Works by and about Scottish historians are included. There are author and author studied indexes as well as a partial list of journals consulted.

0307-9864/1710996   49/710

[53] *Annual Bibliography of the History of Natural History*

The first volume, covering 1982, is published in 1985 by the Depart-

ment of Library Science of the British Museum (Natural History).
Based on its own acquisitions and those of related libraries, more
than 1350 items are included. All the earth and life sciences are
covered comprehensively and certain "fringe" fields less so. Items
are listed by author with a subject index derived broadly from the
Universal Decimal Classification, as well as personal and institutional indexes. It is expected that future volumes will be published late in the year following. A list of over 400 journals
consulted is included.

---- ----/-------   221/446

[54] *Annual Bibliography of Victorian Studies*

This is one of the new breed of computer-produced bibliographies
and is the major bibliographical tool for Victorian England and its
colonies. The most recent volume, that for 1981, includes 3494
items divided into: General and Reference Works; Fine Arts; Philosophy and Religion; History; Social Sciences; Science and Technology;
Language and Literature (by far the largest, arranged by author
studied). There is a very extensive subject index as well as author
and reviewer indexes and a title index which includes both books
and articles. Finally, there is a master list of serials encompassing over 350 titles. A good example of the benefits of a well-
conceived computer application to bibliographical materials.

0227-1400/7140046   294/810/811

[55] *Annual Egyptological Bibliography*

The volume for 1980 was published in 1984 and included over 1000
items classified in several categories: General; Script and Language; Texts and Philology; History; Art and Archaeology; Religion;
Society and Culture; Science and Technology; Country and Surrounding Areas; Nubian Studies. Each entry is accompanied by an abstract
of from 10 to 250 words in English, German, or French. Coverage is
confined primarily to Pharaonic Egypt and contemporary Nubia. There
is an author index and an incomplete listing of journals (some 35)
as well as of collective works. For an attempt to update *AEB* see
[614].

0 85668 278 0/1607404   15/82/549/614

[56] *Annual of Urdu Studies* ("Bibliographical News")

Thirty to forty items were listed by author in the 1983 volume.
Most of the materials are literary in nature with a sprinkling of
relevant historical materials. There are no indexes; none is needed.

0734-5348/7624258

[57] *Annuario bibliografico di storia dell'arte*

Prepared by the Biblioteca dell'Istituto Nazione di Archeologia e

Storia dell'Arte, Rome, this bibliography is much in arrears, the materials for 1974/75 appeared only in 1980. In that volume 5458 items, dealing with the Western art tradition, were arranged in three broad and numerous smaller classifications, the largest being an alphabetical arrangement by artist. There were author, artist, and geographical indexes.

0535-8620/1754037   99/624/639/851

[58]   *Annuarium Historiae Conciliorum* ("Bibliographia")

A brief listing of materials relating to the various Councils in the history of the Catholic Church, with the Council of Trent and Vatican I and II receiving the lion's share. There were about 140 such citations in the two numbers of the 1984 volume. The arrangement is roughly chronological and there are no indexes. Coverage is quite current.

0003-5157/2160680   93/661

[59]   *Antarctic Bibliography*

This is an annual accumulation of the monthly *Current Antarctic Literature* and is prepared by the Library of Congress for the Division of Polar Programs of the National Science Foundation. In the 1983 volume there were over 2500 entries divided among 13 categories and arranged in a series of small sequences by accession numbers, rendering access difficult. While the vast majority of items are of a scientific nature, materials relating to Antarctic expeditions, the history of Antarctic cartography, and relevant political geography are also included. Each item includes an abstract of 50 to 250 words. Titles in foreign languages include an English translation. There are author, subject, geographical, and grantee indexes but no list of journals canvassed.

0066-4626/1064353   630

[60]   *Anthropological Index to Current Periodicals*

Compiled by the Library of the Museum of Mankind in London, *AI* is one of the 3 major anthropological indexes and, now that [61] is to appear only in microfiche, probably the one to be consulted in the first instance. Appearing quarterly, the four numbers of the 1984 volume include nearly 8500 items arranged in six main geographical divisions, each broken into several regional subdivisions, within which the arrangement is alphabetical by author. An annual author index is included with the fourth number of each year. A disadvantage of *AI* is the lack of any master list of journals canvassed, although occasionally issues indicate new and ceased serial titles. Such a master list (of 750+ titles) may be purchased from the Museum of Mankind but such a procedure scarcely enhances *AI*'s use since many journal titles are abbreviated, somewhat unintelligibly, in the individual entries. Nonetheless, an extremely useful tool.

0080-4142/4303138   7/61/429

[61]   *Anthropological Literature*

Compiled by the Tozzer Library of the Peabody Museum, Harvard University, this is the American analog to [60]. More items are included each year, 11,335 in 1983, but its arrangement is less refined than that of [60], all materials being arranged by author
within five very broad categories (Cultural/Social; Archaeology;
Biological/Physical; Linguistics; General/Method/Theory). On the
other hand the indexing is superior since there are joint author,
archaeological site and culture, ethnic and linguistic group, and
geographic indexes as well as a cumulated annual author index.
Like [60] each issue includes new and ceased journal titles and
title changes but there is no master list. Regretably, from 1984
AL will be available only in microfiche and this is certain to
diminish both its usefulness and its use.

0190-3373/4818564   7/60/429

[62]   *Anthropos* ("Zeitschriftenschau")

Each tri-yearly issue contains a rather haphazard modified current
contents arrangement of materials; perhaps 75 to 100 journal issues
are noticed each time. Full title and pages are given for those
titles which are deemed likely to interest readers and it is similar in this way to the practice in [268]. However incomplete, the
listing is fairly current and good for picking up less well-known
publications.

0003-5572/7101399   8/268

[63]   *Antiquaries Journal* ("Periodical Literature")

This does not appear in every issue of *AJ*; the latest (in 1983/2)
covers archaeological literature that appeared in 1982 and 1983 in
a modified current contents format, that is, by journal title. Although coverage is nominally worldwide, by far the greatest emphasis is on materials relating to the British Isles, for which it is
useful in providing access to locally published items.

0003-5815/1481608   71/198/296

[64]   *Antropologica* ("*X* bibliografía antropológica reciente sobre Venezuela")

The ninth such bibliography appeared in the 1981 volume and included some 175 books, articles, and dissertations arranged in a
single author classification. Materials related largely to the
Indian groups of Venezuela but also included some generally theore-

tical or methodological materials as well. There were subject and
ethnic group indexes but no list of journals.

0003-6110/2257607   368

[65] *Aquileia Nostra* ("Bibliografia della X Regio")

The 1980 bibliography contained about 250 entries and reviews relating to the history of northeastern Italy, particularly the region around Venice. The material is arranged by chronological
periods and the reviews are listed separately. A list of 80+ journals consulted is included but there are no indexes.

---- ----/4053931   101/136

[66] *Aquileia Nostra* ("Bibliografia sul Noricum mediterraneo")

In 1980 some 70 items were listed dealing with maritime Noricum,
the Roman province which is modern-day northeastern Italy/north-
western Yugoslavia. The arrangement is entirely by author and
there are no indexes.

---- ----/4053931   136/356/525/619

[67] *Arbog for arbejderbevaegelsens historie* ("Tidsskriftsoversigt")

Each year this lists the contents of a dozen or so Scandinavian
journals that deal with ⌐ cial history and socialism in particular.
Most entries include brief comments. The most recent, covering
1982/83, appeared in the 1983 volume.

0106-5912/-------   498/571

[68] *Arbog for Dansk Skolenhistorie* ("Bibliografi over dansk skolehis-
torie")

The bibliography for 1983 appeared in the 1983 volume and listed
about 175 items relating to Danish educational history. These were
divided into 6 categories by author. There were no indexes.

0107-1661/2398039   171

[69] *Arbok for Trøndelag* ("Bibliografi over trøndersk litteratur og
litteratur med trøndersk tilknytting")

This annual listing encompasses materials dealing with the central
Norwegian province of Sor-Trøndelag (cap. Trondheim). Materials
by authors from the region are also included. The emphasis is
largely but not solely on historical materials.

---- ----/2243422   372

[70]   *Archaeoastronomy* ("In the Current Literature")

Appears in each issue (which themselves are sporadic). In the
1983/1-4 issue there were about 250 items arranged by author preceded by a brief bibliographical essay which discussed a few of
the major titles. The focus is worldwide and is a useful bringing
together of literature in this new field devoted to the apparent
astronomical awareness in pre-scientific societies.

0190-9940/4770512   446

[71]   *Archaeologia Cambrensis* ("Periodical Literature")

Published by the Cambrian Archaeological Association in Cardiff,
this bibliography devoted to archaeological work in Wales is
arranged in a modified current contents format. In the latest
(that for 1983) the contents of 23 issues of 16 Welsh journals as
well as 28 other articles are included. All forms of archeology--
prehistoric, historical, and industrial--are included.

0306-6924/1641359   47/186/198

[72]   *Archaeológiai Értesítö* ("Magyar régészeti irodalom/Bibliographia
Archaeologica Hungarica")

450 to 500 items, largely published in 1982, appear in the 1983
bibliography. These were arranged into classifications dealing
with general topics, prehistoric archeology, classical archeology,
the arrival of the 'Barbarians,' the age of migrations, and "Pro-
tohungarica." In other words, the archeology of Hungary and surrounding areas from the earliest times to *ca.* 900 A.D. was covered.
There was a list of 50+ journals but no indexes.

0003-8032/2829620   229/783

[73]   *Archäologische Bibliographie*

Prepared by the Deutsches Archäologisches Institut in Rome this
is the premier archeological bibliography, at least for those with
an interest in the world of Classical Antiquity. It is both current and comprehensive; the volume covering 1982 was published in
1983 and included 10431 items drawn from over 800 journals, a list
of which is provided. These materials are classified as follows:
Allgemeine; Sammelbande; Personalia; Technik und Material; Topo-
graphie; Museen und Sammlungen; Griechisch-römische Kultur (3600+
items); Andere Kulturen (2300+ items); Rezensionen. There is a
detailed subject index as well as author and reviewer indexes and
an index correlating ancient and modern toponyms.

0341-8308/5857335   328/639

[74] *Archäologische Mitteilungen aus Iran* ("Archäologische Bibliographie")

Appears in each annual number, that for 1981, appearing in 1982 being the most recent seen. In this there were about 200 entries relating to Iran from prehistoric times through the Sasanid period,
that is, until the Muslim conquest in the seventh century, with
"archeological" being broadly defined. These were arranged in a
general and several chronological categories, each divided into too
many sub-divisions, some having only one or two items. Cross-referencing is extensive but there are no indexes.

0066-6033/1481826   4/422

[75] *Archeion* ("Przeglad Zagranicznych Czasopism Archiwalnych/Revue des
périodiques **étrangers d'archivistiques**")

Arranged in a modified current contents format but including annotations (in Polish). The 1983 bibliography covered only 12 journals, most published in 1979 and 1980 and most emanating from central and eastern Europe.

0066-6041/5426876   85/86

[76] *Archeografo Triestino* ("Bollettino bibliografico triestino")

The 1982 volume contained the bibliography for 1981 and included
more than 300 items (many of them newspaper articles) devoted to
various aspects, largely historical, of the Trieste region of Italy/
Yugoslavia. These are listed in a single author sequence but there
is a geographical/personal/topical index as well as a list of about
200 journals canvassed.

---- ----/1741414   356/525/619

[77] *Archief voor de Geschiedenis van de Katholieke Kerk in Nederland*
("Bibliografie betreffende de nederlandse Kerkgeschiedenis")

The bibliography in the 1983 volume included over 400 items on the
history of the Catholic Church in the Netherlands. These were divided into 4 major categories, each in turn subdivided several
times. There were author and subject indexes.

0003-8326/1731148   13/582/640/797

[78] *Architectural Periodicals Index*

This is published quarterly and compiled by the Royal Institute of
British Architects, with the fourth issue being a cumulation of the
previous three. Entries are arranged alphabetically by a host of
subjects and more than 12,000 items appear in 1984. These cover
architecture and its allied arts, construction technology, land-
scaping, and environmental matters among others. Entries are oc-

casionally annotated and titles in foreign languages are translated
into English. Each issue has a personal name index, a list of subject headings (including "Historic buildings," "Gothic architecture," etc.), and a list of periodicals indexed (about 450 annually). The cumulative issue also includes a topographical index.

0033-6912/1588199   102

[79] *Archiv für katholisches Kirchenrecht* ("Literaturverzeichnis")

The bibliography appearing in the 1983 volume included some 400-500
citations to materials dealing with canon law and related subjects.
These were divided into 7 categories and therein arranged by author.
There were no indexes or a list of journals consulted. Current but
not as useful or accessible as some of the other bibliographies in
canon law.

0003-9160/1590581   216/238/669

[80] *Archiv für Liturgiewissenschaft* ("Literaturberichte")

This bibliography appears in most quarterly issues but not *in toto*;
it is divided into nearly twenty categories. For example the 1983
volume includes eleven categories scattered throughout the volume
and encompassing perhaps 1000 to 1200 items, nearly all of which
were briefly annotated. The majority of items deal with the history of the liturgy of the Roman Catholic church: liturgical changes, liturgy and politics, etc. Each year author, onomastic, subject, and biblical passage indexes are provided but this is not an
easy bibliography to use. Items are not numbered and are embedded
in paragraphical mini-bibliographical essays. For 1983 a list of
about 375 journals consulted was also provided.

0066-6386/1731924   454/686

[81] *Archiv für Orientforschung* ("Assyrologie: Register")

This is not a bibliography but an attempt to list all citations to
Assyrian epigraphs in various ways. The most recent attempt, covering 1980 and published in the volume for 1981/82, listed several
hundred such references alphabetically by subject and cuneiform
sign and numerically by modern text designation. Over 500 journals
and collective works were listed.

0066-6440/5758156   82

[82] *Archiv fur Orientforschung* ("Bibliographie")

This along with [584] constitute the major bibliographical resources
for Ancient Near East studies. Materials are classified into:
Mosopotamia; Ancient South Arabia; Iran; Asia Minor; Egypt; Palestine and Syria; Old Testament and Qumran; and General, but not all

are included in each annual volume of *AfO*. For instance, the
latest volume, a double number covering 1981 and 1982, included 550
to 600 for Mesopotamia, roughly the same for Asia Minor, about 45
for Ancient South Arabia, and over 1000 for Egypt and there was no
consistent arrangement among these. Mesopotamia and South Arabia
were arranged by author and the other two were subdivided topically.
There was an author index for Egypt but not for Asia Minor and a
list of journals convassed for Asia Minor but not for the other
three. Despite these peculiarities this is an important bibliography, and users must wish that it could organize itself more systematically.

0066-6440/5758156   22/81/225/584/595

[83] *Archiv für Papyrusforschung und verwandte Gebiete* ("Literarische
Texte unter Ausschluss der Christlichen")

This chronicle of periodical literature on pre-Christian papyrus
texts appears in every almost-annual volume (3 in the past 4 years).
The arrangement is chronological by ancient author and items are
annotated in German. Each issue is dedicated to a specific genre,
e.g., historiography, drama, or poetry. In the 1983 volume were
60 to 70 items in historiography. There are no indexes.

0066-6459/1482000   15/309/310

[84] *Archiv für Reformationsgeschichte*

Each year a separate bibliographical supplement or *Beiheft* is published. The latest, published in 1984, includes 1191 items in 8
categories, the largest being geographical and devoted to Europe
country by country. Materials relate to European religious, political, economic, and social history in the late fifteenth and sixteenth centuries and are frequently annotated (25 to 250 words) in
German, French, or English. There are no indexes, nor is there a
list of journals canvassed.

0341-8375/10044933   232/512

[85] *Archivalische Zeitschrift* ("Zeitschriftenberichte")

Prepared by the Bayerische Staatsarchiv and presented in a modified
current contents format in which items are frequently annotated,
this bibliography covers the field of archival issues and is worldwide in scope. About 100 journals are canvassed each year (1980
seems the most recent). There are no indexes.

0003-9497/1730747   75/86

[86] *Der Archivar* ("Bibliographie zum Archivwesen")

Not dissimilar from [85] in content but markedly so in arrangement.

Materials from 1979 and 1980 are included in the bibliography appearing in 1984. These are arranged in numerous classifications covering various aspects of archival collecting, preservation, utilization, and publicity. Though worldwide in intent, in practice emphasis is on the two Germanies. There are no indexes.

0003-9500/3778607   75/85

[87]   *Archives de Philosophie* ("Bulletin Cartésien")

In 1983/3 were listed some 60 items, mostly published in 1981, dealing with the life, work, and times of René Descartes. Following this list is a bibliographical essay/annotated account of most of the entries. Editions, general studies, studies of Descartes' work and of other relevant work are included. A cumulation of the 1975-80 bibliographies is in progress.

0003-9632/1772219   158/601/602/638/662/675

[88]   *Archives de Philosophie* ("Bulletin de bibliographie Spinoziste")

Prepared by the Association des Amis de Spinoza, this appears in the last issue of each year. That in 1984, which included material largely published in 1983, totalled from 180 to 200 items variously annotated and listed by author in numerous categories. There are no indexes.

0003-9632/1772219   601/602/638/675

[89]   *Archives de sciences sociales des religions* ("Bulletin des périodiques")

This generally appears in the second issue of each year and covers materials published during the preceding year. In 1984 247 items were listed alphabetically by author. The listing is unsystematic and unfocused and it seems impossible to predict what might be included (or excluded). There are no indexes and this must be considered a very minor tool.

0335-5985/1794707

[90]   *Archivo Teológico Granadino* ("Bibliografía")

In 1983 perhaps 200 to 300 items, often extensively annotated, were included. In addition to a "Boletín de Historia de la Teología 1500-1800"(arranged largely by theologian) there were 11 other categories dealing with various aspects of theology, some historical. Emphasis is not surprisingly on Spain and beyond this the "Bibliografía" has little to offer. There are no indexes.

0210-1629/5575038   649

[91]   *Archivum Bibliographicum Carmelitanum* ("Bibliographia Carmeli Ter-
       esiani")

One of two serial bibliographies on the Carmelites (see [242]), the
listing for 1980, published in 1982, included over 1100 items arranged alphabetically by author. There are, however, extensive
cross-references and interspersed subject entries to persons and
places. But no indexes or list of journals.

0570-7242/1739792   242

[92]   *Archivum Franciscanum Historicum* ("Notae Bibliographicae")

The bibliography published in the 1984 *Archivum* totals some 100 to
125 citations arranged by author in two categories ("Franciscana"
and "Varia"). Items are fairly extensively annotated in French,
Spanish, or Italian. There are no indexes.

0004-0665/1513971   142

[93]   *Archivum Historiae Pontificiae* ("Bibliographia Historiae Pontifi-
       ciae")

Prepared under the auspices of the Pontificia Università Gregoriana
in Rome, this is a major tool for the study of ecclesiastical history, particularly of the Papacy. In 1983 there was a total of
3166 items arranged in one general and five chronological classifications, each in turn divided chronologically, geographically, and
topically. Relevant reviews are collected at the end of each of
the major sections. The Papacy is defined broadly and materials on,
e.g., the Byzantine Empire, the Reformation in northern Europe, and
missions are also included. There are author and subject indexes
as well as a list of 650 to 700 journals.

0066-6785/1697126   58/661

[94]   *Archivum Historicum Societatis Iesu* ("Bibliographia de Historia
       Societatis Iesu")

In 1984 this bibliography included over 1000 items arranged in four
categories, the largest dealing with collective and individual biographies of members of the Jesuit order. Occasionally, though not
regularly, some annotation is provided if the title is not sufficiently illustrative. There are author and personal name indexes
but no list of journals.

0037-8887/1513974

[95]   *Argovia* ("Aargauische Bibliographie")

In 1983 there appeared 302 items on the Swiss canton of Aargau,
mostly published in the preceding year. These are arranged into:

Allgemein; Personen; and Orte, Geographische Namen, within each of
which materials are arranged by subject. There are no indexes.

---- ----/1741290   159

[96] *Arizona Quarterly* ("Current Arizona Bibliography")

This bibliography nominally appears twice a year but there was none
in the first three numbers of 1984. Normally, from 40 5o 50 items
on all aspects of Arizona are included arranged by author.

0004-1610/1514101

[97] *Arsbibliografi for dansk maritim historie- og samfundsforskning*

I have not been able to see this bibliography, published by the
Kontaktudvalget for dansk maritim historie- og samfundsforskning,
but the 1983 volume, covering 1982, totalled nearly 60 pages devoted largely to Danish maritime history. It seems then to be both
current and comprehensive.

0107-3109/-------   281/282

[98] *Art and Archaeology Technical Abstracts*

Formerly called *IIC Abstracts*, this is published by the International Institute for the Conservation of Historic and Artistic Works.
It appears twice yearly and includes books, articles, technical
reports, and news items. The two 1984 numbers encompass about
2400 items, annotated (50-150 words) and arranged as follows: General Methods and Techniques; Paper and Archival Materials; Wood;
Fibres and Textiles; Paints and Painting; Glass and Ceramics; Stone
and Masonry; Metals; Photographs and Other Audio-Visual Materials;
Other Natural and Synthetic Organic Materials, most in turn subdivided. Cross-referencing is extensive. This all might easily
be overlooked by historians but there is a great deal on matters
increasingly central to historians' concerns: archeological dating
methods, paleography, for example. Each issue has an author index
and a cumulative subject index appears yearly. In addition there
is a list of 500 to 600 journals with publishing information. The
scope of this alone should surprise and interest historians.

0004-2994/2890414   57/60/61/73/328/612/624/639

[99] *Art Index*

Published quarterly and cumulated annually, this is arranged in the
standard dictionary catalog form--an integrated subject and author
classification, with book reviews listed separately. There is no
discernible emphasis on the historical aspects of art and, while
current, this is not substitute for the most specialized and comprehensive indexes to the history of art and architecture. Some

200 journals are indexed and publication details are provided for these.

0004-3222/1514289   57/100/624/639

[100]   *ARTbibliographies: Modern*

Published twice a year, this index confines itself to art of the nineteenth and twentieth centuries and, even so, manages to include about 8000 items a year. Titles are translated into English and each is briefly annotated. Author and museum/gallery indexes are included, as is a list of journals (about 125 in 1983).

0300-466X/1796113   57/99/624/639

[101]   *Arte Veneta* ("Bibliografia dell'Arte Veneta")

In 1983 about 1500 items were included, divided into: General Works; Architecture generally and by architect; Sculpture generally and by sculptor; Monuments; Painting (which constituted about two-thirds of the total); and Galleries, Museums, and Collections (arranged geographically). There is extensive cross-referencing, but no indexes or list of journals.

0392-5234/1514323   57/65

[102]   *Arts and Humanities Citation Index*

This, along with [724] is one of the first indexes spawned by the electronic age and is capable of arraying information in any number of ways, some of which are relevant here. It it published three times a year and cumulated annually and at longer intervals. It comes in three parts: the Permuterm Subject Index, a paired significant key word index, which cites articles alphabetically under each of the terms and also lists other pairings of the word used as the entry; then there is the Source/Corporate Index, where articles are entered under the name of the author(s); finally there is the Citation Index, designed to tell users who knows them rather that what they need to know. Presently more than 1300 journals in art and architecture; the performing arts; literature; language and linguistics; history; philosophy; and religion and theology are covered by *AHCI* and these are arrayed in various ways in the annual index, including by publisher with details. Materials obviously do not appear here as quickly as in [272] but currency is nonetheless very good. Presently more than 30,000 articles and nearly 50,000 review citations appear each year as well as media information of various kinds.

0162-8445/4122996

[103] Association Internationale pour l'étude de la mosaïque antique.
Bulletin d'Information ("Bibliographie des etudes sur la mosaïque
antique")

Whole numbers of the *Bulletin* are given over to this bibliography.
The latest, published in 1983, covers no fewer than 2050 items
that appeared in 1980 and 1981. Their arrangement is: Bibliographical Works/Collective Works; Festschriften; Colloquia; General
Studies; Thematic Studies; Epigraphic Studies (arranged geographically); Technical Studies; Museums; Expositions; Sales; Countries
(the largest). Many items are annotated, some extensively. There
are author, subject, and geographical indexes and a list of 450 to
500 journals.

---- ----/-------   73/328/354/673

[104] *Ateismo e Dialogo* ("Bulletin bibliographique signalétique")

From 100 to 200 items appear in each quarterly number. These are
divided into: God; Religion and the Sacred; Belief and Unbelief;
Secularization and 'Secularism'; Atheism; Marxism; and Dialogue.
There are no indexes nor a list of journals.

---- ----/5933214   448/469/576

[105] *Augustiniana* ("Bibliographie historique de l'Ordre de Saint-Augus-
tin")

One complete issue every five years is devoted to this bibliography.
The most recent, covering 1975 to 1980, appeared in 1981 and included nearly 1000 items on the history of the Augustinians (for-
mally founded 1256); works on St. Augustine himself are excluded
(see [668]). These are divided into five categories on general
and local history (including monastic houses), biography, and
hagiography. These in turn are subdivided by subject, geography,
or individual Augustinian. There are author/personal name, geographical, and subject indexes but no list of journals.

0004-8003/1697214   668

[106] *Ausgrabungen und Funde* ("Bibliographie zur Ur- und Frühgeschichte")

This usually appears in the sixth (and last) issue of year year.
In 1983 there were 668 items, largely concerned with the archeology
of East Germany and central Europe, which were divided into several
topical, geographic, and chronological classifications. There are
no indexes.

0004-8127/2257965   72/607/758

[107] *Australian Education Index*

Published quarterly and cumulated annually, this is devoted to studies on education in Australia, wherever published. For 1983 more than 3700 items were arranged in 19 categories dealing with various aspects of education and library science. Each issue has author/institution and subject indexes, also cumulated annually. Each year some 175 to 200 journals are canvassed and these are listed in each number (as relevant) and in the annual cumulation.

0004-9026/2071510   111/260

[108] Australian Institute of Aboriginal Studies. *Annual Bibliography*

A separately published and paginated supplement to the Institute's *Newsletter*. That covering 1981/82 and published in 1983 carried 1889 items (books, articles, and pamphlets, theses, and audio-visual materials) listed in a single author arrangement. Subject, onomastic, and geographical (by Australian state) indexes improve access but this still remains difficult. There is also a list of about 300 journals as well as a separate listing of 148 manuscripts.

0004-9344/2445144

[109] *Australian Journal of Historical Archaeology* ("A Bibliography of Historical Archaeology in Australia")

This first appeared in the inaugural volume of 1983, in which about 360 items (including many retrospective ones) were listed. Annual updates are planned; that for 1984 included over 90 items, most published in 1983 or 1984, in an alphabeticaly arrangement by author, and relating to all aspects of historical archeology (including maritime archeology). Books, articles, and unpublished reports are included. There are no indexes or a list of journals.

0810-1868/10154624   358

[110] *Australian Literary Studies* ("Annual Bibliography of Studies in Australian Literature")

That for 1983, published in the May 1984 issue, incorporated more than 500 books, articles, reviews (the largest category) and prefaces largely classified by the authors studied. The listing is not restricted to Australian publications and although the emphasis is largely contemporary, some authors whose works are historically important are also included. There are no indexes.

0004-9697/849640   467

[111] *Australian Public Affairs Information Service*

Published by the National Library of Australia as the Australian

counterpart to [617] and designed to cover scholarly periodical
literature in the humanities and social sciences published in Australia, including some newspapers and government documents. Such
material need not relate to Australia. The main arrangement is
by subject with extensive cross-referencing and thousands of items
are covered each year. *APAIS* is published 11 times a year, with
an author index in each issue, and cumulated annually. More than
200 periodicals are indexed completely and more than 1200 selectively, as well as 100 to 150 collective works and these are listed.

0005-0075/1518859

[112] *Austrian History Yearbook* ("Austrian and German Periodical Literature"/"Austrian and German Books")

Prepared by the Center for Austrian Studies as the University of
Minnesota, the combined 1981/82 volume (published in 1984) contained perhaps 800 to 900 articles published in Germany or Austria
arranged in six general and chronological categories by author.
"American [and Canadian] Publications on Austrian History" is
(for some reason) produced separately and is arranged geographically. Over 300 books published in Austria or Germany are also
listed separately, as are about 300 theses done in Austria on Austrian history since 1520. *En ensemble* the coverage is thorough
but using these bibliographies effectively may require some insights
not available to users. Matters are not helped by the lack of any
indexing.

0067-2378/1518889   3/585

[113] *BC Studies* ("Bibliography of British Columbia")

This appears in every quarterly issue and usually includes from
75 to 100 books, articles, and documents mainly concerning the
history of British Columbia but with a sprinkling of non-historical
material as well. It is extremely current but there are no indexes.

0005-2949/1788002   25/234/235/321

[114] *Balkanike Bibliographia/Bibliographie balkanique*

Materials from 1977 were published in 1981, when 4125 items were
broken down into 8 categories, including history, which was in
turn divided into no fewer than 61 regional and chronological sections. There was an author index as well as a list of more than
200 journals consulted.

---- ----/3315508   153/203/208/677/783

[115] *Baltische Studien* ("Zeitschriftenschau")

About 50 items drawn from East German and Polish journals appear,

in modified current contents form, in each annual issue. These
deal largely with Germany and Poland with some material on the
three ex-Baltic Republics. Scandinavia is not included.

0067-3099/1519098   369/844/854

[116] Baroda. Oriental Institute. *Journal* ("Selected Contents of Oriental Journals")

This appears in every quarterly issue arranged in a modified current contents format by journal title. It is not confined to
Indian journals, but lacks page numbers and includes perhaps the
contents of 30 to 40 journals each time.

---- ----/-------

[117] *Basler Jahrbuch für historische Musikpraxis* ("Schriftenverzeichnis
zum Arbeitsbereich historischer Musikpraxis")

In the 1983 *Jahrbuch* appeared a listing of 647 items divided into
19 categories (the largest dealing with music history and arranged
by composer) published in 1981 and 1982. It covers European music
from the medieval beginnings to *ca*. 1750. There is an author index and a list of 40+ journals consulted.

---- ----/4818899   161/540/625

[118] Bautzen (Germany). Institut für sorbische Volksforschung. *Jahr-
esschrift Lětopis* ("Zeitschriftenbibliographie zur Geschichte der
Sorben und Lausitz")

The most recent, covering 1981, appeared in the 1983/1 number and
included 203 items devoted to the history of the Sorbs (a Slav
minority in East Germany formerly known as the Wends) and the ter-
ritory of Lausitz (Lusatia). These were divided into 3 general
and 5 chronological categories. There were no indexes.

---- ----/-------   119/453/674

[119] Bautzen (Germany). Institut za serbski ludospyt. *Lětopis: rjad
A--rěč a literatura* ("Wuběrkova bibliografija: rěcespyt/Stawizny
literatury")

These separately arranged bibliographies, one devoted to the Sorb
language, the other to Sorbian literature, most recently appeared
in the 1983 volume, where more than 200 items were listed arranged
in several sub-categories. There is a listing of about 25 journals,
but no indexes.

0522-506X/2561854   118/453/674

[120]   *Bayerische Bibliographie*

Produced by the Generaldirektion der bayerischen Staatlichen Bib-
liotheken, this bibliography is much in arrears; the volume for
1974/76 was published in 1981. It included 15,089 items, largely
historical, divided into 11 general categories and a host of smaller ones, covering the period from prehistory to the present and
encompassing books, articles, collective works, and dissertations.
There was a combined subject/personal name/geographical/author
index and a list of some 275 journals which were consulted.

0522-5256/2561721   388/518/596/600/846

[121]   *Béaloideas* ("A Supplementary Bibliography of Irish Ethnology and
Folk Tradition")

Intended to update Caoimhín Ó Danachair's *A Bibliography of Irish
Ethnology and Folk Tradition* (Dublin, 1978), the first bibliography
appeared in the 1980/81 numbers and totalled 302 items in 16 categories and then repeated in a single author list. However, no
listing appeared in either the 1982 or 1983 numbers.

0332-270X/2061331   443/444

[122]   *Beiträge zur Erforschung der deutschen Sprache* ("Literaturhin-
weise")

Each quarterly issue contains a brief listing of books and then
of contents of journals in the field of German languages and linguistics arranged by journal title. Perhaps thirty to fifty journal issues are included each time, virtually entirely from East
Germany and central Europe. There are no indexes.

0232-2714/8434800   157/320/353/437

[123]   *Beiträge zur Konfliktforschung* ("Bibliographie zur Konfliktforschung")

The bibliography for 1982/83 appears in the fourth number of 1983
and consists of about 700 items arranged in: basic work; public
opinion, mass media and propaganda; the powers; and conflicts.
Each of these is further broken down chronologically and/or regionally. Items, which are concentrated on modern European history, are often annotated but there are no indexes.

0045-169X/2045840   21/818

[124]   *Beiträge zur romanischen Philologie* ("Bibliographie zur romanischen
Sprachwissenschaft in der DDR")

A listing of work on Romance philology carried out in the German
Democratic Republic. This is not extensive; only some 400 items

were listed in 1983, divided by Romance language and not including
any indexes.

0005-8181/1208063　　　　　　207/690/769

[125] *Berichte der römisch-germanischen Kommission* ("Archäologie des
Merowingerreiches.　Literaturbericht")

The latest, which appeared in 1980, covers the period from 1976
to 1980.　About 430 items are divided into "Research Themes" (51
extensively annotated items) and archeological sites (381 rather
less extensively annotated items) and these two groupings are
further divided.　There are author, topographical, geographical,
and archeological term indexes.

---- ----/1777487　　　　　　651/666

[126] *Bibliografía Antropológica Argentina*

I have not seen this annual bibliography, begun in 1982 and including anthropological articles published in or about Argentina
or written by Argentine citizens, the latter of dubious value.
An English translation of each title is provided.　*BAA* is published
by Colegio de Graduados en Antropología, Esmeralda 352 1er P.,
(1035) Buenos Aires.

---- ----/-------　　　　　　60/61/62

[127] *Bibliografía Filosofica Italiana*

Prepared by the Centro di Studi Filosofici di Gallarate.　If, as
it seems, the latest of these is that covering 1976 and published
in 1978, it should not be included here.　At any rate, 3251 items
drawn from some 175 journals appeared then, divided into: Encyclo-
pedias and Dictionaries; Bibliographies; Congresses; History of
Philosophy; Philosophy and the Humanities.　The coverage is worldwide but Italy is most thoroughly represented.　There is a combined author/philosopher index.

0409-3372/2810617　　　　　　601/627/638/661

[128] *Bibliografía Folclórica*

The 1984 *Bibliografía*, largely covering 1983 publications, included
225 to 250 items, almost all on Brazilian folkloristics.　These
were grouped by author into ten categories, but without any indexing.

---- ----/3855992　　　　　　439/513

[129]   *Bibliografia Historica Mexicana*

Prepared by the Colegio de Mexico, the 1982 volume included over
2000 items devoted to the history of Mexico from pre-Hispanic
times to the present. These were divided in 32 categories, some
subdivided chronologically or regionally. Occasionally items are
annotated. A list of about 150 journals was included as well as
an author/subject index.

0523-1795/1519744   368/527

[130]   *Bibliografia historii Kościoła w Polsce*

The most recent volume (published in 1982 by the Akademia Teologii
Katolickiej) covers the years 1975/1977. Included are more than
7500 items on the church history of Poland. The major categories
are chronological and diocesan, but other classifications such as
biography, Catholic education, and the Protestant church in Poland
should be of interest. There was a comprehensive author/personal
name index as well as a list of journals canvassed.

---- ----/9759400   131/139/661

[131]   *Bibliografia historii polskiej*

Prepared by the Polska Akademia Nauk, Instytut Historii, the 1984
volume largely included materials published in 1981, a total of
5802 which were divided into reference materials, auxiliary sciences and methodology, and history proper. Each in turn was subdivided into many smaller categories. International in scope,
the history of Poland from prehistory to the present is covered,
but not the Polish experience abroad. There is an author/personal
name/geographical index. Oddly, a list of journals is missing but
this is still the most useful of the host of Polish serial bibliographies devoted to one aspect of history or another.

83 04 01651 6/5915006   139/607/688/766

[132]   *Bibliografia historii śląska*

This is (or was?) published annually. The most recent volume seen
covered 1975 and was published two years later. It included over
2100 items on Silesian history divided in general, chronological,
geographical, and biographical categories, variously subdivided
in turn. There was an author index but no list of journals.

---- ----/2409552   135/452/453/856

[133]   *Bibliografia Missionaria*

Published by the Pontificia Università Urbaniana in Rome, this
annual bibliography, once lagging, is now fairly current, with the

volume covering 1982 published in 1984. This contained 2876 items
in 25 mostly geographical categories. All aspects of mission theory and history and all mission fields of the Roman Catholic church
are included. Coverage of the numerous Catholic missionary organs
could be better but is nonetheless valuable since these are not
picked up by any other bibliography. There are author, personal
name, and subject indexes but no list of journals.

---- ----/4978418   244/435/509/623/858/869

[134] *Bibliografia Republicii Socialiste Romania. Articole din publicatii Periodice şi seriale*

The Rumanian guide to periodical literature, compiled by the Biblioteca Centrala de Stat in Bucuresti, this is a semimonthly listing in all fields, including history. In 1983 a total of 55,870
items were listed, arranged in a host of classifications by Dewey
Decimal system. Each issue contains an author/personal name index and in the last issue of each year is a list of serials canvassed during the year (386 in 1983).

0524-8086/2795005   3/113/153/323/677

[135] *Bibliografia Śląska*

The 1977 bibliography was published only in 1983. In it were
listed over 5400 items covering all aspects of Silesia and arranged in 16 categories, with history being the single largest.
There were author/anonymous work and subject indexes as well as
a list of about 400 journals canvassed.

---- ----/1519751   132/452/453/856

[136] *Bibliografia Storica Nazionale*

Published every two years by the Giunta Centrale per gli Studi
Storici. The most recent volume, which covers 1979 and 1980, was
published in 1982 and included 7502 items in nine general and
chronological categories, the latter subdivided geographically
and topically and covering from prehistory to the present. The
Bibliografia is especially strong on the numerous local history
materials. Not as up-to-date and complete as [150] but inarguably
the principal source for recent materials on Italian history.
There is an author/personal name index and, in the latest number,
a list of more than 400 journals canvassed.

0085-2317/1519754   570/590/604/628/682

[137] *Bibliografía Teológica Comentada del Área Iberoamericana*

Compiled by the Instituto Superior Evangelico de Estudios Teológicos de la Asociación Interconfessional de Estudios Teológicos in

Buenos Aires. The volume for 1981 was published in 1984. It encompassed more than 6600 items arranged in more than 75 categories,
many of which were further subdivided, covering all aspects of
theological and Biblical studies, and church history. All materials published in or about Latin America are included, which means
that the second represents a fairly complete conspectus of its
field while the first represents but a small portion of its field.
Subject/geographical, Biblical, and author indexes are included,
as well as a list of about 400 journals and one of abbreviations
of institutions and organizations.

---- ----/8039908   308/313/466/760/792

[138] *Bibliografia wojewódzlw: krośnieńskiego, przemsyskiego, rzeszow-
skiego i tarnobrzeskiego*

This covers the voivodships of Krosno, Przemysl, Rseszów, and
Tarnobrzeg, which constitute the province of Rzeszów in extreme
southeastern Poland. Apparently the most recent is that covering
June 1975 to December 1976, which was published in 1981. This
comprised about 5600 entries arranged in 16 categories, most subdivided in turn, and covering all fields of knowledge. There were
subject and author indexes as well as a list of about 225 journals
which were canvassed.

---- ----/-------   131/139/661

[139] *Bibliografia Zawartości Czasopism*

Prepared by the Biblioteka Narodowa of the Instytut Bibliograficzny,
this monthly publication lists about 70,000 items published each
year in Poland. All fields are covered and divided in 26 categories. Many of these items eventually reach one of the many specialized Polish subject bibliographies but are likely to appear
here first. There are author, compositor, illustrator, and subject indexes as well as a list of about 50 journals canvassed.

0006-1093/1519756   131/661

[140] *Bibliografie van de literaire Tijdschriften in Vlaanderen en Nederland*

Prepared under the aegis of the Nederlands Letterkundig Museum en
Documentatiecentrum in Antwerp, this is organized in a modified
current contents format listed alphabetically by journal. Coverage is confined largely to belletristic literature in Flemish and
Dutch but occasionally more directly historical materials wander
in. Coverage is extensive but uncountable. There are author,
pseudonym, authors studied, and key word indexes.

---- ----/2802815   141

[141] *Bibliografie van de nederlandse Taal- en Literatuurwetenschap*

Compiled by the Werkgroep voor de Documentatie der Nederlandse
Letteren. The volume covering 1982 (published in 1984) included
5254 items on Dutch and Flemish literature and linguistics gathered from more than 1000 listed journals. These are arranged in
a very complex classification scheme which is outlined at the end.
Roughly speaking, though, about one-quarter of the materials are
devoted to linguistics, the balance to literature. In addition a
supplement includes over 200 items dealing with Frisian language
and literature. Both the main body and the supplement are served
by author and keyword indexes.

0045-186X/2824377   140

[142] *Bibliographia Franciscana*

This appears as a supplement to *Collectanea Franciscana;* the
latest, the fourteenth in the series, covers the years 1974 to
1980 and has appeared so far in three parts since 1982, totalling
almost 8700 items. Of the 8 categories covered to date, much the
largest lists works by or on individual Franciscan authors since
the thirteenth century. No indexes accompany the separate parts.

0010-0749/1771258   92

[143] *Bibliographia Historiae Rerum Rusticarum Internationalis*

Published by the Magyar Mezogazdasagi Muzeum in Budapest, the
Bibliographia attempts to incorporate all materials relating to
rural and agricultural history and related fields, and does so
more fully than any other bibliography. Unfortunately, publication is behind (and may even have ceased); materials for 1975 and
1976 were covered in the volume published in 1979. This included
a total of 5790 items in 10 major and numerous minor categories,
including economic and social history, history of agrotechnics,
prices and wages, agrarian ethnography, and agricultural settle-
ments. A list (obviously incomplete) of 90 to 100 journals is
included and there are geographical and author indexes.

---- ----/2063733   10/348/706

[144] *Bibliographia Internationalis Spiritualitatis*

Prepared by the Pontifical Institute of Spirituality in Rome,
the 1980 bibliography (published in 1983) included over 8800 items
on all aspects of (Catholic) spirituality, broadly defined to include almost any aspect of theology. These were divided into 8
categories (all further subdivided) of which those dealing with
spiritual doctrines, the spiritual life, and the history of spirituality (the largest category) are the most extensive. There are
author/personal name and subject indexes as well as a list of
about 360 journals canvassed. All in all, a major tool insofar

as it encompasses many disparate fields usually considered separately.

0084-7836/6529509   127/601/627/638/661

[145] *Bibliographia Patristica*

BP focuses on the history of the early Christian church (to 787 in the east, 667 in the West) and the volume for 1979 (published 1984) includes nearly 2800 items in the following major categories (each subdivided): Generalia; New Testament and Apocrypha; Authors (two-thirds of the total); Liturgy; Canon Law; History of Dogma; Gnosticism; Patristic Exegesis of the Old and New Testaments. There is also an extensive list of book reviews, an author index, and a list of more than 1500 journals.

0523-2252/1532685   553/670/698/848

[146] *Bibliographia Uralica*

Published by the Eesti NSV Teaduste Akadeemia Keele taja Kirjanduse Instituut in Tallinn, this bibliography is devoted to linguistic literature on the various Uralic languages. In the 1979 volume (published in 1981) more than 1000 items were included divided in 30 major categories (usually specific languages). There are separate author and title indexes for Cyrillic and western languages and a list of journals consulted.

---- ----/3658207   305/513

[147] *Bibliographical Bulletin of the Greek Language/Deltio Vivliographias tes Hellenikes glosses*

This was compiled by the Department of Linguistics of the University of Athens and (it appears) the most recent covered 1976/76 and it may no longer be published. At any rate that volume listed nearly 1000 items, usually briefly annotated, covering the Greek language from Linear A to the present and arranged in over 20 categories. In addition there was an author index and a list of about 200 journals.

---- ----/3405695   39/513/536

[148] *Bibliographie Alsacienne*

Published by the Bibliothèque Nationale et Universitaire de Strasbourg, this is a surprisingly extensive compilation. The volume for 1979/80 (published in 1982) included 6951 items arranged into numerous categories and covering all fields of knowledge, among the largest of which is history. These are accessed by a combined author/personal and place name/subject index.

---- ----/6857628   34/656

[149] *Bibliographie analytique de l'Afrique antique*

After several previous incarnations as parts of journals, the *Bibliographie* is now published separately. Materials are organized in bibliographical essays under seven classifications covering North Africa west of Egypt from prehistory through the Byzantine period. The volume covering 1978/79 was published in 1983 and included several hundred items, an author index, and a list of only 12 journals.

2 7283 0066 6/10903509   39/503

[150] *Bibliographie annuelle de l'histoire de France*

Prepared by the Institut d'Histoire Moderne et Contemporaine of the Centre National de la Recherche Scientifique, this is probably on balance the best of any national historical bibliography. The volume for 1983 (published promptly in 1984) includes 11,571 items on the history of France from the fifth century to the present divided into: Manuels généraux et sciences auxiliaires; Histoire politique; Histoire des institutions; Histoire économique et sociale; Histoire réligieuse; Histoire de la France d'Outre-Mer, Histoire de la civilisation; Histoire locale, with items distributed fairly evenly among all but the sixth and eighth, which are appreciably smaller. Coverage of reference sources is particularly strong. Nearly 2000 journals are canvassed and listed including well over 500 emanating from local history and scientific societies. There is an author index and a very extensive subject index. A *sine qua non* for historians of France and in every respect a model bibliography in terms of currency, access, comprehensiveness, and organization.

0067-6918/1532708

[151] *Bibliographie annuelle des lettres romandes*

Published by the Bibliothèque Nationale Suisse and designed up update earlier compilations on Swiss authors writing in French. Material for 1979 (published in 1982) totalled nearly 1000 items arranged in several categories, but largely alphabetically by author studied. Emphasis is largely contemporary but some historical matter is included as well. There was an author index as well as a list of journals canvassed, both Swiss and foreign.

2 88096 000 2/3248128

[152] *Bibliographia Cartographica*

The volume for 1984 was published in 1985 by the Staatsbibliothek Preussischer, Kulturbesitz für Deutsche Gesellschaft für Kartographie. It totals over 2700 items divided into: bibliographies, general publications, history of cartography, institutions and organizations of cartography, theoretical cartography, cartographic

technology, topographic and landscape cartography, thematic maps
and cartograms, atlases, use and application of maps, reliefs,
and globes. Each of these is in turn subdivided, which is just
as well since there is only an author index. Some 200 journals
which were consulted are listed.

0340-0409/1815334   243/258/401

[153] *Bibliographie d'études balkaniques*

Published by the Centre d'information et de documentation balkaniques, Institut d'études balkaniques Ludmila Jivkova, Sofia.
This is the major historical bibliography devoted to the Balkans
and covers the period from the seventh century to the present.
The volume for 1981 (published in 1983) totals 2207 items in 17
languages arranged in 178 perhaps too disparate topics, some of
which are even further subdivided. In addition,more than 200 reviews are listed separately. Cyrillic titles (a fair proportion
of the whole) are translated into French. There are personal
name indexes for Greek, Cyrillic, and western languages as well
as a geographic index in French. Finally, from 150 to 175 journals are listed.

0523-2376/1532731   114/203/208/677/783

[154] *Bibliographie de l'Afrique sub-saharienne: sciences humaines et*
       sociales

Compiled at the Musée royal de l'Afrique centrale in Tervuren,
this bibliography, once devoted solely to Belgium's former colonial possessions in Africa, has since become broader but the best
coverage still relates to Zaire, Rwanda, and Burundi. The format
is relentlessly fichier and in the 1980 volume (published in 1984),
there were more than 4600 items arranged strictly by author and
arrayed eight to the page, a procedure wasteful of space but perhaps not of preparation. Each fiche includes one or more descriptors. Fortunately there is an extensive subject index as well as
a list of about 350 journals (keyed to the author listing) and
about 125 collective works. Despite its slowness it remains useful for the area of its central focus and for Belgian publications
on Africa generally but otherwise is upstaged by other Africanist
serial bibliographies.

---- ----/2067329   17/18/162/297/426/631

[155] *Bibliographie der Berner Geschichte/Bibliographie de l'histoire*
       bernoise

Prepared by the Burgerbibliothek in Bern. Materials for 1982
were published in 1983, a total of 1311 items in 16 subject categories including biography, local history, church history, literature and fine arts, and folklore. There is a combined author/
subject/geographical index and a list of some 65 journals canvassed.

0250-5673/5034469   159

[156] *Bibliographie der Buch- und Bibliotheksgeschichte*

This is slightly the more current of two extensive serial bibliographies devoted to the history of books, printing, and libraries (see [2]). The volume for 1983 appeared in 1985 and included 4634 items in categories (each subdivided) covering all
aspects of printing history and book production, as well as about
950 reviews. There are author, reviewer, personal name, geographical, and subject indexes as well as a list of from 400 to 450
journals, largely German-language.

0723-3590/9544936   2/833

[157] *Bibliographie der deutschen Sprach- und Literaturwissenschaft*

The field of language and literature is well served by serial bibliographies and this is one of the better ones. The volume for
1983 was published in 1985 by the Schwerprenktbibliothek fur Germanistik, Stadt- und Universitäts in Frankfurt. It encompassed
10,075 items arranged in some 20 categories (largely chronological)
and further subdivided within these, and covering the whole of
the field of German, German-language, and related language literature and linguistics from earliest times to the present. From
650 to 700 journal titles are listed together with the issues of
each that were searched, as were about 120 collected works and 300
collective works. There are personal name and subject indexes.

---- ----/1532717   353/436/437

[158] *Bibliographie der französischen Literaturwissenschaft*

Similar in arrangement and coverage to [157] but dealing with
French and related language materials. The volume for 1983 included 10,020 items arranged in a general and several chronological classifications and a category devoted to French literature
outside France. Each of these is broken down in various ways,
the most common being listings by authors studied in each of the
relevant sections. There are author and subject indexes and a
list of 750 to 800 journals canvassed. Rather anomalously perhaps, this may well be the best single tool for those interested
in current and comprehensive coverage of French language and literature.

0523-2465/2454092   342/343/662

[159] *Bibliographie der Schweizergeschichte*

Prepared by the Schweizerischen Landesbibliothek, Bern, the volume
for 1981 (published 1983) included 2228 items divided in numerous
topical categories and covering all aspects of Swiss history from
the earliest times to the present. The editorial apparatus is
presented in both German and French. Coverage is extensive and
drawn from some 650 Swiss and 550 foreign journals. There is a

combined author/personal name index.

---- ----/1532724

[160] *Bibliographie der Wirtschaftswissenschaften*

Prepared by the library of the Institut für Weltwirtschaft, Universität Kiel. Appearing twice yearly, the perhaps 9000 to 10000 items in each issue are arranged in 18 categories ranging from economic history and economic theory to demography to economic matters generally, and each of these is further divided in an elaborate scheme which is outlined at the beginning of each volume, serving as a table of contents but without page numbers. There are subject and geographical indexes in both German and English as well as author and anonymous title indexes. A listing of about 1000 journals completes the ensemble.

0340-6121/1532728   172/498/571

[161] *Bibliographie des Musikschrifttums*

Compiled by the Staatliche Institut für Musikforschung, Preussischer Kulturbesitz, Berlin. The latest appears to be for 1975, which was published in 1980 and included 6762 items divided into 10 categories, the largest two of which dealt with the history of music and individual composers. There are subject/key word, personal name/author/composer, and title indexes, as well as a list of about 400 journals which were canvassed.

3 7957 1475 3/1532729   117/540/625

[162] *Bibliographie des travaux en langue française sur l'Afrique au sud de Sahara (sciences sociales et humaines)*

Compiled by the Centre d'études africaines of the Ecole des hautes études en sciences sociales, Paris. The volume for 1981 was published in 1983 and included more than 2600 items in French which were arranged into 19 general and geographical categories. Coverage is naturally best for those areas once under French colonial rule but the *Bibliographie* is also useful for the limited circulation materials and monthly publications which it tries to include. Nearly 300 journals are listed together with the issue(s) canvassed, as are about 45 collective works. Finally, there are author and subject indexes.

0248-6202/5627832   17/18/154/297/426/631

[163] *Bibliographie en langue français d'histoire du droit*

Compiled by the Faculté du Droit et Science Politique de Saint-Maur, Université de Paris Val-de-Marne (Paris XII). The most recent volume is that for 1981 published in 1984 and includ-

ing slightly more than 1750 items arrayed entirely by author or
anonymous title, rendering access rather difficult though this is
to an extent mitigated by a very extensive subject index. About
250 journals are listed. It is debatable how coherent a bibliography premised solely on the language of expression can be.

---- ----/1772081   410/413/724

[164] *Bibliographie géographique internationale*

Produced in the Bulletin Signalétique format by the Centre National de la Recherche Scientique in Paris, *BGI* appears four times a
year and a fifth number cumulates all indexes. For 1983 a total
of 6099 items were listed in: General; History; Physical Geography;
Human Geography; World and Multiregional Geography; Europe; Asia;
Africa; Americas; Oceania; and Polar Regions. Each entry is
briefly (25 to 200 words) annotated largely in French but with a
few in English. Subject, place name, and author indexes are included in each issue and cumulated annually. As well, each issue
includes a list of some 200 to 250 journals with issues canvassed
and these totalled some 550 to 600 titles in the 1983 annual cumulation. In its currency, annotation, and indexing this is a major
bibliographical tool in geography.

0067-6993/3448729   276

[165] *Bibliographie Internationale d'Histoire Militaire*

Prepared by the Service Historique of the Bibliothèque Militaire
Fédérale, Bern. The volume for the years 1978/81 was published
in 1983. It comprised 303 items arranged by author and betrayed
a distinctly eastern European bias. Items are annotated in the
best Swiss tradition--in German *and* French. There are chronological, personal/geographical name, and subject indexes.

0378-7869/6472747   21/530/531/818

[166] *Bibliographie Internationale de Démographie Historique*

Once a part of *Annales de Demographie Historique* but now published
separately by the Société de Demographie Historique and the International Association for the Scientific Study of Population. The
volume for 1984 appeared in 1985 and featured 828 items in 10
thematic categories such as population growth, economics and past
populations, and methodology of historical demography, as well as
the various demographic variables. There are author, subject,
geographical, and chronological indexes. The list of journals
regularly canvassed unfortunately appears only in the 1981 volume.

0255-0849/7047746   380/496/610

[167]   *Bibliographie internationale de l'Humanisme et de la Renaissance*

Sponsored by the Fédération Internationale des Sociétés et Instituts pour l'étude de la Renaissance and supported by 25 national committees. The most comprehensive tool in its field, it suffers (not incidentally) from being slow--the volume for 1980 was published only in 1984. This included 8432 items covering the entire array of European civilization in the fifteenth and sixteenth centuries. The arrangement is roughly similar to [39]. The first part, slightly more than half the total, is arranged by author/work studied whereas the second part is arranged in several categories (history, religion, literature, etc.) and these are in turn subdivided as appropriate. There is an author index and a list of about 1800-2000 journals and some 300 collective works.

0067-7000/1423248   316/397/662

[168]   *Bibliographie Linguistique de l'Année/Linguistic Bibliography for the Year*

The most recent volume of this bibliography, sponsored by the Permanent International Committee of Linguists, covers 1981, was published in 1984, and constitutes the major comprehensive linguistic bibliography. The 15,000+ items were divided into 13 categories, generally language families, with the Indo-European languages comprising about one-half the total and general and comparative linguistic practice and theory another one-quarter, and the rest of the world the balance. Each of these major divisions is subdivided, sometimes extensively and usually by individual language. There ia an author index and a list of more than 1000 journals.

---- ----/3363857   169/223/513

[169]   *Bibliographie Linguistischer Literatur*

Prepared by the Stadt- und Universitätsbibliothek in Frankfurt. Despite its generic title and the fact that the volume for 1983 (published in 1984) contains nearly 17,000 items, the coverage of this tool is much **narrower** than that of [168]. In fact, in addition to general linguistics it concerns only English, Germanic, and Romance languages, the first aggregating nearly one-half the total. The two titles seem then to complement each other well although closer study might suggest greater duplication. At any rate each of these categories is broken down into a very large number of smaller categories and a complete table of contents provides easy access to materials. There are subject/personal name and author indexes as well as a list of over 500 journals and publication details on about 175 collective works.

---- ----/5577138   168/223/513

[170] *Bibliographie Luxembourgeoise*

This is in the nature of a national bibliography except that since
Luxembourg is so small, articles as well as recordings are included in addition to books. In sum then it provides reasonably complete access to materials on Luxembourg which were published there.
1503 of these are divided into 21 categories in the 1983 volume.
These cover all fields of knowledge and those likely most to interest historians are literature, history and local history,
archeology, and geography. There are author/anonymous works/re-
cording artist and subject indexes as well as a list of publishers and printers in Luxembourg. Unfortunately each volume includes only updates of a master list of journals which appeared
in 1958.

---- ----/2066422   376/582

[171] *Bibliographie Pädagogik*

The volume covering 1981 materials appeared in 1984 and listed
nearly 12,500 items in a single author/title alphabet, with each
item being provided with a series of key words which are keyed
to extensive subject, personal name, and geographical indexes.
There are also listings of several hundred institutions and of
about 800 journals canvassed. Coverage is global, but the great
majority of materials deals with the Germanies and Austria. Beginning with the 1982 coverage this bibliography is to appear in
3 parts: series A Periodicals (roughly covering as the above);
series B Books; and series C Educational Research.

0523-2678/2190578   219/277

[172] *Bibliographie zur Geschichte der Arbeiterbewegung* ("Bibliographie
ausgewählter Buch- und Zeitschriftenliteratur zur Arbeiterbewegung")

Issued several times a year by the Bibliothek of the Institut für
Marxismus-Leninismus in Berlin. About 600 items appear each year,
each listing being divided into: Classics of Marxist-Leninism;
Theoretical and International Problems of the Labor Movement; the
History of the SED (the ruling party of the German Democratic Republic) and within these the arrangement is by author. Partial
lists of journals, largely Soviet and East German, appear from
time to time, but there are no indexes.

0005-8068/2103356   173/495

[173] *Bibliographie zur Geschichte der Deutschen Arbeitenbewegung*

Compiled by the Archiv der sozialen Demokratie at the Bibliothek
der Friedrich-Ebert-Stiftung in Bonn. The fiche-like entries
(some 1800 in 1983) are divided in ten mostly chronological categories for the history of the labor movement in Germany from the
mid-nineteenth century. Each entry includes the date to which it

primarily refers; most of these fall within the postwar period.
Each quarterly issue has its own subject and author indexes, which
are comulated annually. There is as well a master list of about
400 journals arranged by country that appears in each issue.

0343-4117/3525143   172/495

[174] *Bibliographie zur kunstgeschichtlichen Literatur in Ost- und Südo-
steuropaischen Zeitschriften*

Compiled by the Zentralinstitut fur Kunstgeschichte in Munich.
The 1983 volume includes 1503 items largely published in 1981.
These are divided in 19 general and geographical categories, in
turn subdivided by art form. As its title suggests, it indexes
materials published in eastern Europe (including the Soviet Union
and the Balkans, and though its scope is worldwide once that
criterion is met, emphasis is naturally on the art of these areas
as well. Titles in eastern European languages are translated into
German. There are author, subject, artist, and geographical indexes and a list of about 160 journals organized by country.

---- ----/2629829   57/99/624/639/705/758/851

[175] *Bibliographie zur Literatur und Literaturwissenschaft der DDR*

Dealing with literary research in the German Democratic Republic,
the volume for 1980/81 (published in 1982) contained nearly 1700
items in nearly 50 categories grouped under three broader categories, the largest an arrangement by author studied. The focus
is largely contemporary and on belleletristic materials but (like
[353]) some works of historical interest are also to be found.
There is an author index.

0070-3931/10993556   353/436/437

[176] *Bibliographie zur Symbolik, Ikonographie und Mythologie*

Published annually, the 1984 volume largely covers materials published in 1982. About 300 of these were arrayed in a single author sequence covering the iconographic and pictorial fields, particularly as they relate to belief. Entries were annotated (20
to 250 words) in various languages, largely German. There were
personal name and subject indexes.

0067-706X/932395

[177] *Bibliography of Asian Studies*

The most important tool for Asian history (defined here as Afghanistan and points east), it suffers somewhat from being about three
years in arrears. The volume for 1981 (published in 1985) included 15,000+ items covering the humanities, social sciences, science

and technology. The arrangement is basically geographical by
country and within these by discipline, sometimes further subdivided. There is an author index but for subject access the detailed table of contents must be used. There is also a list of
about 800 journals and over 200 collective works that were consulted.

0067-7159/4285212   799

[178] *Bibliography of Chinese Studies*

Published by the Institute of Asian Affairs in Hamburg, this ori-
ginally was part of the *Deutsche Fernostbibliographie* but since
1982 has been published separately. The 1982 bibliography, published in 1983) listed about 2500 items on the People's Republic
of China, Taiwan, Hong Kong, and Macau. These were arranged in
9 categories, most in turn subdivided. There were no indexes but
a list of more than 60 journals consulted was included.

0724-8415/10639531   655/718/799/861

[179] *A Bibliography of Irish Archaeology*

The first(?) of these, covering 1980 to 1982, was published by the
Ulster Archaeological Society in 1983. It included 368 items on
all of Ireland from prehistory to modern times. About 70 journals
were canvassed.

---- ----/-------   47/839

[180] *Bibliography of Old Norse-Icelandic Studies*

Prepared by the Royal Library, Copenhagen, the volume for 1979/80
(published only in 1984) contained 666 items devoted largely to
literary, linguistic, and historical aspects of Old Norse and Icelandic. These are arranged by author and extensively cross-referenced and are international in provenance. There is a subject index as well as a list of more than 80 journals consulted.

0067-7213/1532759   192

[181] *Bibliography of South Asian Art*

Sponsored by the American Committee for South Asian Art, the bibliography covering 1981/83 appeared in 1985. It included over 1000
entries for American, European, and Indian books and articles relating to South Asian (including Afghanistan and central Asia) art,
architecture, and painting, as well as related fields such as archeology, religion, and numismatics. These are arranged by author in
seven geographical and topical categories. There is a listing of
the nearly 150 journals canvassed but no indexes.

---- ----/-------   50/405

[182] *Bibliography of the English-Speaking Caribbean*

Published twice a year, this is a useful tool because of its currency and attention to ephemeral publications. In 1983 nearly
1400 items were included; all were in English but were drawn from
around the world . These are divided into more than 20 categories
in each issue with a separate section devoted to reviews of relevant books (about 250). There are author, reviewer, and geographical indexes in each number.

0276-6949/7378859   199/240/241

[183] *Bibliography of the History of Medicine*

Compiled annually by the National Library of Medicine, the several
thousand entries are arranged in three ways. First biographical
items are listed by biographee; then there is a subject arrangement divided into about 300 subject headings, most further subdivided; finally there is an author arrangement, which repeats some
bibliographical details. There is also a separate list of nearly
200 diseases which are indexed, both individually and brought together in the "Diseases and Injuries" category. Items are drawn
from the computerized data base HISTLINE.

0067-7280/1532763   278

[184] *Bibliography of Works in the Philosophy of History*

This is published every five years as a *Beiheft to History and
Theory*. The years 1978 to 1982 were covered in a *Beiheft* to the
1984 volume, which includes over 2100 items on the philosophy of
history and historiographical issues in European languages. These
are arranged by year and then by books and articles within. There
is an author index and a brief subject index.

0018-2656/3458029   394

[185] *A Bibliography on Foreign and Comparative Law*

These are annual "supplements" to cumulative bibliographies published at approximately five-year intervals. That for 1982 (published in 1985) includes over 6200 items in 10 categories, each
further subdivided. Many sections are devoted in part to the history and historical aspects of the several forms of foreign and
comparative law. Regretably, as "supplements" these annual volumes lack indexes of any kind as well as lists of journals canvassed; these appear only in the cumulative editions.

0067-7329/1532766   45/548

[186] *Bibliotheca Celtica*

Prepared by the National Library of Wales. The most recent bibliography appeared in 1981 and covered the years from 1973 to 1976
so currency is not its strong feature. However, it is comprehensive and about 5000 items were included. It once covered the
larger Celtic world but is now confined to Wales. Entries are
classified into about 20 categories, each in turn subdivided.
There is an author/personal name index and a list of 350-400 relevant journals. The next volume is intended to cover the years
1977-80.

0067-7914/2067361   47/191/820

[187] *Bijdragen en Mededelingen betreffende de Geschiedenis der Neder-
landen* ("Kroniek")

Most numbers feature 50 to 75 pages of briefly annotated entries
on Dutch local history, totalling perhaps 150 items each time.
They are arranged topically and chronologically. There are no
indexes.

0165-0505/1532933   13/396/640/797

[188] *Biography* ("A Current Bibliography on Life-Writing")

None has appeared since 1982 when about 50 items were listed dealing with various aspects of the art of biography.

0162-4962/4092559   864

[189] *Biological Abstracts*

This is published twice monthly and organized into about 80 separate categories of which a few (evolution, public health, physical anthropology and ethnobiology) may be of interest to historians. Some 360,000 abstracts of (75 to 300 words) were included
in 1984, drawn from more than 9500 journals, a list of which is
compiled each year. Each issue has author and keyword-in-context
indexes, which are cumulated annually. The latter is densely and
almost unintelligibly arrayed but access is enhanced by the organization into the 80 discrete units mentioned above.

0006-3169/1536423

[190] *Blätter für deutsche Landesgeschichte* ("Landesgeschichtliche Zeitschriftenschau")

This appears once each year, covering material from the previous
year and into the current year. It is arranged in a modified current contents format, with journals being indexed selectively and
grouped geographically (and without regard to title) by journals

published in Germany, Austria, and elsewhere. The number of articles covered probably runs to more than 700 each year but since
there are no indexes, easy access is impossible but this bibliography is valuable because it is comprehensive and current. It may
be worth noting that the *Blätter* often features other more or less
specialized and non-recurring bibliographies.

0006-4408/11490109   457

[191] Board of Celtic Studies. *Bulletin* ("Llyfryddiaeth Llenyddiaeth
       Gymraeg")

This first appeared in 1982 and included over 1000 items relating
to Welsh literature. Categories are chronological and within by
author. They are annotated but in Cymry. There are personal name/
anonymous title and subject indexes. Given the slowness of [186]
this is a welcome addition.

0142-3363/1775132   47/186/820

[192] *Bokmenntaskrá Skírnis. Skrif um Íslenskar Bókmenntir Síðari Tíma*

Published as a supplement to *Skírnir*, this covers Icelandic literature, largely the work of living authors but extending back occasionally as far as the sixteenth century. The bibliography for
1983 included perhaps 1200 to 1500 entries as well as a list of
over 150 journals in all languages which were canvassed. Materials are arranged into 5 categories of which (as usual) by far the
largest is the alphabetical arrangement by author studied. There
are no indexes.

---- ----/1696982   180

[193] *Borneo Research Bulletin* ("Bibliography")

Prepared by the Borneo Research Council and appearing twice a year,
the most recent bibliography (which appeared in the September 1984
number) had 30 items (the range recently has been from 15 to 30)
arranged by author and devoted largely to the natural sciences but
including whatever historical writings there happen to be.

0006-7806/968186   177/324/403

[194] *Brabantse Bibliografie*

The bibliography for 1981 was published in 1982. Arranged according to the Universal Decimal Classification and covering all
fields of knowledge as they relate to North (Dutch) Brabant. Over
1200 items were listed in this way. In addition there are author,
geographical, personal, and key word indexes as well as lists of
some 60 local and about 100 other journals.

---- ----/10573604   654/676

[195] *Brandenburgische Literatur*

The volume covering 1980 was published in 1984 by the Wissenschaft-
liche Allgemeinbibliothek des Bezirkes Potsdam. It comprised nearly 1600 items divided into 11 categories covering all aspects of
the Brandenburg, with history *per se* comprising about one-third of
the total. There are author and subject indexes and a list of
nearly 200 journals (included as part of the main numerical sequence).

0232-6639/11487024   453/523/853

[196] *Braunschweigisches Jahrbuch* ("Bibliographie zur braunschweigischen
Landesgeschichte")

Recently this has run to about 500 items on the Brunswick area of
Germany each year divided into some 10 chronological and topical
classifications, with the largest devoted to local history and arranged alphabetically by place name. There are no indexes nor a
list of journals consulted.

0068-0745/3109122   550/556/557

[197] *Brigham Young University Studies* ("Mormon Bibliography")

For 1981 (published in 1982) there were 367 items arranged by:
Arts and Literature; Contemporary; Biographical and Family History;
Inspirational; History; Doctrinal; Bibliographical; Indexes. There
were no indexes or list of journals. The coverage is broad, including Mormon missionary efforts in Oceania and elsewhere.

0007-0106/7656568   293

[198] *British Archaeological Abstracts*

Compiled by the Council for British Archaeology, this appears
twice a year. For 1984 (covering July 1983 through June 1984)
there were 1944 items drawn from over 250 journals, both British
and non-British as well as perhaps 100 collective works. There is
also a list of unanalyzed publications. Materials are organized
chronologically and topically within and a grid provided as a table
of contents ensures easy access. *BAA* now incorporates part of
Archaeological Bibliography of Great Britain, which ceased in 1980;
perhaps as a result, it no longer lives up to its title since only
a very few entries are now provided with any annotation. This,
though, is less important than its excellent currency.

0007-0270/1537129   63/71/296

[199] *British Bulletin of Publications on Latin America, the Caribbean,
Portugal and Spain*

Compiled by the Hispanic and Luso-Brazilian Council in London and based on its acquisitions. It appears in April and October of each year and consists of about 30 pages arranged by country, with brief annotations provided for the books included. It is obviously very selective but useful for newspapers, magazines, and similar publications.

0007-036X/1537142   182/211/240/241/262/368

[200] *British Education Index*

Compiled by the Bibliographic Services Division of the British Library, this appears quarterly and is restricted to English-language materials published in the British Isles. Perhaps 5000 to 6000 items are included each year. These are arranged in a subject and in an author arrangement, each incorporating bibliographical details so that complete access is possible by two different routes. For 1984 more than 300 journals were canvassed and listed. Educational history is a minor but not insignificant component of coverage.

0007-0637/1537230   171/219/260/277/724

[201] *British Humanities Index*

A general index not likely to be of surpassing value to historians but useful for materials outside the generally recognized historical mainstream. This appears quarterly and is arranged by subject with an author index only in the cumulated annual volume. Some 350 to 400 popular and scholarly journals are regularly canvassed.

0007-0815/1537252

[202] *British Journal of Industrial Relations* ("A Bibliography of British Industrial Relations")

The bibliography for 1982 appeared in 1984, consisting of nearly 1100 items. The focus is largely contemporary but relevant historical materials are not excluded. The bibliography is divided into: General; Employes--Industrial Attitude and Behaviour; Employee Organisation (the most historical category); Employers and Their Organisation; Labour-Management Relations; the Labour Force, Labour Markets and Conditions of Employment (over one-half the total); the State and its Agencies. Materials are arranged in different ways among the categories but there are no indexes.

0007-1080/1782012   423

[203] *Bulgarian Historical Review* ("La littérature historique bulgare")

This appears in alternating quarterly numbers, covering the previous six months. Ordinarily from 200 to 250 items are included, largely on the history of Bulgaria, with titles translated into

French.   There are no indexes.

0324-0207/1794570

[204] *Bulgarian Historical Review* ("Publications parues à l'étranger sur l'histoire de la Bulgarie")

This alternates with [203] and encompasses materials on Bulgarian history published outside the country.   Typically from 150 to 250 items are included each time divided into 8 categories.   There are no indexes.

0324-0207/1794570   114/153/203/674

[205] *Bulgarski Ezik* ("Bibliografiia na Bulgarskata ezikovedska litera-tura")

This listing of materials on literature and linguistics (largely Bulgarian; nearly all South Slav) for the first half of 1982 ap-peared in the 1982/6 number and included 988 items divided in 9 categories, most subdivided.   There was an author index but no list of journals.

0005-4283/1537686   508/513/551

[206] *Bulgarski Folklor* ("Bulgarska folkloristicna literatura")

The bibliography for 1979 included from 150 to 175 items on Bul-garian folklore divided into several categories, most importantly theory and method; history of folkloristics; folk narratives; folk music; and ethnic arts and crafts, as well as a separate listing of reviews.   There were no indexes but a brief listing of journals and collective works consulted was included.

---- ----/2859757   205/513

[207] *Bulletin Analytique d'Histoire Romaine*

Published by the Groupe de Recherche d'Histoire Romaine of the Université des Sciences Humaines de Strasbourg, the lateness of this tool (the two volumes covering 1973/74 were published in 1982 and 1984) might well merit its exclusion.   However, the fact that its nearly 5000 entries are accompanied by abstracts and the breadth and comprehensiveness of its coverage render this valuable without being current.   Entries are arranged into: sources (two-thirds of the total and largely archeological rather than textual); general history; and regional history.   Each of these is in turn subdivided many times.   There is an author/personal name/geographical index and a list of more than 1500 journals canvassed.   Roman history and that of the Empire and neighboring areas is covered from the beginnings of the city or the beginnings of the association with Rome until the end of the western empire.

0525-1044/2728544   39/73

[208] *Bulletin analytique de bibliographie hellénique*

Published by the Institut Français d'Athènes, the *Bulletin* suffers
from its tardiness; the volume covering 1973 was published only in
1980. However, it retains importance since it surveys a field not
otherwise given much attention by serial bibliographies. For 1973
over 2600 items were included into five broad classifications (Literature; Sciences; Humanities; Scholarly Books; Translations) with
the first three being further subdivided. Annotations of 50 to
100 words were provided in most instances. This was followed by a
modified current contents analysis of more than 500 journals arranged by discipline. There were author indexes for each of the
two major sections but no subject access other than that provided
by the arrangement itself.

---- ----/1537688   3/39/114/153/323

[209] *Bulletin analytique de documentation politique, économique, et
sociologie contemporaine*

Compiled by the Fondation National des Sciences Politiques in Paris,
this appears monthly and totals 5500 to 6000 citations each year.
Items are grouped alphabetically by country with a further division
for international and comparative studies and are briefly annotated
in French. Each year a separate list of journals (2517 in 1983)
is issued as well as a skeletal and largely useless subject index.
Despite its title, quite of bit of historical material finds its
way into the listings in *Bulletin analytique*.

0007-4071/1337034

[210] *Bulletin analytique de linguistique française*

Compiled by the Institut national de la langue française in Nancy
and published six times a year, this deals largely with the purely
linguistic aspects of the French language but with some attention
to its historical development. Recently, from 2500 to 3000 entries
are included each year arranged in 20 categories, most further subdivided. There are author and subject indexes as well as a list
of about 150 journals in each issue.

0007-408X/943730   168/169/223/513

[211] *Bulletin Bibliographique Amérique Latine*

Compiled by GRECO 26 of the Centre National de la Recherche Scientifique on the order of the various *Bulletin Signalétiques* but
much smaller. The 1984 volume, covering 1983, included 554 items
in 13 categories, with a welcome emphasis on theses, reports, and
other limited distribution materials. About 85% of the materials
are in French and most are briefly annotated. There are subject,
geographical, and author indexes and a list of about 75 journals,
nearly all of them published in France. A supplement to the

Bulletin called *Bibliographie des Publications Françaises sur l'Amerique Latine* is drawn from the Fichier FRANCIS, a data base of 900,000 entries from which all the *Bulletin Signalétique* entries are taken. In fiche format, this draws together several hundred items on Latin America which have already appeared in one of the *BS*s. History is poorly represented.

0292-8515/8527555   230/262/368/378/865

[212] *Bulletin d'Arabe Chrétien* ("Publications récentes")

In 1984 only about 50 items were included for materials relating to the Christian Arabs of the world. These were annotated and listed by author, without any indexes.

---- ----/2962969   218

[213] *Bulletin de Théologie Ancienne et Médiévale*

Published as a supplement to the journal *Recherches de théologie ancienne et médiévale*. The volumes for 1981 and 1982 each included about 400 variously annotated items (some of which attained review length), mostly in French, a few in English. These are organized in a roughly chronological fashion from the early Christian Fathers to the fifteenth/sixteenth centuries and, it appears, randomly within these. There is an author index in each number, not enough to provide easy access.

---- ----/4865666   90/313/675/795/858

[214] *Bulletin des études portugaises et brésiliennes* ("Revue des revues")

Prepared by the Institut Français de Lisbonne. In the 1981/82 volume (published in 1983) were listed by journal title the contents of 300 to 400 journals, mostly published in Portugal and Brazil and all dealing with these one or another aspects of these two cultures, including their history. Most items are briefly annotated in Portuguese or French. Journals are arranged alphabetically by title but there are no indexes.

0379-4954/3657263   199/421/611/646

[215] *Bulletin of Hispanic Studies* ("Review of Reviews")

Selected contents of journal issues appear in each quarterly issue, totalling about 400 a year. These are organized on the modified current contents approach and deal largely with Spanish literature from the fifteenth century on. Oddly, page numbers are not included, preventing the user from determining at least one important aspect of a citation.

0007-490X/1198524   31/213/246/513/573

[216]   *Bulletin of Medieval Canon Law* ("Select Bibliography")

Prepared by the Canon Law Society of Great Britain and Ireland, the most recent bibliography appeared in 1982 and included 250 to 350 entries, sometimes briefly annotated, devoted to the development of canon law during the Middle Ages. These are arranged into 16 classifications and there is an author index.

0146-2989/1537764   79/238/669

[217]   *Bulletin of the Comediantes* ("Bibliography of Publications on the *Comedia*")

The bibliography for 1983 and 1984 (appearing in the Winter 1984 number) included nearly 900 items on Spanish (and Portuguese) Golden Age drama, particularly the genres known as comedia de capa y espada and comedia de ruido. Except for a miscellaneous category, these were listed alphabetically by playwright, with works on Calderón totalling nearly one-third of the whole. There were no indexes nor any list of journals canvassed.

---- ----/3665651   215/531

[218]   *Bulletin on Islam and Christian-Muslim Relations in Africa* ("Abstracts")

Published quarterly by the Centre for the Study of Islam and Christian-Muslim Relations in Africa, Selly Oak Colleges, Birmingham, U.K. Each issue includes from 75 to 100 abstracts arranged by African country and running to 25 to 100 words each. These are largely from denominational publications and might relate to past or present relations between the two religions. There are no indexes but there is a list of about 125 journals, with publication details, itself very useful, given the nature of many of them.

0264-1356/10246270   212

[219]   *Bulletin Signalétique 520: sciences de l'éducation*

Like all *BS*s, published by the Centre National de la Recherche Scientifique, Paris. For 1984 there are over 5000 entries, most of them quite current. These are arranged in nearly 20 topical categories, including history and philosophy of education and others of historical interest, and are briefly annotated. Each issue has an author index and subject indexes in both French and English. Each year a supplementary key word index is issued designed to facilitate computer searching. Indexes are cumulated annually along with a list of 250 to 300 journals canvassed.

0223-341X/4212845   171/724

[220] *Bulletin Signalétique 521: Sociologie-Ethnologie*

Published quarterly by the Centre de Documentation de Sciences
Humaines of the Centre National de la Recherche Scientifique,
Paris. In 1984 there are over 4000 entries for both sociology and
ethnology (which are listed separately). The first is divided in
16 sections, some subdivided, and the second into 8 sections, each
subdivided. Each issue includes a list of journals (about 900)
and author and subject indexes, all cumulated annually.

0007-5566/4477964   209/432

[221] *Bulletin Signalétique 522: Histoire des Sciences et des Techniques*

Prepared by the Centre de Documentation Sciences Humaines of the
Centre National de la Recherche Scientifique, Paris. In 1984
there were over 3200 entries divided into general; mathematical
sciences and techniques; physical sciences; technology; earth sciences; and natural sciences (including medicine) and each of these
is subdivided in various ways. Most items are very briefly annotated and there are subject indexes in French and English and an
author index in each quarterly issue and these are cumulated into
a supplementary number annually. Various numbers of about 400
journals are canvassed each year; these too are listed in each
issue and cumulated annually.

0007-5574/1569995   446/706/789

[222] *Bulletin Signalétique 523: Histoire et Sciences de la Litterature*

Published quarterly by the Centre de Documentation Sciences Humaines of the Centre National de la Recherche Scientique, Paris.
Over 6500 briefly annotated citations are included in the 1984
volume, drawn from over 500 journals. These are classified in a
host of categories under three general rubrics: generalities; sciences of literature; and history of literature. Each item is
briefly annotated. There are subject, author, and author studied
indexes and a list of journal numbers consulted. Each of these
is cumulated annually. Emphasis is very much on European literature, almost to the exclusion of all others. Asiatic literatures
are not included at all.

0007-5582/1569996   513

[223] *Bulletin Signalétique 524: Sciences du Langage*

Published quarterly by the Centre de Documentation Sciences Humaines of the Centre National de la Recherche Scientifique, Paris.
In 1984 more than 3000 items were listed (a substantial decrease
from previous years). These are divided into 19 classifications,
including sociolinguistics and ethnolinguistics; classification
of languages; and historical linguistics. Many entries are very
briefly annotated. Each number features author, subject, and

language indexes and a list of journals consulted (various issues
of more than 300 titles each year) and these are all cumulated
annually. Unlike most of the *BSs*, *BS 524* does not stand up well
to its competition either in coverage or in organization.

0007-5590/1569997   168/169/513

[224] *Bulletin Signalétique 525: Préhistoire et Protohistoire*

Issued quarterly by the Centre de Documentation Sciences Humaines
of the Centre National de la Recherche Scientifique. In 1984
there were about 3700 entries, most of them briefly annotated.
The arrangement is largely geographical, with separate general
and methodological sections. Europe is most thoroughly covered
but relatively meager attention is paid to Classical Antiquity,
which does not fall within its definition of protohistory and
which in any event is very well covered by [73] and [207]. Culture, site, subject, and author indexes which appear in each issue
are cumulated annually, as is the list of nearly 400 journals canvassed.

0181-1894/2721717   73/328/352

[225] *Bulletin Signalétique 526: Art et Archéologie--Proche Orient, Asie,
Amérique*

Published quarterly by the Centre de Documentation Sciences Humaines of the Centre National de la Recherche Scientifique, Paris.
About 2000 annotated entries were included in 1984 devoted to material relating to the Ancient Near East; the Islamic World; south,
central, southeast, and east Asia; and the New World. Typically,
about one-third of the total relates to ancient Egypt, and almost
nothing to the New World, making this a useful substitute for
[55], which are several years behind. The annotations are generally somewhat more extensive than in other *BSs*, sometimes running
to several hundred words. In each number there are author and
subject indexes as well as a list of journals consulted (about
250 titles a year) and each is cumulated in a special annual supplement.

0007-5612/2721739

[226] *Bulletin Signalétique 527: Histoire et Sciences des Religions*

Published quarterly by the Centre de Documentation Sciences Humaines of the Centre National de la Recherche Scientifique, this
is the most extensive of the various *BSs* and related bibliographies, running to about 9000 entries in 1984. The arrangement is
largely by religion, with both doctrinal and historical aspects
covered. Although all the world religions as well as the minor
religions are covered, this is essentially an index to writings
on Christianity, to which fully 80% of the entries refer. Judaism
and Islam merit only about 5% each, the balance devoted to the

rest of the religious universe. Entries are briefly annotated.
There are separate indexes to each of the major religions and three
smaller ones devoted to the religions of the rest of the world.
These and the list of serials canvassed (over 1000 each year) are
cumulated annually. Despite the emphasis on Christianity, this
BS is probably less important than some other tools in the well-
populated field of religious serial bibliographies.

0180-9296/5301340   102/623/635/636/707

[227]   *Bulletin Signalétique 528: Bibliographie Internationale de Science
Administrative*

Published quarterly by the Centre de Documentation Sciences Humaines of the Centre National de la Recherche Scientifique, Paris.
Over 3600 items are listed in 1984 which are classified into: administrative science; history; methods of administrative science;
administrative structures (the largest); the civil service; administrative modes of action; administrative control; public enter-
prises. Each of these is further subdivided, sometimes quite extensively. There is probably little here to engage the historian's
attention, although each section includes some historical and regional items of possible interest. There is a subject index in
Franch, a key word index in English, and an author index. Each is
cumulated annually as is the list of journal titles canvassed (over
350 a year).

0150-8695/5067580   298/616/617

[228]   *Byzantinische Zeitschrift* ("Bibliographische Notizen und Mitteilungen")

This, the major tool devoted entirely to matters Byzantine (from
325 to 1453), appears once a year. In 1984 from 3000 to 3500 items
were included, some annotated. These are divided into eleven classifications (each subdivided), with history proper and art history
being the largest and others including theology, geography, and
the various auxiliary historical sciences. Arrangement within each
section is roughly chronological. Arrangement details are important because there is no table of contents, indexes, or list of
journals, unfortunately mitigating its comprehensive coverage.

0007-7704/1537961   39/229/314/434/524

[229]   *Byzantinoslavica* ("Bibliographie")

This appears in each semi-annual number, the latest (1984/1) running to between 900 and 1000 items which are divided into: Byzan-
tinology; Languages; Belle Lettres and Folklore; Historical Sources; History; Auxiliary Historical Sciences; Geography, Ethnography, and Topography; Art and Archeology; Byzantine-Slav Relations;
Cyril and Methodius; Byzantine Relations with Other Countries. An
author index appears in the second number of each year but there
is no list of journals. Many items are annotated in one language

or another. Although focusing on Byzantium in the Balkans, other
areas are included sporadically.

0007-7712/1537962   114/153/228

[230] *CLASE. Citas latinoamericanas en sociología y economía*

Produced by the Centro de Información Científica y Humanistica of
the Universidad Nacional Autónoma de México, this is a Latin American variant of the classic current contents approach. Each quarterly issue has a list of journal arranged in various ways, followed by xerographic table of contents pages of various Latin American journals, and concluded by key word, author, and citation indexes. Both "sociology" and "economics" are defined broadly.

0185-0903/4972598   211/262/378/776

[231] *Cahiers de Civilisation Médiévale* ("Bibliographie")

The "Bibliographie" is published as an annual supplemental issue
to *CCM*. The 1984 number included 2739 citations arranged alphabetically by subject with extensive corss references and a separate
section of reviews to items from previous bibliographies. Europe
and Islamic North Africa from the tenth through the twelfth centuries (and occasionally beyond) are covered. Materials are drawn
from about 700 journals and over 100 collective works but only a
partial list of the former is provided. There is an author index.

0007-9731/1538035   434/524

[232] *Calvin Theological Journal* ("Calvin Bibliography")

This appears once a year and in 1984 totalled 350 to 400 citations
arranged into: Bibliographies; Calvin's works; Calvin's life and
work; Calvin's theology; Calvin's aesthetics; Calvin's social,
ethical, and political views; Calvin's influence; Calvinism. Most
are further subdivided. Although the emphasis is clearly on Calvin himself, materials relating to Geneva or the Reformation more
generally are also included. There are no indexes.

0008-1795/1774859   84/159/512/862

[233] *Campania Sacra* ("Bibliografia")

Compiled by the Pontificia Facoltà Teologica dell'Italia Meridi-
onale in Naples. 117 items on the ecclesiastical and theological
history of Campania (the area of which Naples is the chief city)
for 1977/78 were published in the 1980 volume. These were briefly
annotated and were arranged largely by the various geographical
regions of Campania. There are no indexes.

---- ----/5078380   570/682

[234] *Canadian Ethnic Studies* ("Bibliography")

Prepared by the Research Unit for Canadian Ethnic Studies of the
University of Calgary. That which appeared in the 1983/3 issue
encompassed 300 to 350 items on all the various ethnic groups
(largely immigrant) of Canada except the Inuits (Eskimos), perhaps
because they are covered by [321]. These are arranged by author
in 13 classifications. There are no indexes.

0008-3496/1553089   237/321/630

[235] *Canadian Historical Review* ("Recent Publications Relating to
Canada")

This appears in each quarterly issue, is very up-to-date, and constitutes the major Canadian historical bibliography. About 400
items appear each time and these are arranged in several chronological and geographical categories. Unfortunately, there are no indexes.

0008-3755/1553108   11/25/51/113/657/803

[236] *Canadian Review of Comparative Literature* ("Revue des revues")

This comprises the September issue of each year and is drawn from
about 135 journals, which are listed. The 1984 bibliography totaled 332 items, each annotated (40 to 200 words) and arranged under: histoire et relations littéraires; théorie littéraire et méth-
odes d'études littéraires; and littérature et les autres artes.
Coverage is international, though obviously quite selective. There
are author and subject indexes.

0319-051X/1727228

[237] *Canadian Slavonic Papers* ("Canadian Publications on the Soviet
Union and Eastern Europe")

The December number usually carries material from the preceding
year. The most recent (1984 for 1983) included about 400 in 11
topical classifications, arranged by author, the largest being devoted to Slavs and other eastern Europeans in Canada. There are
no indexes or list of journals.

0008-5006/1553234   3/323

[238] *Canon Law Abstracts*

Published semi-annually, this normally lists 200 to 250 items each
time. These are annotated in English (50 to 300 words) and divided into general and historical topics as well as (and the largest
category) a listing of recent decisions arranged according to the
5 books of canon law. There are no indexes but a list of about

60 journals is included.

0008-5650/1774890   79/216/669

[239] *Caraka: A Newsletter for Javanists* ("Recent Publications")

This newsletter appears once or twice each year, each time contain-
ing 30 to 40 items on Java, sometimes briefly annotated, and in
all languages (most commonly Dutch).

---- ----/-------   177/324/403

[240] *Caribbean Studies* ("Current Bibliography")

This includes materials on Caribbean and circum-Caribbean nations
and when it appears (it has been sporadic recently) may contain
several hundred entries. Not all areas, however, are necessarily
included in each bibliography. Its emphasis is contemporary and
it is particularly good on statistical, official, and ephemeral
materials. About 50 journals, largely published in the Caribbean,
are regularly canvassed. There are no indexes.

0008-6533/844091   182/199/241

[241] *Carindex: Social Sciences*

This has been published semi-annually by the Association of Caribbean University, Research, and Institutional Libraries and is designed to serve as a subject guide to Caribbean periodical literature in the social sciences. Materials are arranged in a host of
subject entries in each number and an author index appears annually.
The September 1980 number is the latest to appear but there are
plans to bring this index up to date and maintain it. In the latest available issue about 90 Caribbean journals, periodicals, and
newspapers were canvassed and listed, with publication details.

0250-7617/4294320   182/199/240

[242] *Carmelus* ("Bibliographia Carmelitana")

The second Carmelite bibliography, this one is compiled by the
Sezione Bibliografica dell'Istituto Carmelitano in Rome and published as a separate issue. That for 1983, published in 1984, included over 1400 items with occasional brief annotations. These
are divided into 14 categories (most subdivided), including history and collective biography, missions, and literature. Many
entries are devoted to St. Teresa de Avila. There is an author/
anonymous work index but no list of journals.

0008-6673/1715907   91

[243]   *Cartographica* ("Recent Cartographic Literature")

70 to 100 items appear in each issue, divided into topical and geographical categories and with an emphasis on European publications. There are no indexes.

0317-7173/6809484   152/258/401

[244]   *Catholic Historical Review* ("Periodical Literature")

Devoted to the history of Catholicism generally, this bibliography appears in each quarterly issue and aggregates to 700 to 800 items annually divided into: general and miscellaneous; ancient; medieval; Reformation and Counter-Reformation; Seventeenth and Eighteenth centuries; Nineteenth and Twentieth centuries; America; Latin America. There are no indexes or any list of journals.

0008-8080/1553555   93/245

[245]   *Catholic Periodical and Literature Index*

Published bi-monthly by the Catholic Library Association, this index canvasses nearly 150 Catholic journals in search of "currently significant subjects" and also includes work by Catholic authors. These entries are arranged in an .integrated author and subject arrangement totalling several thousand annually. In many ways then, this is not a comprehensive bibliography of Roman Catholicism but it does provide several kinds of information: publishing details on the journals it covers; extensive details on Papal encyclicals and addresses; and a very extensive listing of book reviews. The *Index* is cumulated bi-annually.

0008-8285/2065864   93/244

[246]   *Celestinesca* ("Repertorio bibliográfico")

A brief listing of 15 to 25 items appears in most semi-annual numbers. These relate to the sixteenth-century derived form of Spanish novel known as the *Celestina*.

0147-3085/3136935   215/217

[247]   Centre d'etudes himalayennes. *Liste des documents acquis en 19--*.

The Centre is a component of the Centre National de la Recherche Scientifique in Paris, and while this is nominally an acquisitions list, it is extensive enough to be reasonably considered as an annual bibliography of its subject. It covers the Himalayan countries, with particularly heavy emphasis on Nepal. In 1984 about 1150 items were included: 1000 in the "Human Sciences and Development" and another 150 in the natural sciences. In each case the listing was by author under individual country. There are no in-

dexes but a list, incomplete, of about 30 journals "regularly received" is included.

---- ----/8102003   177

[248] *Chaucer Review* ("Chaucer Research")

Materials are usually included in the bibliography of the following
year, thus 1983 items appeared in 1984. This is largely a deriva-
tive listing, to the extent that most items are drawn from the most
recent [513]. In 1984 some 450 to 500 entries were classified into:
current research; completed research; miscellany; and publications.
Materials on both Chaucer and later writers influenced by his work
are noted. There are no indexes.

0009-2002/1553931   513/770

[249] *Chicano Periodical Index*

The most recent covers the years 1979 to 1981 and was published in
1983. This included over 11,500 items on Hispanic Americans,
largely drawn from Chicano periodicals. A Chicano thesaurus was
followed by a detailed subject arrangement based on it. There
were also author and titles indexes and a list of about 150 Chicano
journals, periodicals, and newspapers with publishing information.
This is expected to appear annually beginning with the volume for
1982.

0 8161 0393 3/9508486   402

[250] *Chinese Science* ("Chinese Researches in the History of Science and
Technology")

The first of these (and so far the last), covering 1982, appeared
in the November 1983 number of this irregular journal. Over 100
Chinese-language titles were listed by author, with titles translated into English. This was preceded by a bibliographical essay
briefly summarizing the most important items. Both natural and ap-
plied sciences are covered from the earliest period to 1919. There
are no indexes.

0361-9001/2441331   446/482

[251] *Christianity and Literature* ("Bibliography")

Appearing in each quarterly number, materials (usually from 100 to
125 and annotated) on various aspects of the relations between literature and Christianity are arranged into several chronological
classifications. Boundaries are fluid and almost anything might
appear. There are, however, no indexes, although a listing of perhaps 40 to 50 journals canvassed appears in each number.

0148-3331/3128374

[252] *Cîteaux* ("Conspectus Bibliographicus")

This appears in each quarterly issue and generally includes about 100 sometimes extensively annotated items on a particular aspect of Cistercian affairs, e.g., spirituality or monastic history, the former arranged largely by individual, the latter by abbey. There are no indexes and access can be difficult.

0009-7497/2099069   144/256

[253] *Články v českých časopisech*

This monthly publication lists all articles in Czech periodicals and other serial publications, totalling over 50,000 annually in recent years. These are arranged in 31 categories, each subdivided, some many times, and including all fields of knowledge. In each issue are author and personal name indexes and a list of journals canvassed, which runs from 300 to 500 separate titles each month.

0006-1115/9224812   3/323

[254] *Classical and Modern Literature* ("Bibliography of the Classical Tradition")

Compiled by the Institute for the Classical Tradition at Boston University, the first of these appears in the Spring 1985 number and covers publications from 1980 to 1982 (from 1983 coverage will be on an annual basis). It is intended to encompass research in the history, assimilation, and transmutation of the Greek and Roman heritage in medieval and modern times and is divided into: (a) Classical references and (b) post-Classical cross-references. The first, arranged alphabetically by ancient author referred to and by various subjects, totals 1057 items, while the latter is arranged into a host of topical and geographical categories arranged alphabetically and serving as an index to the first part. Most items in the first section are very briefly (10 to 30 words) annotated. In addition there is an author index, separate listings of the rubrics adopted in the two main listings, and a list of nearly 100 journals canvassed.

0197-2227/5986688

[255] Coburger Landesstiftung. *Jahrbuch* ("Coburger Bibliographie")

This appears in the last number of each year and typically runs to 200 to 300 items (books, articles, recordings) on the city of Coburg. These are arranged in 4 categories by author. There are no indexes or any list of journals.

0084-8808/3529429   120/846

[256]   *Collectanea Cisterciensia* ("Bulletin de spiritualité monastique")

These appear in most quarterly numbers, totalling up to 200 items
per year, which are annotated up to about 1000 words. Coverage is
not confined to Cistercian monasticism but the classification is
rather aimless and, though there is an author index each year,
there is no subject index, rendering access problematical.

---- ----/3296921   144/252

[257]   *Colorado History. An Index to Articles in Colorado Magazines*

Compiled annually by the Reference Department of the Boulder Public
Library, the latest volume covers 1981 and includes some 100 items
ordered alphabetically by a variety of subject headings. A list of
19 journals was also included, but there were no indexes.

---- ----/8721451   25

[258]   Comité français de cartographie. *Bulletin* ("Bibliographie")

This is a minor but quite current listing of 20 to 40 items in each
issue. These are arranged by title in French and non-French classifications and, in theory at least, attempt to address the entire
field.

0588-618X/1564287   152/243/401

[259]   *Comparative Criticism* ("Bibliography of Comparative Literature in
Britain")

Materials for 1981 were included in the 1984 volume under 6 categories ranging from Biblical criticism to individual authors and
from Homer to the present. There are from 200 to 225 of them and
all are likely to have appeared one or more times in the several
other serial bibliographies devoted to one or another aspects of
literature.

0144-7564/6119311

[260]   *Comparative Education Review* ("Comparative Education Bibliography")

Published in two numbers each year and only about six months behind in its coverage. Each listing contains about 225 to 250 items
in six topical (adult and non-formal education; comparative education; general; educational planning and reform; general studies on
comparative education; higher education) and seven regional classifications, highlighting the Third World. There are no indexes.

0010-4086/1564552   171/219/277/724

[261]   *Comparative Romance Linguistics Newsletter*

The entire Spring 1984 issue was devoted to this bibliography and
included perhaps 1500 entries divided into: General Romance; Catalan; French; Galician; Italian; Occitan; Portuguese; Rheto-Romance;
Romanian; Sardinian; Spanish; and Romance-based Creoles. Within
these arrangement is by author and there are no indexes. There is,
however, a listing of about 300 journals, largely published in Europe. Coverage ranges from very current (some 1984 items) to very
dated (items from the mid-1970s).

0010-4167/2626462   168/169/223/513

[262]   *Contents of Periodicals on Latin America*

Published by the Institute of Interamerican Studies, Graduate
School of International Studies, University of Miami. This appears
in the classic current contents xerographic format but with the
advantage of being arranged in alphabetical order by journal title.
There is a completely unnecessary table of contents but no indexes.
More than 70 journals were included in the most recent issue. This
competes with (and complements) [230] and [776].

0882-2743/10634073   211/230/378/776

[263]   *Contents of Recent Economic Journals*

This is publsihed weekly by the Library Services of the British
Department of Trade and Industry. Each issue features photocopies
of about a dozen tables of contents as well as a (more useful) list
of working papers received by the Library of the University of War-
wich. In this history is largely defined out of economics. A list
of about 300 English-language journals habitually canvassed is included in each issue.

---- ----/3989952   304/408/430/468

[264]   *Correo de Linguistica Andina* ("[Mas] publicaciones")

The latest listing (in the issue of March 1984) carried about 30
items on all aspects of ancient Andean civilizations but especially
on history, ethnohistory, and linguistics. These were arranged by
author. Though small, the listing is quite current and canvasses
several fairly obscure publications well. In its field it antici-
pates other tools (e.g., [368]) by a year or more.

---- ----/9447859   368/645

[265]   *Cuadernos de Estudios Gallegos* ("Bibliografía de Galicia")

This appears every 2 or 3 years; the latest appeared in 1981 and
included about 1700 items published in or about Spanish Galicia.

These were divided into 9 topical classifications by author. A
list of about 30 important journals was included, but there were
no indexes.

0210-847X/2067860   421

[266]   *Cuban Studies/Estudios Cubanos* ("Bibliography/Bibliografía")

This appears in each semi-annual issue and recently has totalled
from 250 to 350 items arranged in 24 classifications and dealing
with all aspects of Cuban life and history from *ca.* 1850 to the
present. It is strong on dissertations and papers delivered at
meetings.

0361-4441/1665872   240/241/368

[267]   *Cultura Neolatina* ("Schedario")

The most recent was spread over the volumes for 1981 and 1982 and
totalled some 400 to 500 items, often quite extensively annotated,
dealing with late medieval and early modern Romance literature,
including both books and articles. Characteristically, the entries
were several years behind. There were no indexes but a list of
about 125 journals was included.

0391-5654/1228234   254/397/524/689/761

[268]   *Current Anthropology* ("Recent Publications")

This is a random listing, in a modified current contents format, of
recent books, collective works, and articles on almost anything related, however remotely, to anthropology. It is useful for its
currency, for the fact that obscure publications are frequently included, and because it translates titles into English. Fifty pages
a year might be devoted to this listing, which would mean upwards
of 1000 titles. There is no attempt at indexing.

0011-3204/1565600   7/60/61/62/429

[269]   *Current Bibliography of Surrey*

Prepared by the Local Studies Library of the Surrey County Library,
this appeared annually through the 1982 coverage, after which it
is to be published every two years. That for 1982 listed over 500
items relating to Surrey arranged alphabetically in a host of geographical, personal name, and topical headings with extensive cross-
referencing. Some pamphlets and newspaper articles as well as books
and journal articles are included. There are no indexes or a list
of journals but a list of publishers' addresses is included.

0140-0940/11648050   47/752/838

[270] *Current Bibliography on African Affairs*

Published four times a year (although issues are occasionally combined), this features bibliographical essays, retrospective bibliographies, book reviews, and a fairly large (the latest has 587
items) current bibliography. This last is divided into more than
20 general and geographical classifications and is particularly
strong on "current awareness" materials, weekly and monthly magazines, and reports. Items are occasionally very briefly annotated.
An author index is included in each issue but no list of journals.

0011-3255/1565605   19/644

[271] *Current Contents: Africa*

Compiled by the Abteilung Afrika of the Stadt- und Universitätsbibliothek, Frankfurt, this is produced in the classic current
contents format with photocopies of about 1000 journal contents
pages each year drawn from a corpus of around 300 journals and arranged more or less in alphabetical order. This is especially valuable for the numerous German and Russian journals which it canvasses and will be even more useful once the quality of reproduction
improves. There are no indexes.

0721-5207/5383526   17/18/19/270/297/426

[272] *Current Contents: Arts and Humanities*

This is a weekly compilation of table of contents pages from journals in the arts and humanities (defined to include art and architecture; performing arts; literature; language and linguistics;
history; philosophy; religion and theology). Journals are grouped
randomly within these categories in each issue, but there is also
an alphabetical listing of the journals appearing each week. In
addition each issue features a key word index to article titles;
an author index (with addresses in many cases); a list of organizational acronyms; a list of publishers' addresses; and the contents
of selected collective works. In early January and early July appears a list of the more than 1300 journals now being canvassed.
In late January, May, and September a cumulative list of journals
canvassed in the previous four months is included as a supplement.
All titles are translated into English but without including the
wording in the original language. The surpassing value of this and
its counterpart [275] is their currency. It is not uncommon for
the tables of contents of issues of journals to appear here before
the issue itself is available.

0163-3155/4359443

[273] *Current Contents of Academic Journals in Japan: Humanities and
Social Sciences*

The last issue seen covered 1978 and incorporated the contents of

about 250 journals. Nearly 4300 entries were classified into 39
categories, under which they were arranged by authors. Ten to
fifteen of these categories related directly or indirectly to historical matters. All titles were translated into English, with
the language of the original indicated. There was an author index
as well as a list of the journals canvassed.

0386-7293/8521181   177/442/799

[274] *Current Contents of Periodicals on the Middle East*

Compiled by the Shiloah Center for Middle Eastern and African Studies at Tel Aviv University, this appears six times a year and each
issue contains 50 or more photocopies of contents pages arrayed in
alphabetical order. Contents pages of collective works are also
occasionally included. There are no indexes. American periodicals are featured prominently, lessening its utility for American
users, who will have better alternatives. Coverage includes Israel, North Africa, and the Islamic Middle East.

---- ----/7936376   330/528/529

[275] *Current Contents: Social and Behavioral Sciences*

This, the counterpart of [272] covers sociology/anthropology/ling-
uistics; social issues and philosophy; psychology; psychiatry; public health and social medicine; rehabilitation and special education; education; library and information science; geography, planning, and development; law; economics and business; management.
Although the categories are different many of the contents pages
from [272] also appear here in the same week, none more than in
history. Otherwise, the format and features of this publication
are identical to those of [272] except that the contents of many
more collective works appear here.

0092-6361/1565614

[276] *Current Geographical Publications*

This encompasses additions to the research catalog of the American
Geographical Society. This, along with [164] is certainly one of
the major serial bibliographies in geography. The 10 issues per
year probably total more than 10,000 items, which are arranged in
about 15 thematic and 12 regional classifications plus a separate
section on maps. It is very current and comprehensive but difficult to use since there is no indexing. There is, however, a list
of journals consulted for each number, typically 150 to 200 titles.

0011-3514/1479917   348/724

[277] *Current Index to Journals in Education*

Published monthly by the Educational Resources Information Center
(ERIC) in Washington and cumulated every two years. Recently,
from 17,000 to 21,000 items have appeared each year. Materials
are arranged in various ways. First is a main entry index in which
all items (with annotations) are grouped under several categories.
This is followed by a much more refined index which features hundreds of subjects arranged alphabetically. Then there is an author
index and a journal contents index. The last three are keyed to
the numerical sequence of the main entry index, the only place
where bibliographical details are provided, including ERIC accession number and major and minor descriptors which assist in computerized database searching. Materials with historical content
are few but what there is can be determined readily and the entries
are extremely current. A listing of nearly 800 journals rounds out
each issue; these include publication details.

0011-3565/1565633   171/219/724

[278] *Current Work in the History of Medicine*

Compiled by the Wellcome Institute for the History of Medicine in
London, this appears four times a year and of late has included
from 8,000 to 10,000 entries annually. The main arrangement is a
subject index of great refinement but which, unfortunately, does
not include any geographical headings. There is an author index,
a list of authors' addresses, and a separate listing of new books
in the field. Together with [183] this provides a comprehensive
and enviably current coverage of recent work in the history of medicine.

0011-3999/1565701   183/706

[279] *Czasopismo geograficzne/Geographical journal* ("Spis najnowszej
Polskiej literatury geograficznej")

About 150 to 200 items drawn from Polish publications are included
in each quarterly issue. These are divided into physical geography,
economic geography, historical geography, regional geography, and
cartography. There are no indexes or list of journals. One might
reasonably suspect that few of these items reach the more universal
serial bibliographies in geography such as [164] and [276].

0045-9453/1565750   634

[280] *Czasopismo prawno-historiczne* ("Materialy do polskiej bibliografi
historicznoprawne")

This appears in the first number of each year. That for 1983 totalled 907 items in the field of legal history in the Polish language and classified into, among others, history of law, history of
legal doctrines, canon law, and the courts. There is an author/

anonymous title index.

0070-2471/4289745   410

[281] *Dania Polyglotta*

Published annually, this includes material in and on Denmark (including Greenland and the Färoes) in languages other than Danish
as received by the Royal Library in Copenhagen. Over 2000 of these
were listed in the 1983 volume, divided into several categories
based on (but not identical with) the Dewey Decimal Classification.
There is an author/anonymous title index.

0070-2714/3910750   282/283/284/285

[282] *Dansk artikelindeks: aviser og tidsskrifter*

Each year this includes several thousand items published in Danish
newspapers and journals covering all aspects of knowledge, largely
of course as they relate to Denmark. Materials are arranged according to the Dewey Decimal Classification, which is outlined at the
beginning, and are drawn from over 600 journals, which are listed.
There is an author index as well as a very extensive subject index.

0106-147X/8325590   281/283/284/285

[283] *Dansk Litteraturhistorisk Bibliografi*

Compiled by the Bibliographic Section of the Royal Library, Copenhagen, the volume covering 1976/77 was published in 1983. This included over 1300 items on Danish literature from the Middle Ages
to the present divided into several general, chronological, and
regional categories and including Greenland and the Färoe Islands
within its purview. There is an author/personal name index and a
list of about 300 Danish and non-Danish journals which were canvassed.

0108-2299/1799988   281/282/284/285

[284] *Dansk Økonomisk Bibliografi*

Compiled by the library of the Handelshøjskolen in Copenhagen, the
volume covering 1982/1983 was published in 1984 and comprised over
2900 items arranged in nearly 50 classifications. Perhaps one-
fifth to one-quarter of these have a historical component and nearly
all deal in whole or part with Denmark. There are author and subject indexes but no list of journals consulted.

87 17 03434 5/1207290   281/282/283/285

[285] *Dansk Udenrigspolitik Arbog* ("Bibliografi over litteratur udkommet i 19-- om dansk udenrigspolitik")

The bibliography for 1983 included some 600 items arranged in 4 major categories, 2 of them subdivided. Emphasis is on Danish foreign relations since 1945 and largely with other western European countries. Weekly and monthly periodicals are particularly well covered but there is no list of these nor any indexes.

87 7318 216 8/9561455   281/282/283/284

[286] *Dante Studies* ("American Dante Bibliography")

The most recent, that for 1981, appeared in the 1981 volume and included about 200 translations, critical studies, and reviews, most of them annotated briefly (20 to 250 words). In addition, one or more reviews of about 25 books were listed. Only materials in American publications are included.

0070-2862/2240452   23/450/524/684

[287] *Delaware History* ("Bibliography of Delaware History")

That in the Fall/Winter 1983 number covers publications of 1981/82 and included about 60 books, articles, and pamphlets arranged by author or anonymous title. There were no indexes.

0011-7765/1566099

[288] *Demos. Internationale Ethnographische und Folkloristische Informationen*

Despite its title this is confined almost entirely to materials on the folklore and ethnography of the countries of eastern Europe. Each quarterly issue features about 100 extensive (up to several hundred words) abstracts in German of books and articles, which are divided into far more categories than is convenient or necessary. Each year the fourth number includes an author/personal name index as well as a list of journals and collective works canvassed.

0011-832X/3720605   206/327/439/513/802

[289] Deputazione di storia patria per l'Umbria. *Bollettino* ("Segnalazioni bibliografiche")

The bibliography for 1982, published in 1984, included over 1000 entries on the Umbria region of central Italy, most of which were annotated. These were classified according to prehistory; history; philology; literature; art; music; geography; political, social, and economic science; the Franciscans; biography; bibliography; and guides. There are no indexes or list of journals.

0300-4422/1421099   92/136/142/450/570/682/684

[290]   Deutsche Schillergesellschaft. *Jahrbuch* ("Schiller-Bibliographie")

This appears every three or four years. The latest, published in
the 1983 *Jahrbuch* and covering 1979 to 1982, consisted of more than
500 items concerned with Friedrich Schiller, his life, work and
times. These are divided into 8 categories, most sub-divided in
turn. Only German-language materials, wherever published, are included. There is an author index but no list of journals consulted.

0070-4318/1258453   12/355/436/484/832

[291]   *Deutsches Archiv für Erforschung des Mittelalters* ("Besprechungen
und Anzeigen")

This appears twice a year and provides fairly extensive discussions
of the contents of books, journal issues, and collective works.
Materials might relate to any aspect of the Middle Ages but are arranged (in no particular order) into 7 categories covering the various subdisciplines of history and totaling 150 pages or more of
each issue. Of these the largest deals with sources and textual
criticism. There are no indexes so that specific access is virtually impossible.

0012-1223/1566509   434/524

[292]   *Développement culturel/Livres et articles parus en 19--: répertoire
bibliographique*

The listing for 1981 was published in 1984 and included over 1100
items divided into 15 categories such as: cultural politics; archives; mass communications; libraries; museums; and culture and
society, as they relate to France. These are frequently briefly
annotated. There are indexes of publishers, organisms and collect-
ivities, authors, and key-words. In addition about 250 journals
which were analyzed are listed.

---- ----/7828800   865

[293]   *Dialogue* ("A Survey of Current Literature")

This is included in each quarterly issue and usually includes
about 300 items divided into more than 60 categories and covering
Mormonism throughout the world. There are no indexes.

0012-2157/1566589   197

[294]   *Dickens Quarterly* ("The Dickens Checklist")

Appearing in each quarterly issue, this typically includes 60 to
100 items on Dickens, his work and times. These are listed in several categories and are not indexed and, while journal titles are
abbreviated, no list of them appears.

0742-5473/10362455   54/513/810/811

[295] *Dioniso* ("Bibliografia")

Devoted to the ancient theater, this bibliography appears irregularly. The latest appeared in the 1978 volume and totalled somewhat more than 500 items in three classifications, with the majority devoted to the ancient Greek theater. In addition there is a
brief section devoted to theaters and amphitheaters surviving from
antiquity. There are no indexes.

---- ----/7429224   39

[296] *Discovery and Excavation in Scotland* ("A Scottish Bibliography")

Published annually by the Scottish Group of the British Council
for Archaeology. The 450 to 500 entries for 1983, published in
1984, were arranged in one general and three broad chronological
classifications, within which the arrangement seems fairly adventi-
tious. There are no indexes or a list of journals.

0419-411X/3835786   63/198/710

[297] *Documentatieblad*

Published quarterly by the Afrika Studiecentrum in Leiden, each
number includes 500 to 600 abstracts of Africanist literature, much
of it historical, and arranged in broad geographical classifications.
These are drawn from 150 to 200 journals as well as collective works.
The list of journals is cross-listed with the abstracts, which are
themselves largely in English, with some in French and a few in
other languages. In addition there are geographical and subject
indexes.

0166-2694/-------   17/18/19/154/271/426

[298] *Documentation politique internationale*/International Political Science Abstracts

This is published six times a year by the International Political
Science Association and recently has aggregated from 6000 to 6500
abstracts annually. These are divided into six rather broad categories: political science--methods and theory; political thinkers
and ideas; governmental and administrative institutions; the political process; international relations; and national and area studies. These are arranged by author with no further subdivisions.
Abstracts of 50 to 100 words are in the languages of the article
being abstracted. There is a subject index in English in each number, which is not cumulated, and an annual author index.

0020-8345/1753679   1/209/431/617

[299]   *Early China* ("Annual Bibliography")

This appears in each annual issue. That in the 1982/1983 number
covered about 250 items. These deal with pre-Han China, are in
western languages, and are classified by art and archeology; history; religion and philosophy; literature; philology and linguistics; science; and miscellaneous. Books, articles, and reviews
are included, but there are no indexes. This bibliography covers
a field not well represented in any other serial bibliography in a
western language.

0362-5028/2292773   177/655/718/861

[300]   *East Central Europe/L'Europe du Centre-Est* ("A Selected Bibliography
of Articles and Books in the Social Sciences Published in Hungary")

Published annually, the listing in 1984 covered 1981 publications,
including nearly 300 articles and about 100 books. Books and articles are listed separately and materials are arranged in several
categories but only a few items concerned the historical output of
Hungarian scholarship. Twenty-five journals were canvassed and
listed.

0094-3037/2287340   3/14/29/112/323/783

[301]   *East Central Europe/L'Europe du Centre-Est* ("A Selected Bibliography
of Articles and Books in the Social Sciences Published in the German
Democratic Republic")

This annual bibliography canvasses about 20 East German journals
and in 1984 (covering 1983) it included some 175 to 200 items, most
very briefly annotated and arranged into 8 categories including
history, military, and ideology. In general the items relate to
East Germany although some have a larger perspective.

0094-3037/2287340   3/172/323/453/457/847

[302]   *East Midlands Bibliography*

Published quarterly the the East Midlands Branch of the Library
Association, this covers Derbyshire, Nottinghamshire, Leicestershire,
Rutland, Northamptonshire, the Soke of Peterborough, and parts of
Lincolnshire. Materials are arranged in a combination Dewey Decimal and geographical arrangement. In recent years some 700 to 800
items have been included, most of which are historical to one degree
or another. Very comprehensive annual and quinquennial indexes are
also published but there seems to be no list of journals canvassed.

0029-2885/6232503   838

[303] *Economic History Review* ("List of Publications on the Economic and
       Social History of Great Britain and Ireland")

       Usually appears once a year; materials appearing in 1983 were listed
       in the 1984/4 number and included about 1300 items which are divided
       into 18 categories covering all the usual aspects of social and econ-
       omic history. There are no indexes.

       0013-0117/1883400   160/408/430/468

[304] *Economic Titles/Abstracts*

       This is published twice monthly based on materials compiled by the
       Library and Documentation Centre of the Netherlands Foreign Trade
       Agency, The Hague. From 14,000 to 15,000 abstracts (50 to 100
       words) appear each year, in French, English, and German. These
       are drawn from more than 2000 journals, which are not listed.
       Each issue has a subject index, which is cumulated annually but is
       difficult to use since there are 24 numerical sequences used each
       year. Economic history is not well represented, but coverage of
       what there is is broad and quick.

       0303-4879/1101574   209/263/408/430/468

[305] Eesti NSV Teaduste Akadeemia. *Toimetised* ("Bibliograafia")

       The 1983 bibliography carried information on 1025 works devoted
       to the social sciences published by members of the Estonian Acad-
       emy of Sciences. Virtually all are on Estonian matters and prob-
       ably represent nearly the entire universe of such materials. These
       are divided into about a dozen categories and are in Russian or Es-
       tonian. There are author and personal name indexes in both Eston-
       ian and the Cyrillic alphabet and a list of some 20 journals, pre-
       sumably provided merely as a piece of information.

       0373-6431/-------   115/146/844/854

[306] *The Eighteenth Century: A Current Bibliography*

       Prepared by the American Society for the Eighteenth Century and
       somewhat slow, the volume covering 1981 appearing only in 1985.
       In this there are listed some 4500 to 5000 generously annotated
       (up to about 1500 words) entries covering Europe from 1660 to 1800
       and classified into: printing and bibliographical studies; histori-
       cal, social, and economic studies; philosophy, science, and relig-
       ion; fine arts; literary studies; and individual authors, which
       constitutes nearly one-half the total. All but the last are ar-
       ranged alphabetically by author. There is an author/editor/review-
       er index, but no subject index, very much a desideratum for the
       first five sections. Nevertheless, a tool unmatched in its rich-
       ness of detail.

       0161-0996/3834722   306/513/711/872

[307]   *Elbogen* ("Malmö-litteratur")

This appears in each annual number; this latest, in the 1983 volume, lists 428 items in 15 categories (many subdivided) covering
all fields of knowledge as they relate to the Malmö region of
southern Sweden. There was an author index but no list of journals
canvassed.

0345-2786/11660464   364/375/393/780

[308]   *Elenchus Bibliographicus Biblicus*

The volume for 1981 was published in 1984. It comprised nearly
14,000 entries arranged in 21 classifications, largely by groups
of Biblical books, but also including the Biblical world and the
history of Biblical criticism among others. Most categories are
extensively subdivided. Titles in non-Roman languages are translated, usually into English. There are lists of the Hebrew and
Greek letters, an author index, and an index to Biblical citations,
as well as a list of about 1300 journals and nearly 200 collective
works from which entries were drawn. Cross-referencing is frequent.
In the heavily-populated field of Biblical bibliography the *Elenchus* stands out for its comprehensiveness and ease of consultation,
if not yet quite for its currency. It is certainly a *sine qua non*
for Biblical scholars, Ancient Near East historians, historians of
religion, and others.

0392-7423/10172921   313/440/406/488/553/578/635/636

[309]   *Enchoria* ("Demotistische Literaturbericht")

Materials for 1980 to 1983 were published in 1983 and comprised
183 annotated (in German) citations and about 20 reviews, each
arranged by author, and dealing with Demotic Greek, the language
of Ptolemaic and Roman Egypt. There are no indexes and the system
of abbreviations used is not explained.

0340-627X/1852497   15/83

[310]   *Enchoria* ("Koptologische Literaturbericht")

The latest, from 1977/1979, was published in 1982. It included
434 citations divided into 17 categories ranging from magic to the
plastic arts as they related to Coptic Egypt.

0340-627X/1852497   15/83

[311]   *Encomia* ("International Courtly Bibliography")

Published by the International Courtly Literature Society and devoted to the secular literature of the early Middle Ages. The bibliography for 1982 appeared in the Fall 1984 number and totalled

819 items, including a large leaven of reviews. Most of these are briefly annotated and are organized rather inconveniently by the country in which the item was published and within these by texts, editions, and translations; critical and historical studies; and reviews. Coverage is uneven; for example, Spain has only one entry, which cannot reflect the work being done there. In some mitigation author and subject indexes are included.

0363-4841/2479293   434/513/524/580/747

[312] English Place-Name Society. *Journal* ("Bibliography")

The most recent seems to be that for 1979/80, which appeared in the 1981/82 volume. It comprised 70 or so entries arranged by author and 15 reviews, all dealing with place name research on the British Isles. There were no indexes.

---- ----/1567971

[313] *Ephemerides Theologicae Lovaniensis* ("Elenchus Bibliographicus")

This is compiled by the Universiteitsbibliotheek of the Katholieke Universiteit, Leuven, and appears as a separately paged supplement to the *Ephemerides*. It is a major tool, encompassing over 9900 items in 1984 deovted to all fields of theology, including the Bible (the largest section) but excluding church history per se (though the history of non-Christian churches is addressed). They are divided into 10 categories and a host of subdivisions. There is an author index and an index to the history of theology. However, the list of journals canvassed appeared last in the 1980 volume!

0013-9513/1568110   313/440/466/488/553/578/635/636

[314] *Eranos* ("Bibliografisk översikt")

This bibliography appears in every other year of the annual, the most recent being that in 1984, covering 1982 and 1983. It is a rather random sampling of the literature on Classical Antiquity, classical philology, and the Byzantine era and comprised about 250 to 300 items, with the largest number dealing with paleography. Each division is a brief discussion of one or more works on a particular topic (e.g., Cyprus or the history of Athens) so that there is no attempt to cover the entire field systematically. Annotations are in Swedish and English and there is an author index.

0013-9947/1568151   39/73/315/354

[315] *Eranos* ("Classical and Medieval Philology, Classical Archaeology, and Ancient History in Sweden")

This appears every other year and is concerned with the publications

of Swedish scholars in these fields. In the latest (1984 for 1982/
83) about 250 items are arranged by Swedish university and include
both published and forthcoming items. Access is unecessarily difficult since there are no indexes, but the materials included are
likely often to escape the more general bibliographical sources.

---- ----/1568151   39/73/315/354

[316] *Erasmus in English* ("Recent Publications")

This newsletter customarily contains a listing of 30 to 50 items
in English on Erasmus arranged by author. Given the tardiness of
such larger bibliographies as [167] this can be useful for its currency despite its limited focus.

0071-1063/1956845   167/397/524

[317] *Essener Bibliographie*

Compiled by the Staatsbibliothek in Essen, this is devoted to materials on the city and area of Essen in the Ruhr region of West Germany. The bibliography for 1977 (published in 1979, the latest for
which I have specific knowledge) seems, to judge from its size, to
have included from 1000 to 1200 items, doubtless appropriately organized and indexed.

0071-1462/-------   115/457

[318] *Essex Archaeology and History* ("Periodical Literature")

The bibliography in the 1983 volume listed about 100 items on Essex
history and archeology, arranged under "Essex" and then alphabetically by locality. Most of these appeared in 1982, with some earlier. Articles and monographs in series are included. There are
no indexes.

---- ----/2319614   63/198/752

[319] *Ethnomusicology* ("Current Bibliography, Discography, and Filmogra-
phy")

Each quarterly number contains a listing of 500 to 600 books, articles, theses, records, tapes, films, and videotapes in the field,
which are arrayed in several geographical categories. There are
no indexes but the refinement of organization makes searching relatively easy under normal circumstances.

0014-1836/4184114

[320] *Etudes Germaniques* ("Revue des revues")

The contents of 30 to 50 journals, mostly French and German and arranged by journal title, appear in most quarterly issues. The emphasis is on literary materials.

0014-2115/1568352   353/436/437

[321] *Etudes/Inuit/Studies* ("Bibliography")

The latest of these, totalling several hundred items on Inuit (Eskimo) matters, appeared in 1980. Since then there has been the occasional interim "Survey of Periodicals" or "Review of Articles" with 20 to 40 briefly annotated entries each time.

0701-1008/3887274   234/630

[322] *Euhemer* ("Polska bibliografia religioznawstwa")

This bibliography covers materials on "the science of religions" published in Poland. 1980/81 was covered in the bibliography in the 1983 volume and included about 500 items divided into 10 categories such as the sociology and philosophy of religion; ethnoreligion; ecumenism; and the history of religion in all parts of the world (the largest classification). There are no indexes or any list of journals.

0014-2298/2701333   226/635/636/637

[323] *European Bibliography of Soviet, East European, and Slavonic Studies*

Compiled by the Institut d'études slaves of the Ecole des hautes études en sciences sociales in Paris, with help from libraries in Berlin and Birmingham, this is the European counterpart of [3] but is somewhat tardier to appear. Materials for 1979 appeared in the 1984 compilation, which comprised 5827 items covering social science and humanities literature about the Soviet Union and eastern Europe published there or in western Europe. These are classified into: the U.S.S.R. and Eastern Europe; the U.S.S.R.; and Eastern Europe, each divided into the same 12 categories, each in turn subdivided in various ways. There is an author index and a list of more than 1000 journals canvassed.

0140-492X/3953056   3/237/674

[324] *Excerpta Indonesica*

Prepared by the Centre for Documentation on Modern Indonesia of the Koninklijk Instituut voor Taal-, Land- en Volkenkunde, Leiden. It appears twice a year covering the preceding year or two. Abstracts (50 to 200) words are in English; 283 of these appeared in the

1984/2 number and were divided into nine Dewey Decimal-based classifications. There is a combined author/subject index and a master
list of more than 350 journals.

0046-0885/1967125   177/403

[325]   *Explicator* ("A Checklist of Explication")

The winter number of this journal is given over to the checklist.
The latest (that of Winter 1984) covered 817 materials largely
published in 1982. These are arranged alphabetically by author
or screenwriter studied and includes English-language sources from
the sixteenth century to the present, with an emphasis on the later
end of this spectrum. Some of the materials involve historical
work or literary work with historical implications. There are no
indexes but a list of more than 100 journals is included.

0014-4940/1327211

[326]   *Ezhegodnik germanskoi istorii/Annual of German History* ("Raboty
sovetskich i zarubeznych istorikov po germanskoj istorii")

The bibliography for 1982 (consisting largely of East German rather
than Russian publications) was published in 1983. It totalled
about 600 entries on German history divided into: General Works;
Medieval History; Modern History; Contemporary History (the largest); German Cultural History; Historiography; and Bibliographical and Reference Works. There are no indexes nor a list of journals (whose abbreviations in the bibliography are left unexplained).
The value of this is likely to reside almost solely in the Russian-
language materials it includes.

0531-8866/2319692   3/453/457/849

[327]   *Fabula* ("Bibliographische Notizen")

20 to 30 briefly annotated items on folklore and related fields
appear in each semi-annual issue, including both books and articles.
Useful for German-language materials in particular.

0014-6242/1568717   439/513

[328]   *Fasti Archaeologici*

Published under the aegis of the International Association for
Classical Archaeology, this is designed to be the definitive bibliography in its fields, a role it shares with [73]. Although
larger than [73] it suffers from the debilitating tardiness that
is often associated with comprehensiveness; the volumes carrying
materials published in 1975 and 1976 were published only in 1982.
These comprised no fewer than 18,630 items divided into six major
categories: general and reference works (2645 items); prehistoric

and classical Greece (2821 items); pre-Roman Italy (1796 items); the Hellenistic world and the eastern Roman provinces (2496 items); the Roman West (6979 items); and Christianity and late Antiquity (1893 items), each subdivided in numerous ways. Many items are annotated, in various languages and sometimes at length. There are ancient/modern author, geographical, subject, lexical, and literary/epigraphic source indexes as well as a list of fewer than 200 journals--only those used often enough to be abbreviated. In sum, a tool fine enough to set users wishing that it were more current.

---- ----/1568954   73/328/762

[329] *Felix Ravenna* ("Principale bibliografia su Ravenna")

This bibliography, devoted to Ravenna from pre-Roman through early medieval times, appears sporadically. The most recent seen, which appeared in 1979, included about 220 to 225 items arranged alphabetically by author, with no indexes or lists of journals.

0391-7517/1569082   136

[330] *al-Fihrist: majalla fasliyya mutakhassisa fi al-tawthiq wa l-fahrasah*

An attempt to provide an Arabic counterpart to [529] this includes materials from about 220 monthly and quarterly Arabic-language journals. The 1000 or so entries in each quarterly issue are listed in a overly-refined library-oriented subject arrangement, with an author index and a list of journals. All aspects of Islam, including Islamic history, are covered.

---- ----/8227795   274/528/529

[331] *Finisterra* ("Bibliografia geografica de Portugal continental")

The bibliography for 1979 (appearing in the 1980 volume) listed 232 items dealing with continental Portugal. These were usually annotated briefly and arranged into general; historical; physical geography; human geography; regional geography; and teaching, most of these being in turn subdivided. There was an author index.

0430-5027/1385271   421

[332] *Florida Historical Quarterly* ("Florida History in Periodicals")

This appears in the July number each year and lately has included 75 to 100 items on Florida history, anthropology, and archeology arranged by author. There are no indexes.

0015-4113/1569457   476/631/837

[333] *Folk og Kultur* ("Dansk folkekultur 19--: en selektiv bibliografi")

The 1985 bibliography listed over 250 items divided into 16 categories (some further subdivided) on such matters as folk history;
folklife; material culture (the largest); and buildings. There
are no indexes nor a list of journals.

0105-1024/1998813   283/335

[334] Foreningen til norske fortidsminnesmerkers Bevaring. *Arbok* ("Bibliografi")

This covers writings on all aspects (architecture, preservation,
historical function, etc.) of historic buildings, particularly
churches, in Norway. Each year the bibliography runs from 300 to
600 items arranged alphabetically by locality or, if necessary, by
subject, with a separate list of reviews. There is an onomastic
(author, personal and corporate name) index as well as a list of
about 50 Norwegian journals consulted.

0071-7436/1569740   581

[335] *Fortid og nutid* ("De kulturhistoriske museers årsskrifter 19--: en
oversigt")

This listing in the 1984 volume included the contents of issues of
14 journals published by Danish museums and covering various aspects
of Danish material culture, emphasizing the past two or three centuries.

---- ----/1569856   283/333

[336] *Fortid og nutid* ("De lokalhistoriske årbøger 19--: en oversigt")

The most recent, covering 1983 and published in 1984, lists the
contents of about 30 Danish local history journals, arranged alphabetically and then by journal title. There are no indexes.

---- ----/1569856   281/282

[337] *Fra Himmerland og Kjaer Herred* ("Litteratur om Himmerland og Kjaer
Herred")

Materials on the history of the Himmerland and Kjaer Herred regions
of Denmark from 1983/84 was included in the 1984 listing. This
totalled about 175 to 200 items grouped into several categories,
the largest of which dealt with local history and was arranged by
locality. Pamphlets and other ephemeral literature were particularly well covered.

---- ----/6202383   281/282/336

[338] *Fra Holbaek Amt* ("Et udvalg af litteratur om Holbaek Amt")

The bibliography for 1982 in the 1983 volume included some 35 items
on the history of Holbaek province in Denmark, arranged into general,
local history, and personal history. There are no indexes.

87 87575 03 5/6175091   281/282/336

[339] *Fra Ribe Amt* ("Et udvalg af historisk litteratur om Ribe Amt")

The volume for 1983 included about 150 items on the history of the
Ribe province of Denmark largely published in 1982. These were
divided into numerous categories, principally by locality. There
were no indexes.

0046-4864/6167044   281/282/336

[340] *Fra Viborg Amt* ("Viborg litteratur")

In similar fashion to the several other Danish provincial bibliographies this lists and briefly annotates material on (in this case)
the province of Viborg in northern Jutland. Perhaps 30 to 50 items
typically appear in each annual update. There are no indexes.

0085-0853/-------   281/282/336

[341] *Die Frauenfrage in Deutschland. Bibliographie*

The first of a new series of this title was published in 1983 and
largely covered materials appearing from 1980 to 1982. Over 2700
of these were arranged into 15 categories, most further subdivided.
All aspects of women's experience in Germany are covered, including
"the woman in history" and collective and individual biographies.
There are author/personal name and subject indexes but no list of
journals canvassed.

0344-1415/10470511   772/834

[342] *French 17. An Annual Descriptive Bibliography of French 17th Century
Studies*

Compiled by the 17th Century French Division of the Modern Language
Association, the 1984 volume largely covers materials which appeared
in 1983. These are arranged under: bibliography, linguistics, and
history of the book; artistic, political, and social background;
philosophy, science, and religion; literary history and criticism;
authors and personages (the largest and arranged by author studied);
and research in progress. These probably total 1000 to 1200 entries, many of which are annotated. Citations to reviews of included works are also provided, as is a list of 200 to 225 journals.
Regretably there are no indexes and this renders *French 17* far less
useful than it might otherwise be since none of the six broad sec-

tions is in any way subdivided except that on authors.

0191-9199/4633102   158/662

[343] *French XX Bibliography*

Published annually by the French Institute/Alliance Française, New
York, this covers French literature (fairly closely defined) from
1885 to the present. For 1983 over 7800 items were listed, mostly
from the years 1980 to 1983. These were classified into: general
subjects; author/subjects (arranged by name of author and constituting three-quarters of the total); and cinema. Each of these is
further subdivided. There are no indexes for each year but for
each five issues author, author as subject, and anonymous work indexes are cumulated. There is no list of journals.

0085-0888/2014769   158/662

[344] *French Periodical Index (Répertoriex)*

This is a computer-generated index of 35 French-language popular
periodicals, typically weeklies and monthlies. Entries are presented in a single integrated author/subject arrangement and there
is frequent cross-referencing. Most materials are contemporary in
nature although a few specifically historical journals are included.
There is a list of journals but no indexes.

0362-5044/2294165   150/379

[345] *Genealogical Periodical Annual Index*

The most recent, covering 1980 and published in 1984, totaled some
8300 entries, arranged alphabetically by surname or by locality
(U.S. states, subdivided by counties). Wherever possible, personal
entries included the birth, marriage, or death date. There is a
list of more than 150 journals canvassed, together with publication
data.

0072-0593/4205809

[346] Genootschap voor Geschiedenis Gesticht (Brugge). *Handelingen*
("Boekenschouw lopende bibliografie van de geschiedenis van het
oude graffschap Vlaanderen en de provincie West-Vlaanderen")

The bibliography for 1981 included 752 items on Flanders broadly
classified into the auxiliary sciences, general history, and economic and social history, each in turn subdivided, and with the last
being more than one-half the total. There was an author index and
a list of about 100 journals consulted.

---- ----/-------   499/654/676

[347]   *Geo Abstracts B: Climatology and Hydrology*

Published six times a year and cumulating some 3500 items in 1984.
There are 14 categories for climatology and meteorology and another
11 for hydrology, with each item being briefly (20 to 100 words)
annotated. Author and geographic indexes are published annually
but do not appear in each issue. Foreign titles are translated
into English. Historical climatology and other fields of interest
to historians are included.

0305-1900/1826765   526

[348]   *Geo Abstracts C: Economic Geography*

This appears six times a year (with about 2500 items appearing in
1984), is annotated (50 to 100 words) and divided into 23 categories including economic geography; agriculture; labor, capital,
and income; and regional studies. Author and regional indexes
appear in the sixth number each year but there is no list of journals. Foreign titles are translated into English.

0305-1919/1432868   164/276/349/724

[349]   *Geo Abstracts D: Social and Historical Geography*

Published six times a year and carrying a total of about 3000 items
in 1984. These are annotated briefly (50 to 100 words) and are divided into some 20 categories including historical geography; field
experience; documentary evidence; political geography; and methodology. Like the other *Geo Abstracts* series, this tends to be Anglo-
centric in both its coverage and its data base. Also like them,
foreign titles are translated into English.

0305-1927/2240494   164/276/349/724

[350]   *Geophysics and Tectonics Abstracts*

Published 6 times a year, in 1983 some 4100 abstracts (50 to 150
words) of articles were published. These were divided into 15
categories, of which those most likely to interest historians are
age determination, seismology, and volcanology. An annual index
incorporating subject, author, and geographical listings is published.

---- ----/8883289   98

[351]   *Georgia Historical Quarterly* ("Georgia History in 19--: A Bibliography")

One year is usually covered in a late issue of the following year.
Recent bibliographies have run from 750 to 800 items and are arranged by author under "General Books and Articles" and "Genealog-

ical Source Material." A list of about 25 journals is included
but no indexes.

0016-8297/1751094   25/476/631/837

[352] *Germania* ("Zugänge der Bibliothek")

This lists materials acquired by the Römisch-Germanischen Kommission
and appears in each semi-annual issue, normally including items published in the equivalent six-month period of the previous year.
Each is an extensive listing, first of books and parts of collective works and then of articles by journal title, of general archeological sources, with an emphasis on early Europe and the Ancient
Near East. Coverage is particularly good for the numerous localized
journals.

0016-8874/2032669   81/584

[353] *Germanistik. Internationales Referatenorgan mit bibliographischen
Hinweisen*

A major tool for the field of German language and literature, this
appears quarterly and accumulates about 7000 to 8000 items annually,
many of which are annotated. These are classified into more than
30, mostly regional and chronological, categories and once a year
a list of some 300 modern editions of medieval German texts is provided. The 1984 numbers cover 1983 and 1984 publications. Each
issue lists the journals canvassed for that issue and more than
400 titles are canvassed during a year. Author and subject indexes
are published each year but none are included in the quarterly
issues.

0016-8912/1696129   320/436/437

[354] *Gnomon* ("Bibliographische Beilage")

Published as a supplement in alternate issues and recently totalling
about 600 entries on classical philology and history arranged in
seven categories, including ancient authors; philosophy and history;
and epigraphy. Largely drawn from German-language materials, this
listing is very current but lacks indexing.

0017-1417/1160828   39/73/314

[355] *Goethe-Jahrbuch* ("Goethe-Bibliographie")

The listing of materials for 1981 appeared in 1983. It included
429 items divided into "Primary Literature" and "Secondary Literature," each in turn further subdivided. Coverage extends beyond
Goethe to include the German Enlightenment generally. There was
an author index.

0323-4207/1796254   12/290/436/484/832

[356] Goriški Letnik. *Zbornik Goriškega Muzeka* ("Ocene in poročila/[Reviews and Reports]")

Material is organized in a modified current contents format, by journal title. Journals which appeared from 1979 to 1981 were listed in the 1982 reports and included some 30 titles which included material on the history of the northeast Italy-northwest Yugoslavia region.

0350-2929/8026371   66/76/525/619

[357] *Göttinger Jahrbuch* ("Bibliographie zur Geschichte und Landeskunde von Göttingen und Südniedersächsen")

This includes materials related to the history and geography of Göttingen and its neighborhood. About 200 items are normally listed in seven categories, including one devoted to the university. There are no indexes or list of journals.

0072-4882/2042594   550/556/557

[358] *Great Circle* ("Select Bibliography of Publications on Marine Archaeology")

A page or two in each semi-annual issue of this journal, published by the Australian Association for Maritime History, is devoted to this bibliography. Presumably the emphasis is on Australian and Oceanic publications.

0156-8698/10502009   109

[359] *Groningse Volksalmanak* ("Bibliografie betreffende de geschiedenis en taalkunde van de provincie Gröningen")

This normally includes about 200 items on the province of Gröningen in the Netherlands. These are divided into several categories devoted to particular aspects of history (maritime, legal, ecclesiastical, political, etc.) and these are generally in turn subdivided. There are no indexes or list of journals.

---- ----/9249226   13/187/396/640/797

[360] *Le Guetteur Wallon* ("Bibliographie historique de la province de Namur")

In 1982 this bibliography encompassed some 15 pages and was devoted to the history of Namur and its region in Belgium.

---- ----/-------   654/676

[361]   *Guide to Indian Periodical Literature (Social Sciences and Humanities)*

Published quarterly by the Indian Documentation Service in Gurgaon, this is a general index to Indian periodical literature, and as such features the usual integrated alphabetical subject and author arrangement, with extensive cross-referencing. Several thousand items are included in each issue and during the course of a year about 550 journals and several newspapers are canvassed. Usefully, a list of publishers' addresses is included.

0017-5285/1751626   177/405

[362]   *Guide to Social Science and Religion in Periodical Literature*

Published twice a year, the *Guide* appears in a single large subject entry arrangement and is devoted largely to contemporary or doctrinal issues, but does include materials on their historical background. It is particularly valuable for its coverage of the many weekly publications in this field. There are no indexes but there is a list of more than 100 journals regularly canvassed.

0017-5307/1784945

[363]   *Hadtörténelmi közlemények* ("Bibliografiája")

This bibliography on military history is divided in two parts: Hungarian and foreign. The bibliography published in 1984 (largely covering 1981) listed over 700 of the former and 800 of the latter, each divided into about 40 categories. There are author and topical indexes as well as a list of some 75 journals canvassed.

0017-6540/2430456   21/165/530/531/818

[364]   *Halland* ("Halland i litteraturen")

357 citations to 1982 literature on the province of Halland in southern Sweden appeared in the 1983 volume. Arranged into 20 categories, some subdivided, they dealt with all aspects of Halland, including church history, topography, biography and genealogy, and literature. About 20 journals are listed but there are no indexes.

0347-4364/5161254   307/365/483/780

[365]   *Hälsingerunor* ("Nyutkommen litteratur om Hälsingland")

Each year 20 to 30 items, largely books, on the Hälsingland area of southern Sweden are listed, with each item briefly annotated.

0440-0585/5192117   307/364/483/780

[366] *Hamburger Beiträge zur Numismatik* ("Besprechungen")

From 750 to 1000 items published in 1973/75 are included in the
most recent bibliography, published in 1982. Books, articles, and
collective works are canvassed and most items are extensively annotated. Coverage is confined largely to Classical Antiquity and
medieval and modern Europe. An author index, as well as a list of
about 100 journals which were consulted, are included.

0072-9523/3230938   369/457/808

[367] *Hamburger Bibliographie zum parlamentarischen System der Bundesre-
publik Deutschland*

The latest, covering 1979 and 1980, included 1250 to 1300 items
arranged in 19 categories. These dealt with World War II, the post-
war West German political party system, and parliamentary government, both national and regional, in west Germany. There is an
author/personal name index as well as a list of 50 to 60 journals.

0340-8949/5188325   774/812

[368] *Handbook of Latin American Studies*

This is the major tool for the humanities and social sciences in
its field. Edited by the Hispanic Section of the Library of Congress, volumes covering the social sciences and humanities respec-
tively are published alternately. In the former are included anthropology, economics, education, geography, political science,
and sociology; in the latter art, film, history (including ethnohistory), language, literature, music, and philosophy. Each also
has a special section on bibliographical and other reference works.
The latest social studies volume (largely covering 1979 and 1980)
comprised 8408 items, while that on the humanities (largely 1980
and 1981) totalled 7762 entries, with in each case the major categories being subdivided by geography and chronology. Items are
annotated, often critically. Each volume includes an author and
a subject index as well as a list of the journals canvassed, running to about 600 titles in each instance.

0072-9833/1751732   199/211/230/262/368/386/776/865

[369] *Hansische Geschichtsblätter* ("Hansische Umschau")

This appears in each annual issue and recently has comprised perhaps 400 to 500 references to materials dealing with the history
(particularly, but not exclusively, the economic history) of the
Hanseatic League and northern Europe generally (including Russia)
in the late medieval and early modern period. These are divided
into seven topical, chronological, and geographic categories, under which items are listed in no apparent order. Each item is annotated, sometimes quite extensively. There is an author index
and a list of about 150 journals consulted.

0073-0327/1623679   115/366/854

[370]   *Hardsyssels Arbog* ("Udvalg af litteratur om Ringkøbing")

This is concerned with the Ringkøbing area in western Jutland, Denmark. Materials for 1981 and 1982 were included in the 1983 listing, which included between 200 and 300 items on various aspects of the past and present of the area, arranged into several categories.

0046-6840/-------   281/282/336

[371]   *Hegel-Studien* ("Abhandlungen zur Hegel-Forschung")

Some 450 to 500 items on Hegel published in 1981 and earlier were listed in the 1983 volume in a single alphabetical arrangement by author. Most items are briefly annotated in one language or another, most often German. There are no indexes, rendering specific access difficult.

0073-1587/1751937   184/601/602/638

[372]   *Heimen* ("Ny lokalhistorisk litteratur")

The bibliography for 1983 appeared in the 1984/2 number and included about 200 items on Norwegian local history arranged geographically into 20 categories by province. There are no indexes.

0017-9841/1751952   565/567

[373]   *Helinium* ("Bibliographie archéologique: Belgique, Pays-Bas, Grand Duché de Luxembourg")

The bibliography for 1983 appeared in 1984 and totalled nearly 1000 items and was divided in 10 categories--some general, one biographical, the rest chronological. The period covered ranges from the Paleolithic Age to *ca.* 1000 A.D. There are no indexes or lists of journals.

0018-0009/1890322   13/125/376/640/654/676

[374]   *Hellēnikē Theologikē Bibliographia*

This was first published in 1979 (covering 1977) as a supplement to *Theologia*. Each volume totals about 300 pages and so (presumably) includes 2000 or more items largely concerned, one would imagine, with the history and theology of the various churches of eastern Christendom. It would be reasonable to assume that the bibliography is divided and subdivided into numerous categories and that it also includes appropriate indexes as well as a list of journals canvassed.

---- ----/10630730   208/448/509

[375]   *Hembygden* ("Dalslandlitteratur")

Concerned with the former Dalsland area of southwestern Sweden (now
part of Älvborg province), for 1984 this included several hundred
items on various aspects of the area's past and present arranged
into several classifications.

0346-6132/1782982   780

[376]   *Hémecht* ("Bibliographie d'histoire luxembourgeoise")

Prepared by the Bibliothèque Nationale, this is essentially the
historical items from [170] abstracted and published separately.
In 1983 647 items, mainly from 1982, were listed and divided into:
bibliographies; auxiliary sciences; general history; and cultural
history. Religious and monastic history were particularly well
represented. There is an author index but no list of journals.

0018-0270/2412470   170/424/582

[377]   *Hessische Bibliographie*

This is compiled annually by the Stadt- und Universitätsbibliothek,
Frankfurt am Main. The bibliography for 1982 (published in 1984)
included 9800 items on all aspects of Hesse, with history strongly
emphasized in all categories. Materials are divided into three
categories: regional; local (alphabetically by place); and topical
(divided into over 30 classifications). There was an author index
as well as a combined geographical/person/subject index and a listing of over 900 journals canvassed.

0171-1423/6116595   190/457/545

[378]   *Hispanic American Periodical Index*

This appears annually and includes perhaps 6500 to 7000 citations
arranged alphabetically according to Library of Congress subject
headings but with a separate listing for book reviews. All fields
are covered as they apply to all of Latin America. There is an
author/editor index as well as a list of about 250 journals, for
which publication details are given.

0270-8558/3864464   262/368/776/865

[379]   *Histoire de l'Education* ("Bibliographie d'histoire de l'education
française")

Compiled by the Service d'histoire de l'education of the Institut
National de recherche pédagogique in Paris, this appears in the
August issue each year. In 1983 there were listed over 1400 items
arranged into nine broad categories and numerous subdivisions. Only
items concerned with education in France were included. There were

author, geographical, and persons cited indexes, but no list of
journals.

0221-6280/7602855   171/219/277/724

[380]   *Histoire Sociale/Social History* ("A Current Bibliography on the
History of Canadian Population and Historical Demography in Canada")

The most recent example of this bibliography (for 1983 and appearing in the 1984/2 number) listed about 75 items drawn from other
Canadian bibliographies and arranged geographically. Some 60 journals (not listed) were canvassed.

0018-2257/1586704   160/166/610

[381]   *Historia* [Santiago] ("Fichero Bibliografico")

Materials for 1979/80 were listed in 1981 and comprised about 250
briefly annotated items divided into several general and geographical categories, of which the largest by far was that on the history of Chile, although the rest of the world is (very) nominally
represented. A list of more than 30 journals, nearly all Chilean,
is provided, but there are no indexes.

0073-2435/2080066   368

[382]   *Historia Agriculturae*

Occasionally a volume of this series is devoted entirely to the
bibliography of Dutch agrarian history. The latest (Vol. XV published in 1983) covered 1978 to 1980 and includes no fewer than
200 works of reference separately listed by author, followed by
more than 600 items on Dutch agricultural history, also listed by
author, with occasional cross-references. There was a very undif-
ferentiated geographical index and a subject index, as well as a
list of over 200 journals canvassed.

0439-2027/3289288   13/143/348/706

[383]   *Historical Abstracts*

This is published quarterly in two series: A (covering the period
from 1450 to 1914) and B (from 1914 to the present). Each of these
carry nearly 10,000 entries in 1984, dividing them into general,
thematic, and geographical categories. Each entry contains an abstract of 40 to 100 words and as well an indication of the date(s)
to which the entry principally refers, and each major category is
subdivided in various ways. The first two issues of each year
carry author and very detailed subject indexes, which are cumulated
annually along with that for the third issue, and published separately. Over 2000 journals are canvassed each year and a list of
these is included in the annual cumulative index of each series.

Obviously not comprehensive in any of the fields it covers, this is useful because of its massive subject indexing, translation of all foreign titles into English, and abstracts.

0363-2725/1000359

[384] *Historical New Hampshire* ("Other Publications in New Hampshire History")

This brief listing (fewer than 30 items recently) appears once each year and is arranged by author.

0018-2508/1752126   25/464/631/837

[385] *Historical Records of Australian Science* ("Bibliography of the History of Australian Science")

101 items published in 1982 appeared in the 1983 volume arranged by the various fields in both science and technology. There was author index.

---- ----/7511064   111

[386] *Historiografía y Bibliografía Americanistas* ("América en la bibliografía española: reseñas informativas")

The most recent (for 1982) appeared in 1984, listing 162 items in 16 categories and devoted largely to colonial Spanish America. There were no indexes and most of the entries will have already appeared in other relevant bibliographies.

0439-2477/1772572   262/368

[387] Historischer Verein für die Pflege der Geschichte der ehemaligen Fürstbistums Bamberg. *Berichte* ("Schrifttum zur Geschichte von Stadt und Hochstift Bamberg sowie der Randgebiete")

That included in the 1981 *Berichte* included over 1000 items on the history of Bamberg, West Germany, and vicinity. These were arranged in 11 categories, each in turn subdivided. There were author and subject/personal name/geographical name indexes but no list of journals consulted.

---- ----/2093159   120/388/518/846

[388] Historischer Verein für Mittelfranken. *Jahrbuch* ("Literaturschau fur Mittelfranken")

The 1982/83 volume listed about 400 items on the history of the area in Bavaria around Nürnberg. These are listed by author with no indexes and no list of journals.

---- ----/1752146

[389] Historischer Verein fur Schwaben und Neuburg. *Zeitschrift* ("Neues
Schrifttum zur Landeskunde Bayerisch-Schwabens")

The 1984 bibliography comprised about 200 items on the Swabian
area of western Bavaria and was arranged in three categories, the
largest dealing with personal and family histories. There is also
a brief listing of items under journal title.

0342-3131/2134167   120/845

[390] Historisk Samfund for Praestø Amt. *Arbog* ("Litteratur om Praestø
amt")

The listing for 1983 in the 1984 volume included about 30 annotated
entries divided in local history and personal history, and dealing
with the Praestø region of southeastern Sjaelland in Denmark.

0107-6868/5274612   281/282/336

[391] Historisk Samfund for Sorø Amt. *Arbog* ("Litteratur om Sorø amt")

The 1983 bibliography in the volume for 1984 included about 20 annotated citations on the history of the Sorø region of southwestern
Sjaelland in Denmark.

---- ----/1587544   281/282/336

[392] *Historisk Tidskrift för Finland* ("Finlandsk historisk litteratur")

In 1984 appeared about 250 items on all aspects of Finnish history
listed separately by works of reference, books, and articles, and
arranged within each category by author. There were no indexes.

0046-7596/1697075   777

[393] *Historisk Tidskrift for Skåneland* ("Skånelandslitteratur")

The third number of each year lists materials published in the preceding year on the Skåneland area of southernmost Sweden (chief
cities Malmö and Kristianstad). In 1983 the bibliography encompassed 10 pages and so probably 100 or more items arranged into
various categories.

---- ----/1752154   307/780

[394] *History in Africa* ("Comparative Bibliography")

This appears in each annual number and recently has run to 1000 to
1200 items concerned with the methodology of history generally but
excluding Africa. The arrangement is entirely by author and there
are no indexes, the assumption apparently being that users will

want the opportunity to become aware of all items in the listing.

0361-5413/2246846   184

[395] *History of Economic Thought Newsletter* ("Some Recent Articles")

This appears in each semi-annual issue and recently has run to from
75 to 125 items listed by author. There is no pretense at being
comprehensive but the listing is quite current, with some items
being listed within weeks of appearing in print.

0440-9884/2243299

[396] *Holland. Regionaal-historisch Tijdschrift* ("Regionaal-historische
bibliografie van Holland")

Recently this bibliography, prepared by the Historische Vereniging
Holland in Dordrecht, has averaged some 25 pages per year. To
judge from its title and place of publication it deals with the
province(s) of South and/or North Holland in western Netherlands.

---- ----/-------   13/187/640

[397] *Humanistica Lovaniensia* ("Instrumentum Bibliographicum Neo-Latinum")

About 300 to 350 items are listed in the 1983 volume,
largely from 1982 and dealing with various aspects of Neo-Latin
literature and source criticism. These are divided into: general;
poetics; drama; oratory; inscriptions; and recent Latin. There
are no indexes or lists of journals.

90 6186 155 1/1781417   167/267/316/689

[398] *Hume Studies* ("The Hume Literature for 19--")

The most recent appeared in late 1982 and included about 80 items
arranged by author and devoted to Hume, his work and his times.
Most of these would already have appeared in such bibliographies
as [601] and [638].

0319-7336/2442960   306/601/638

[399] *ICSSR Journal of Abstracts and Reviews: Geography*

Published by the Indian Council of Social Science Research, that
published in 1983 for 1981 included about 200 abstracts ranging
from a few sentences to more than a page. These were divided into
26 categories, all dealing with Indian geography and drawn from
about 50 listed journals. There were author and geographical indexes.

0250-9687/4221276   164/276/348

[400]   *ICSSR Journal of Abstracts and Reviews: Political Science*

Published by the Indian Council of Social Science Research, this
appears semi-annually and totals about 300 abstracts each year,
dealing largely with the Indian sub-continent but with some attention to other areas of the Third World. The latest, covering 1982,
was divided into 6 categories, with abstracts of from 100 to 200
words. There is a separate list of reviews, an author index, and
a list of 24 journals, all Indian.

0250-9660/5504479

[401]   *Imago Mundi* ("'Imago Mundi' Bibliography")

Materials in historical cartography published from 1981 to 1983
appeared in 1984. These included about 175 items, nearly all
books, and in all languages. There is an author/personal name index.

0308-5694/2227740   152/243/258

[402]   *Immigrants and Minorities* ("Current Bibliography of Immigrants and
Minorities")

About 500 items published in 1982/3 appeared in the 1984 bibliography, divided into general, theoretical, and comparative studies;
and regional and national studies, with worldwide coverage, and
each in turn subdivided. There were no indexes.

0261-9288/9309620   24/26

[403]   *Indeks Majalah Ilmiah Indonesia/Index of Indonesian Learned Journals*

Compiled by the Indonesian National Scientific Documentation Center
in Jakarta, the most recent, which covered the first half of 1982,
was published in 1984. It included 1725 items drawn from 202 journals (which were listed). The preponderance of these related to
the natural and biological sciences, but history and the social
sciences accounted for about 150 to 200 items. Titles in Indonesian were translated into English, and there were author and subject
indexes.

0216-6216/10355089   177/324

[404]   *Indeks Majalah Malaysia/Malaysian Periodicals Index*

Published twice yearly by the Perpustakaan Negara Malaysia in
Kuala Lumpur, for 1982 more than 5000 items were listed, covering
every subject, with history and allied fields reasonably well represented. A subject arrangement in dictionary catalog form is
followed by an author index repeating the same information in

another form. A list of 176 Malaysian journals canvassed is provided, with publication details.

0126-5040/3347214   177/417/719

[405] *Index India*

Compiled by the Rajasthan University Library, Jaipur, this index includes only English-language articles on India published in Indian and foreign journals. Even so, for the first half of 1981 (published in 1983), it listed 16,428 items, of which 526 were classified as history, although many more would also be of interest. The history materials were organized into 11 chronological and topical categories, with many relating to epigraphy, numismatics, and archeology. Book reviews and dissertations are also included, as is a list of 1000 to 1100 journals consulted and author and subject indexes. Given the excessive slowness of [50], this must be considered the major bibliographical tool for Indian history.

0019-3844/1774363   50/116/177/361

[406] *Index of Articles on Jewish Studies/Reshimat maamarim be-madae ha-Yadhadut*

This is based on [488], whose editors compile it, and drawn from materials received by the Hebrew National and University Library in Jerusalem. Materials for 1982 were published in 1984 and included 3776 items in all languages and classified into: Bibliography; Manuscripts; Old Testament; Apocrypha, Dead Sea Scrolls, Early Christianity; Mishnah, Talmud, Midrash, Halakhah and Jewish Law; Spiritual Trends in Judaism; Liturgy; Literature; Language; Jewish History outside Israel; Culture and Sociology; Eretz Israel; and the State of Israel. References are based on about 100 Hebrew-language and 500 other journals, as well as 150 collective works. There are review, onomastic, and author indexes for materials in both Hebrew and in other languages.

---- ----/10166775   412/463/488

[407] *Index of Conference Proceedings Received*

This monthly compilation lists the titles of conference proceedings volumes received by the British Library Lending Division, aggregating to about 16,000 titles annually. Materials are listed alphabetically by key words drawn from the proceedings' or organizations' titles in whatever the language of the conference happened to be. Titles of individual papers are not included (for at least some of these see [418]) but ISBN or ISSN numbers are provided wherever possible. Monthly issues are cumulated yearly (as well as at longer intervals) but otherwise there is no indexing. History and its neighbors are not particularly well represented.

0305-5183/3703373   418

[408]   *Index of Economic Articles in Journals and Collective Volumes*

Published by the American Economic Association, this index is
rather slow, with materials for 1979 being published in 1984. The
Index is an "adjunct" of [468], drawing its materials from it and
reordering them. Perhaps 18,000 to 20,000 entries are included
in the 1979 listing. These are first arranged in a rather complicated classification system (which requires 15 pages to describe)
and then repeated in an author arrangement. Only items in English
or with English summaries are included. There is much (though difficult to measure) on economic history and comparative economics.
A list of about 250 journals and 350 collective works is included
as well as a topical index to the classification schema.

0536-647X/1752732   209/263/304/430/468

[409]   *Index to Canadian Legal Periodical Literature*

This appears quarterly and is cumulated in each successive issue
throughout the year. There are separate subject and author arrangements, each of which provides bibliographical details, as
well as case and book review indexes and a listing of subject headings. Each number lists more than 100 Canadian journals, each with
publishing information.

0316-8891/2247419   185/413/548/724

[410]   *Index to Foreign Legal Periodicals*

Despite its title this quarterly publication (cumulated annually)
of the American Association of Law Libraries includes journals
globally but indexes only materials on comparative, international,
and municipal law which do not relate to the United States, United
Kingdom, or the British Commonwealth. These are arranged alphabetically in a multitude of subject headings, with articles in
Oriental languages translated into English. There are author/re-
viewer and geographical indexes as well as a list of about 350
journals canvassed.

0019-400X/6121706   185/413/548/724

[411]   *Index to Indian Legal Periodicals*

This is published twice yearly by the Indian Law Institute in New
Delhi. Each year about 3000 entries are included, arranged in
nearly 100 categories in a combined author/subject heading arrangement, with a separate book review index. Historical matters are
covered as appropriate, but this is not a prominent part of the
bibliography.

0019-4034/1752937   185/413/548

[412] *Index to Jewish Periodicals*

This appears twice yearly and offers an integrated author/subject index to more than 40 English-language periodicals in the fields of Jewish studies. Both scholarly and popular journals are represented.

0019-4050/1048671   406/463/488

[413] *Index to Legal Periodicals*

This canvasses more than 400 English-language journals, arranging materials in an integrated subject/author index. It totals several thousand entries a year, covers all fields of law, appears monthly, and is cumulated annually. The journals covered are listed, together with publication details.

0019-4077/1585611   410/548/724

[414] *Index to New Zealand Periodicals*

Prepared by the Bibliographic Unit of the National Library of New Zealand; coverage for 1982 appeared in 1983. Several thousand items in all fields (including book reviews) are listed by subject in dictionary catalog format, with author cross-references. More than 200 journals are listed, with those from New Zealand provided with publication details.

0073-5957/11382448   467

[415] *Index to Periodical Articles by and about Blacks*

The volume for 1982 was published in 1985 and included several thousand citations to literature about Blacks, very largely Black Americans, arranged in a dictionary catalog format. Coverage is especially good for weekly and monthly periodicals. Materials in history are minimal. Cross-referencing is extensive and a list of about 30 journals, with publication details, is provided.

0161-8245/3565220

[416] *Index to Periodical Articles Related to Law*

This canvasses journals (mostly outside the field of law) not covered by [410] and [413] for materials on the relationship of the social and behavioral sciences with law. Several hundred items appear each year and include such areas as archival law and legal history. Each quarterly listing in cumulated into the following quarter resulting in an annual cumulation. There are no indexes but a list of about 125 journals is included.

0019-4093/988168   410/413

[417] *Index to Periodical Articles Relating to Singapore, Malaysia,
       Brunei, ASEAN: Humanities and Social Sciences*

The first of these, covering 1980/82, was published in 1984 by the
National University of Singapore Library. This included citations
to about 6200 articles. The major arrangement is by Library of
Congress subject heading, of which there are hundreds. In addition,
there is a listing of book reviews and an author index. There is
also a list of about 120 "core" journals canvassed, most of them
published in the three countries covered.

0217-6920/11962974   177/404/417/419

[418] *Index to Social Sciences and Humanities Proceedings*

Recently this has indexed the contents of over 800 conference proceedings, being published quarterly and cumulated annually. All
the contents of each volume are listed fully, but the volumes themselves are listed in no particular order, though numbered. There
are, however, author/editor, sponsor, meeting location, corporate,
and key word indexes to facilitate access. It is hardly systematic;
almost anything can appear but its easy access and currency make
it a useful browsing tool providing the user is in possession of a
magnifying glass.

0191-0574/4785721   407

[419] *Index to South African Periodicals*

Compiled by the Johannesburg Public Library, this has appeared only
in microfiche format since 1980 and within that by fiche-card, making it a singularly difficult tool to use efficiently. The most
recent, which covered 1982, covers from 450 to 500 scholarly, technical, and general South African periodicals (for which a listing
is provided) in all fields, with the sciences being particularly
strongly represented. Entries are arranged in a single alphabetized author/subject arrangement. Reviews (of works by South Afri-
cans only) are grouped together under "Books." There are no indexes.

---- ----/1752748   17/18/426

[420] *Indice de Materias de Publicaciones Periodicas Bautistas*

This is published annually by the Instituto Biblico Bautista Mexicana in San Antonio, Texas and is concerned with the Baptist experience in Latin America. The volume for 1983 (published in 1985)
contains several hundred entries arranged in a very large number
of subject classifications integrated with authors in a single alphabetical arrangement. Materials are largely concerned with contemporary theological issues among Spanish-speaking Baptists.
Twenty-six Spanish language Baptist journals are canvassed and
listed. There are no indexes.

0 311 19860 0/5669855   751

[421] *Indice Histórico Español*

This is normally published 3 times a year, although the most recent
number covered the entire year 1980 and was published in 1984. It
included 1982 items briefly annotated (25 to 200 words) and divided
into seven major chronological and geographical categories and a
host of minor ones. Spain (and to some extent Portugal) is covered
from prehistory to the present and the Spanish overseas territories
from their discovery until independence. This is the only tool
devoted entirely to Spanish history and it is regretable that it is
now being published so far in arrears and without indexes (or lists
of journals) of any kind. Withal it remains useful.

0537-3522/1753053   90/199/215/515/667

[422] *Indo-Iranian Journal* ("Publications Received")

Despite its title, this represents a fairly extensive bibliography
of recent materials on early Buddhism and Indo-Iranian history and
linguistics. 800 to 1000 items were arranged entirely by author
in the December 1983 number. No listing has appeared since but
this would be a valuable tool if it continues.

0019-7246/1929743   4/74/226

[423] *Industrial and Labor Relations Review* ("Recent Publications")

This appears in each quarterly number, usually running to about
300 entries divided into 14 categories and without any indexing.
There is a minor historical dimension to several of the classifications.

0019-7939/1753069   202/495

[424] Institut archéologique de Luxembourg. *Bulletin* ("Bibliographie
luxembourgeoise")

This is concerned, not with the Grand Duchy of Luxembourg, but with
the province of Luxembourg in southeastern Belgium (capital Arlon).
The bibliography for 1980, which appeared in 1982, comprised nearly
300 items arranged in a single author sequence, with virtually
every item of a historical or biographical nature. There are no
indexes, nor a list of journals consulted.

0020-2177/2697567   654/676

[425] Institut Napoléon. *Revue* ("Bibliographie napoléonienne")

Each semi-annual number features a brief annotated listing (25 to
50 items) of recent publications on Napoleon and his era. There
are no indexes.

0020-2371/1995151   150

[426]   *International African Bibliography*

Compiled by the Library of the School of Oriental and African
Studies, University of London, this appears quarterly. In 1984
over 3000 items were listed, being divided in each issue into general and then geographical categories (Egypt excluded; offshore islands included). All fields of knowledge are covered but with an
emphasis on the arts, humanities, and social sciences. Each entry
includes one or more not very useful subject tracings and each issue has a subject index based on these; there is an annual author
index as well. More than 1000 journals are "scanned" but no list
of these is provided. Currency is good but historians are likely
to find the African section of [631] both more extensive and more
current.

0020-5877/1588491   16/17/18/19/154/271/297

[427]   International Arthurian Society. *Bibliographical Bulletin*

This appears annually and in the volume for 1982 552 items were
listed, most of them annotated. These are arranged, rather unhelp-
fully, by country of origin and within these categories by texts,
translations or adaptations; critical and historical studies; book
reviews; and theses. Medieval epic literature in general and the
Arthurian cycle in particular are covered. There are author and
subject indexes as well as a list of about 225 journals canvassed.

0074-1388/1771689   580/622/747

[428]   *International Bibliography of Historical Sciences*

One of a series of UNESCO-sponsored bibliographies, this was once
pre-eminent in its fields but has since fallen on lean times. This
is partly owing to its tardiness (1976/77 being published in 1984)
and to the fact that it has failed to take notice of the burgeoning
historiographical production in and on areas outside Europe and
North America. The 1976/77 volume contains 7176 items arranged in
more than 20 categories, of which only 250 deal with the Third
World *in toto*. There are author/personal name and geographical
indexes. It is hard to imagine that there can be more than a few
items in this latest volume that historians could not have learned
about, and much earlier, from any number of other serial bibliographies.

0074-2015/1753415

[429]   *International Bibliography of the Social Sciences/Anthropology*

The 1981 volume was published in 1985 and comprised almost 7800
items in a complex classification scheme adequately outlined at the
beginning. Anthropology is generously defined and there is a good
deal of historical material listed, even if defined relatively
traditionally. Titles of articles not in English or French are

translated into one of these languages. There is an author index
and excellent subject indexes in both English and French, as well
as a list of more than 500 journals which were canvassed. Coverage
of Third World topics and publications is particularly strong.

0085-2074/1753416   7/8/60/61/62/268

[430] *International Bibliography of the Social Sciences/Economics*

The volume for 1982 was published in 1985. In it, and arranged in
a complicated classification scheme, were listed exactly 12,000
items (a good increase from previous years), including a strong
economic history component scattered throughout the numerous
divisions and sub-divisions. There is an author index as well as
subject indexes in both French and English. About 800 canvassed
journals are listed. This complements the several other serial
bibliographies in economics and economic history in its extensive
coverage of Third World affairs.

0085-204X/1753414   209/263/304/408/468

[431] *International Bibliography of the Social Sciences/Political Science*

The volume for 1981 was published in 1984 and included 7109 items
(up 2000 from the previous year) arranged in an elaborate classification which is outlined at the beginning. Coverage is global,
with particularly good coverage of Third World and development
matters. Titles not in French or English are translated. There
is an author index and subject indexes in French and English, as
well as a list of about 500 journals which were consulted.

0085-2058/1832048   1/209/298/616/617

[432] *International Bibliography of the Social Sciences/Sociology*

The volume for 1980 was published in 1982 (there may have been
others since) and listed 6259 items in a complex classified arrangement, which is outlined at the beginning. Topics likely to be of
particular interest to historians include history of sociology;
historical demography; and comparative social structures. Titles
not in French or English are translated. There is an author index
as well as subject indexes in both French and English. Finally,
650 to 700 journals which were canvassed are listed.

0085-2606/1753417   209/220

[433] *International Development Abstracts*

This appears six times yearly and in 1984 totalled about 3000 abstracts (50 to 200 words) on various aspects of development. In
each issue these are divided into more than 20 categories, including demography, population, migration; economic history; and inter-

national relations. An *International Development Index* is published
each year as well, a cumulative author, subject, and geographical
index to the preceding year's abstracts plus some relevant abstracts
drawn from the various *Geo Abstracts* series.

0262-0855/9041428   44

[434] *International Medieval Bibliography*

Published semi-annually by the School of History of the University
of Leeds, this is intended to encompass all aspects of medieval
Europe and the Byzantine empire from *ca.* 500 to *ca.* 1500. For
1983 over 7500 items were listed, divided into more than 40 categories, both topical and regional. These were drawn from over 1000
journals,and nearly 170 collective works were consulted as well.
Lists of both are provided. Topics or a range of dates are usually
indicated for each entry. An author index and a "general" (largely
onomastic) index are porvided for each volume. This, along with
[524] are the standard tools for medieval studies.

0020-7950/1783429   231/291/524/539

[435] *International Review of Mission* ("Bibliography on World Missions
and Evangelism")

Prepared by the Scottish Institute of Missionary Studies, this appears in each quarterly issue, aggregating to over 1000 items each
year. These are divided into several general topics and then by
mission field. Included are such fields as the history of missions,
theology of missions, and ecumenism. Items are occasionally briefly
annotated but there are no indexes and no list of journals searched.

0020-8582/5471196   133/242/509/623/858/869

[436] *Internationale Bibliographie zur deutschen Klassik, 1750-1850*

Prepared by the Nationale Forschungs- und Gedenkstatten der klas-
sischen deutschen Literatur in Weimar, this annual volume deals
with German life and letters roughly for the century after 1750.
The volume for 1978 was published only in 1983 and included 4181
items arranged generally and then by individual author, nearly 250
of which are represented separately and who in sum constitute about
two-thirds of the total. Several hundred book reviews are listed
separately. There is a single combined author/author studied/sub-
ject index as well as a list of over 500 journals that were canvassed.

---- ----/1586051   12/290/355/484/832

[437] *Internationale Germanistische Bibliographie*

The volume for 1982 was published in 1984; it included more than

23,000 items divided into 28 categories (about one-half of which are directly or indirectly historical). These are mostly chronological and are subdivided variously. There is an author index and an extensive subject index, as well as a listing of 750 to 800 journals and more than 400 collective works consulted. This constitutes a useful addition to the several bibliographies already concerned with Germanistics.

0721-4561/8290895   320/353/436

[438]   *Internationale Jahresbibliographie der Festschriften*

The first volume, covering 1980, was published in 1982. Materials were first listed alphabetically by name of honoree (whether institutional or individual), with contents of each listed (though without page numbers). This was followed by a listing by author, again without page numbers. Finally there are brief (and inadequate) subject indexes in German and English. In all, more than 10,000 separate papers are included. All fields are covered but effective subject access is very limited.

3 7648 1276 1/9299653

[439]   *Internationale Volkskundliche Bibliographie*

Produced by the German Folklore Society in cooperation with the Modern Language Association, this is the major bibliographical tool for folk studies (but see [513]). The volume covering 1979/1980 was published only in 1985 and included some 8800 items divided into 21 categories, most further subdivided, sometimes extensively. Among others these included: geographical and ethnographic units; popular beliefs; folk medicine; folktales, myths, and legends; and other folk literature. There are subject indexes in German and English (and a French subject index is imminent) as well as an author index. In addition, more than 1000 canvassed journals are listed.

0074-9737/1716093   288/327/513

[440]   *Internationale Zeitschriftenschau für Bibelwissenschaft und Grenzgebiete*

The volume covering 1981 included more than 3200 entries, most of which were briefly annotated. These were divided into 13 categories covering the Bible *per se*, the history and archeology of the Biblical world, and Biblical criticism from ancient times to the present. There is an author index (but no subject index) and a list of about 400 journals canvassed. Perhaps not quite as useful as [308] but a good example of the abundance of excellent tools available to Biblical and allied scholars.

0074-9745/1753790   308/313/466/488/553/598/847/848

[441] *Internationales Archiv für Sozialgeschichte der deutschen Literatur*
("Auswählbibliographie")

The 1983 bibliography selectively covered materials published
largely in 1981 and 1982. Over 1300 items are classified in 15
categories, most in turn sub-divided. These relate generally to
the relation of literature and society, and include such subjects
as "everyday life" and ephemeral literature. There are no indexes
but there is a list of more than 2000 journals canvassed.

0340-4528/2592741

[442] *An Introductory Bibliography for Japanese Studies*

This covers the humanities and social sciences in alternate years,
with materials from the former for 1978/79 being published in 1984
and the latter for 1977/78 in 1982. Each volume takes the form of
several bibliographical essays in English in the relevant disciplines (humanities: history; archeology; religion; intellectual history; language; literature; art history/social sciences: law; political science; international politics; sociology; geography; cultural anthropology; education) followed by a listing of relevant
Japanese titles, some annotated. Each volume has author and subject indexes. While not a bibliography *sensu stricto*, it remains
the best entrée into recent work in Japanese history for non-Japan-
ese speakers.

---- ----/5421473   177/273/799

[443] *Irish Economic and Social History* ("Select Bibliography of Writings
on Irish Economic and Social History")

That in the 1983 volume includes 425 to 450 items mostly published
in 1982. These were arranged in a single alphabetical arrangement
by author, with no indexes or list of journals. Both "economic"
and "social" are generously defined and the entire range of Irish
history is touched on, with predictable emphasis on modern and recent times.

0332-4893/3680172   47/121/701/839

[444] *Irish Geography* ("Recent Geographical Literature Relating to Ireland")

Of late this has included some 200 to 300 items annually arranged
into: general; geomorphology; climate, soils, and biogeography;
historical and cultural geography; and social, political, and
economic geography. Listings are fairly current but there are no
indexes or list of journals.

0075-0778/2143946   47/179/839

[445] *Irish University Review* ("IASAIL Bibliography Bulletin")

Concerned almost exclusively with Irish literature or works by
Irish authors, the latest bibliography (for 1983) included about
1000 items arranged largely by author studied and including books,
articles, and reviews. The materials are largely criticism of
contemporary literature but historical studies are included. Citations are drawn from journals worldwide but no list is included;
nor are there any indexes.

0021-1427/1160264   9/49/513/841

[446] *Isis* ("Critical Bibliography of the History of Science and Its
Cultural Influences")

Published as a separately-paginated supplement to *Isis*, the bibliography for 1983 contains 2771 items which are divided as follows:
general references and tools; science and history from specific
points of view; and history of specific sciences (about 70% of the
whole), including all the physical and exact sciences (and pseudo-
sciences) as well as medicine and technology, less extensively
(for which see [706] and [789]). All of these are subdivided in
numerous ways. Also listed are reviews of more than 1000 books.
Coverage is current and includes material noted through September
of the previous year. There is an author/personal name index and
a list of more than 500 relevant journals.

0021-1753/1638942   221/706/798/845

[447] *Islam and the Modern Age* ("Islam and Islamic Studies: An Annual
Bibliography of Articles")

Based on a canvassing of periodicals and newspapers received by the
Zakir Husain Library, New Delhi, a total of 64 such journals, of
which a list is provided. Materials for 1981, which appeared in
the last issue of 1982, totalled about 1200 to 1500 items, all in
English. These were divided into a section on Islam generally and
another (dominated by India and Pakistan), devoted to regional
studies, each of which is further subdivided. There are no indexes.

0021-1826/1774507   6/330/542/621

[448] *Istina* ("Chronique des périodiques")

This appears in nearly each quarterly issue, although not uniformly
since it rotates through a series of subjects from one number to
another. Generally speaking, materials relating to ecumenism are
included, with (it appears) special attention to the eastern Christian churches. Materials are arranged in a modified current contents
format by journal title, and in each issue from 15 to 40 journals
might be analyzed. Most items are provided with brief annotations
in French. There are no indexes.

0021-2423/1754024   374/576/589

[449] *Istorijski Glasnik* ("Bibliografija Jugoslavije")

The most recent, which appeared in the 1983 annual volume, covered
materials published in 1981 and earlier. Some 750 to 800 items
were classified into: prehistory; Yugoslav history (in 8 chronological subdivisions); non-Yugoslav (but still Balkan) history (only
12 items); auxiliary historical sciences; and miscellaneous. There
is a list of about 30 relevant journals but no indexes.

0021-2644/10655882   3/114/153/323

[450] *Italian Studies* ("Works of Italian Interest Published in Great
Britain")

The most recent, covering 1982, appeared in 1984 and included perhaps 250 books and articles on various Italian matters, largely
literature and history. These were divided into 6 categories, each
of which has historical aspects, and arranged by author thereunder.
There were no indexes and a very brief list of journals canvassed.

0075-1634/1604960   136/684

[451] *Ivra* ("Rassegna bibliografica")

The most recent volume is that for 1980 and its bibliography totals
some 1300 items on ancient and Roman law divided into 19 categories
ranging from Babylonian through early medieval law and with an emphasis on interpreting the ancient sources. The contents of major
journals and collective works are listed separately. Some items
are annotated in varous languages, occasionally extensively. There
is an author index and an index of ancient sources.

0021-3241/2092801   494

[452] *Jahrbuch der schlesischen Friedrich-Wilhelm-Universität zu Breslau*
("Literatur zur schlesischen Landeskunde")

Material for 1981 appeared in the 1982 volume and included 361 German-language items in 11 categories arranged by author or author
studied and dealing with Silesia. Items on history and literature
comprise more than 80% of the total. A list of 59 journals was one
of the categories. There are no indexes.

0448-1348/2199737   132/135/453/856

[453] *Jahrbuch für die Geschichte Mittel- und Ostdeutschlands* ("Zeit-
schriftenumschau")

The volume for 1984 listed perhaps 2500 items published in 1982
and earlier and divided into general (subdivided largely chronologically) and geographical classifications, the latter encompassing
Berlin, Brandenburg, Mecklenburg and Pomerania, East and West

Prussia, Saxe-Anhalt, Thuringia, Saxony, Sorbia, Silesia, and bor-
der and interstitial areas. Within these materials are listed by
journal title. There is a list of about 600 German and 275 foreign
journals but no indexes, rendering access to materials, especially
genres of materials, somewhat difficult. Nevertheless an important
tool for its field. In addition about 400 books are listed by
author or title in an "Ergänzungsbibliographie."

0075-2614/4737243   3/172/301/323/849

[454] *Jahrbuch für Liturgik und Hymnologie* ("Literaturbericht zur Liturgik")

Each year perhaps 400 items are included in a series of short bibliographical essays dealing with the liturgy in early and modern
times arranged in four categories generally sub-divided. There is
also a similar but smaller report on hymnological literature.
There is an author/personal name index but no list of journals.

0075-2681/1782829   80/686

[455] *Jahrbuch für Wirtschaftsgeschichte* ("Bibliographie wirtschaftsges-
chichtlicher Literatur der DDR")

This appears in the second and fourth numbers of each year, totaling about 500 entries per year dealing with economic history literature published in the German Democratic Republic. This is classified into ten general and chronological categories dealing with
economic history from antiquity to the present, with an emphasis
on the socialist countries. There are no indexes and, all in all,
this is not a particularly useful tool since it covers no subject
comprehensively.

0075-2800/1782983   160/303/408/430/468

[456] *Jahrbuch zur Geschichte Dresdens* ("Bibliographie")

The bibliography in the 1984 volume included separate listings of
dissertations (about a dozen) and articles (30-35), the latter arranged by author. There are no indexes.

0419-7291/1786460   452/695

[457] *Jahresbericht für deutsche Geschichte*

Compiled by the Zentralinstitut fur Geschichte of the Akademie der
Wissenschaften of the German Democratic Republic, this appears bi-
annually and is the standard continuing bibliography of German history before 1945. The volume for 1980 and 1981 (published in 1983)
contained 10,718 items divided into give general and chronological
categories, each of which is further subdivided in a number of ways.
There are author/anonymous title and subject indexes but no list of
journals.

0075-286X/1754151   3/115/172/301/323/453/849

[458]   *Jämten* ("Ny litteratur om Jämtland och Härjedalen")

This annual listing includes books and articles on various aspects of the province of Jämtland (capital Ostersund; and incorporating the former province of Harjedalen) in west-central Sweden. Some 40 to 50 entries are arranged in several categories but without indexing or a list of journals canvassed.

---- ----/4785359   780/874

[459]   *Jewish Law Annual* ("Survey of Recent Literature")

In 1981 about 220 items were listed in a series of alphabetical categories ("Abortion" to "Usury"). Each item is annotated, sometimes extensively and materials from Old Testament times to the present are included.

---- ----/4553741   406/412/488

[460]   *Jezik in Slovstvo* ("Slovenistika")

About 525 to 550 items published in 1982 were included in the 1983/84 volume. These dealt with Slovene language and literature and, though materials in all languages were included, the vast majority were in Slavic languages. Materials are arranged alphabetically by author under the two categories of "language" and "literature" and there are no indexes; thus access is difficult.

0021-6933/2086105   449/721/860

[461]   *Jihočeský sborník historický* ("Jihočeska národopisna bibliografie")

The bibliography for 1979, appearing in the 1983 volume, included about 80 items on the Jihoceský region of western Czechoslovakia (capital Ceske Budejovice). These were divided into 13 categories, of which the largest dealt with social and ethnic processes, and place and personal onomastics. There were no indexes but a short list of journals canvassed was included.

---- ----/2897604   759/852

[462]   *Journal Asiatique* ("Bibliographie samaritaine")

The listing in 1983 covered materials from 1980 to 1983 and included 118 items divided into 13 categories including history and geography; relations with Christians and other Jews; the Pentateuch; and epigraphy. There are no indexes or list of journals.

0021-762X/1782245   463/768

[463]   *Journal for the Study of Judaism* ("Review of Articles")

Arranged by journal title in a modified current contents format, articles (slightly annotated) on Judaism and the Jewish people from the Persian through the Roman periods were drawn from about 100 different journals in 1983. There are no indexes.

---- ----/1800061   406/412/488/768

[464]   *Journal of American History* ("Recent Articles")

In each quarterly issue there are 400 to 500 articles listed by journal title and arranged in 23 general and five regional classifications. Coverage is very current (although, unfortunately, page numbers are not provided) and this, together with [631] are the best 'early warning' serial bibliographies in United States history.

0021-8723/1782332   25/631/837

[465]   *Journal of Arabic Literature* ("Annual Bibliography of Works on Arabic Literature Published in the Soviet Union")

The most recent of these (for 1979/80 in the 1983 volume) included citations to 88 critical studies and translations, both books and articles, published in Russian, with Russian titles translated into English. All aspects of Arabic literature are covered. There are no indexes.

0085-2376/1783632

[466]   *Journal of Biblical Literature* ("Collected Essays")

Although not systematic, this represents an up-to-date listing in each quarterly issue of the contents of 10 to 25 recent collective works in Biblical studies. Given the prominence of the genre in this field this, though modest, remains useful.

0021-9231/1782210

[467]   *Journal of Commonwealth Literature* ("Annual of Commonwealth Literature")

The second number of each year is given over largely to this bibliography. The materials are divided into: General; East and Central Africa; Western Africa; Australia; Canada; India; Malaysia and Singapore; New Zealand; Sri Lanka; Pakistan; and South Africa. These very markedly in content, scope, and format; some (e.g., South Africa) are extensive bibliographies, whereas others (e.g., western Africa) are sketchy and ignore critical studies almost entirely. Not to be compared to the major bibliographies in this field, particularly [513].

0021-9894/1623556   110/236/467

[468]   *Journal of Economic Literature* ("New Books: Annotated Listing"/
"Current Periodicals")

JEL is published quarterly by the American Economic Association.
Each issue is a complex of bibliographic information organized in
a number of ways. First 200 or more books are divided into a number of classifications and briefly annotated (75 to 200 words).
This is followed by a list of journals in alphabetical order and
in modified current contents format. Then these are re-arranged
in the same classification scheme as the books. Finally, certain
of the articles listed in these two indexes (perhaps one-third to
one-half) are arranged in this same classification and provided
with abstracts of up to 100 words, which are prepared by their
authors. Finally, there is an author index, keyed to the numbers
of the classification system. Since items themselves are not numbered, it is difficult to estimate the number of items, but it
would be reasonable to estimate that, typically, from 1500 to 2000
articles are listed each time, of which 750 to 1000 are abstracted.
All fields of economics and economic history are covered.

0022-0515/1788942   209/263/304/408/430

[469]   *Journal of Ecumenical Studies* ("Ecumenical Abstracts")

This ordinarily appears in the first and third issues of each
year. 100 to 120 citations are arranged by country and then by
journal and are accompanied by abstracts of 50 to 200 words. Emphasis is largely on the contemporary period. There are no indexes.

0022-0558/1754547   448/576

[470]   *Journal of Forest History* ("Biblioscope")

Listings of 40 to 60 articles appear in each quarterly issue.
Though nominally global, in practice the great majority of these
are concerned with the U.S. and Canada. They are arranged by author and there are no indexes.

0094-5080/1793553

[471]   *Journal of Garden History* ("Current Bibliography of Garden History")

The listing in 1984 included more than 500 entries, divided into
15 categories and largely comprising materials published in 1982
and 1983. Among categories of interest are: biohistorical studies;
country houses and villas; economic activities; literary, poetical,
and philosophical context; and individual architects, botanists,
and gardeners. Coverage is global but with emphasis on the British Isles. There are no indexes or any list of journals canvassed.

0144-5170/7132577   78

[472] *Journal of Glass Studies* ("Check List of Recently Published Books
and Articles on Glass")

Based on material received at the Corning Museum of Glass Library,
this annual bibliography has recently run to about 1250 to 1500
items. There are brief sections on general and technical studies,
but more than 80% of the materials are devoted to the history of
glass. These are classified chronologically, then geographically,
and finally by style. All periods from prehistory are included
except the contemporary period, which is covered by the bibliography
in *New Glass Review*. "Substantive" book reviews are also included.
There is no list of serials or any indexes.

0022-4250/1605749   103

[473] *Journal of Mississippi History* ("Publications Relating to Mississippi")

This appears in each quarterly issue, generally includes fewer
than 40 items arranged by author, and does not attempt to be systematic (though still useful). There are no indexes.

0022-2771/1782329   464/476/631/837

[474] *Journal of Modern Literature* ("Annual Review Number")

Materials for 1982/83 amounting to 3500 to 4000 items appeared as
the November 1983 issue. Included are scholarly and critical
studies on English-language literature of the Modernist period and
these are classified into: reference and bibliography; literary
history; themes and movements; regional, national, and ethnic literatures; comparative studies; criticism of modern literature generally; criticism of fiction; criticism of poetry; criticism of
drama; criticism of film; and individual authors (three-quarters
of the total). There is a combined author/author studied/reviewer
index but no list of journals.

0022-281X/949853

[475] *Journal of Palestine Studies* ("The Arab-Israeli Conflict in Periodical Literature")

Appears sporadically and usually includes 200 to 250 items in Arabic and in western languages devoted to all historical and contemporary aspects of the Arab-Israeli conflict. These are divided
into five categories plus a separate listing of book reviews.
There is a list of more than 150 journals consulted but no indexes.

0377-919X/1784372   274/330/528/529

[476] *Journal of Southern History* ("Southern History in Periodicals")

Listings for the year appear in the second number of the following
year. In 1985/2 about 700 items were listing in the following categories: general; bibliography and historiography; Blacks and slavery; legal and constitutional history; economics; military and na-
val history; politics and government; religion; science and medicine; social, cultural, and intellectual history; urban history.
There are no indexes or a list of journals. Coverage is very current, making this the most important regional serial bibliography
for the United States.

0022-4642/1782314   25/332/351/464/473/534/813/837

[477] *Journal of Sport History* ("Journals Survey")

Recently this has appeared in each quarterly issue on a rotating
basis, with 40 to 50 brief (100 to 200 word) abstracts on 3 or 4
topics over a year's time. Among those covered are: the ancient
and modern Olympic Games; methodology and theory; sports in antiquity; sport in the southern hemisphere; Australian sport; European
sport; and U.S. sport (broken into various categories, usually by
individual sport), as well as leisure and dance. Each bibliography
also features a "New Titles" section of unannotated entries, some
of which eventually are abstracted. There are no indexes nor is
there a list of journals canvassed.

0094-1700/1793987   754/755/873

[478] *Journal of the Early Republic* ("Recent Articles")

This listing appears twice yearly, covering materials on American
history from 1789 to 1850. These are arranged by journal title,
usually total about 100 items each time, are coded to about 25
topics, and are reasonably current. There are no indexes.

0275-1275/7088630   25/464/631/837

[479] *Journal of Transport History* ("Bibliography of Transport in Other
Periodicals")

This appears in the September issue every other year; that in 1983
covered materials which appeared in 1981 and 1982 and featured a
brief bibliographical introduction followed by a list of about 70
items arranged in 9 categories covering various aspects of land,
sea, and air transport. There are no indexes.

0022-5266/1754849

[480] *Journalism History* ("Communication History Abstracts")

Fewer than 20 of these appeared in the Spring-Summer 1983 number, largely concerned with the United States, arranged by author, and briefly annotated.

0094-7679/1795320

[481] *Juzhnoslovenski Filolog* ("Bibliografija")

The bibliography appearing in the 1983 volume covered 1981 and earlier and included nearly 1700 items on Yugoslav linguistics and allied fields. These were divided into 14 categories of which the largest dealt with Serbo-Croatian, but all South Slavic languages are covered. There is an author index (by page numbers even though the entries are numbered. . .) and a list of about 80 journals consulted.

0350-185X/1605317   29/168/169/504/513/551

[482] *Kagakushi Kenkyū* [Journal of the History of Science, Japan] ("Annual Bibliography")

In the 1983 volume there were listed 1400 to 1500 items arranged in 20 categories covering science, technology, mathematics, electronics, transportation, and medicine in past and present Japan. All listings are in Japanese and there are no indexes.

0022-7692/7195545   250/446

[483] *Kalmar län. Arsbok för kulturhistoria och hembygdsvård* ("Litteratur om Kalmar")

This lists material relating to the city and county of Kalmar in southern Sweden as acquired by the Kalmar Stadsbibliotek. For 1981 (published in 1982) about 60 items were listed, largely books and some dating back several years. These were divided into a general and several regional/local classifications. There were no indexes.

---- ----/5001603   780

[484] *Kant-Studien* ("Kant-Bibliographie")

This appears every two or three years. The most recent covered 1979 and 1980 and appeared in the 1983 volume. Included were about 650 items arranged in 5 categories, of which that devoted to Kant, his life and works, comprised nearly the entire total. This, like the other categories, is arranged by author and since there are no subject indexes, efficient access is lacking. There is, however, a list of nearly 50 journals that have been canvassed.

0022-8877/1782290   12/355/371/436/601/602/638

[485] *Keats-Shelley Journal* ("Current Bibliography")

The 1984 bibliography (which covered 1982 publications) included
338 items divided into 5 categories concerning Keats, Shelley,
Byron, Hazlitt and Hunt and their "circles." There is an author/
personal name/title index as well as a list of more than 60 journals canvassed.

0453-4387/1800245   513

[486] *Khosana* ("New and Recent Publications")

Published by the Thailand/Laos/Cambodia Studies Group of the Southeast Asia Council of the Association of Asian Studies, this appears twice a year, each time featuring a listing of some 400 to
500 items on the three countries plus sections on minorities and
on refugees, with materials on Thailand predominating. All disciplines are covered but there are few entries for materials not in
English. There are no indexes or list of journals; nevertheless
this bibliography is both quite current and an improvement on other
tools in its field.

---- ----/3898235   177

[487] *Kinyras. Bibliography of Ancient Cyprus*

Published annually, the latest (for 1979) appeared in 1982 and included 423 items arranged in: bibliography; history of Cypriot
studies; ancient sources; religion; geography and anthropology;
history; archaeology (with history the largest); and philology.
Materials on Cyprus in all languages from prehistory to the mid-
seventh century A.D. are included. There is a list of about 50
journals consulted but no indexes (although an author index for
1974 to 1978 was included with the 1978 compilation).

---- ----/9353939

[488] *Kiryat Sefer*

Published quarterly by the National and University Library, Jerusalem. In 1983 nearly 6000 items were listed and were arranged in
some 25 categories, mostly subdivided. These covered all fields
including science and technology, the Jews in diaspora, and the
Bible, as well as the expected areas. Scope is international but
most items (and all commentary) are in Hewbrew, but with an English
table of contents. Each year separate Hebrew/Yiddish author; Hebrew titles; Arabic author; and non-Hebrew author indexes are issued. There is, however, no list of journals analyzed. From
Kiryat Sefer is taken [406].

0023-1851/1755169   406/463

[489] *Kölnische Bibliographie*

Materials for 1976 to 1978 were included in the volume published
in 1980. Here more than 2000 items were listed and divided into
13 categories covering all fields of knowledge, with history and
its related fields the best represented. Most of the larger categories were further subdivided. Both Cologne and the area dominated by it historically are included. There is an author/editor
index but no list of journals.

0454-9007/2277635   190/828

[490] *Konsthistorisk Tidskrift* ("Svensk Konsthistorisk Bibliografi")

The most recent, which appeared in the 1982 volume, included about
750 items (mostly from 1979 to 1981) on the history of Swedish art,
architecture, the book arts, as well as such allied fields as pho-
tography. These were divided into a host of topical and geographical categories and most entries were briefly annotated (10 to 100
words). There were no indexes or a list of journals canvassed.

0023-3609/1755241   624/639/851

[491] *Kritikas Gadagrāmata* ("Grāmatas un publikācijas periodikā")

This bibliography of Latvian literature and (to a lesser extent)
language appears in each annual volume. That in 1983 largely covering 1981 contained some 700 to 800 entries arranged by general
topics, by genre, and by authors studied and covered all periods,
though preponderantly the nineteenth and twentieth centuries.
There were no indexes nor any list of journals.

---- ----/5166300   115

[492] *Kulturberichte aus Niederösterreich* ("Niederösterreichische Bibliographie")

This bibliography (not seen) covers the Niederösterreich province
of northeastern Austria (capital Vienna) and is based on materials
received by the Niederösterreichische Landesbibliothek in Vienna.
The 1981 listing published in 1982 included more than 300 items,
probably arranged in several categories and covering not only history but other aspects of the region.

0023-5121/-------   112/585/829

[493] *Kwartalnik Historii Nauki i Techniki* ("Bibliografia Bieżąca Historii Nauki i Techniki")

This appears in each quarterly issue and lately has totalled from
1500 to 2000 items annually relating to the history of science and
technology in Poland. These are arranged in 7 categories based on

the various scientific and technical fields and include only material published in Poland. There are no indexes or lists of journals.

0023-589X/2263350   221/446/706/789

[494] *Labeo* ("Rassegna bibliografica di storia romana")

This appears in most issues and usually constitutes 200 or more
items arranged in some dozen categories and dealing with the history of ancient Rome, particularly its legal history. Coverage is
fairly current but there are no indexes or list of journals.

0023-6462/4173021   451

[495] *Labor History* ("A Bibliography of American Labor History")

This appears once a year, covering materials published in the previous year. Typically, 200 to 300 of these will be listed, arranged in general and chronological/regional categories. There
are no indexes or a list of journals.

0023-656X/1755402   172/348

[496] *Latin American Population History Newsletter* ("Recent Publications")

75 to 100 items on Latin American historical demography appear in
each semi-annual issue arranged into several categories. There
are no indexes.

---- ----/4481832   160/166/610

[497] *Latviešu valodas kultūras jautājumi* ("Bibliogrāfija")

This is a minor affair compared to [491]; in 1984 only about 20
items were included, largely on Latvian linguistics.

0130-0059/8694504   491

[498] *The Left Index*

Published quarterly, this index draws material from more than 60
journals with a Marxist, radical, or left perspective. These are
listed in each number. In this way about 1800 items are listed
annually, first by author and then by subject. In addition there
is an index of book reviews and a journal index keyed to the author
entries. There is no particular focus to the materials other than
any determined by their source; emphasis is on contemporary issues.

0733-2998/8574892

[499] *De Leiegouw* ("Bibliografie 19-- van de Geschiedenis, Taal- en
Volkskunde in het Kortrijkse")

That in the 1982 volume, covering in general 1980 and 1981, included more than 300 items on the history of the city and region of
Courtrai in Belgium. Materials were divided in 8 categories, covering such aspects of history as religion, art, genealogy, and
language/literature. There were author/personal name and geographical indexes.

0459-0023/4366036   346/654/676

[500] Leo Baeck Institute. *Year Book* ("Post-War Publications on German
Jewry")

Materials from 1983 and earlier appeared in the 1984 volume. There
were more than 1000 of these devoted to the history of Central
European Jewry since 1933 and arranged into 10 classifications
including general history; research and bibliography; the Nazi
period; and other chronological categories. Most items are in German but Hebrew materials are also included. There is a combined
author/subject index but no list of journals.

0075-8744/1035634   367/659/774/831

[501] *Leuvense Bijdragen* ("Inhoud van Tijdschriften")

Appearing in the final number of each year, this is a listing by
journal title of the contents of perhaps 100 to 125 journals dealing with Germanic philology and related subjects. Unfortunately
page numbers are not included. There are no indexes.

0024-1482/5301522   769

[502] *Libyan Studies Bulletins: Current Awareness Service*

Prepared by the Libyan Studies Centre in Tripoli, this appears
annually and is arranged in a current contents format, with western
and Arabic language journals listed alphabetically and separately.
Much of Islamic North Africa is covered (if only incidentally).
Most recently about 60 western-language and more than 250 Arabic
journals were canvassed and these are listed. There are no indexes.

---- ----/-------   41/42/519

[503] *Libyca* ("Bibliographie Maghreb-Sahara")

The bibliography for 1976 (in the 1977 volume, the latest seen)
contained over 400 items on Libya and the surrounding area. These
dealt mainly with prehistory and anthropology (social and cultural
anthropology constituting three-quarters of the whole). There
were no indexes, nor a list of journals.

0459-3030/1136789   149

[504] *Limbă Română* ("Bibliografia romanescă de Linguistică/Bibliographie roumaine de linguistique")

The latest seen covered 1976 and appeared in the 1977 volume. It featured 1770 items (including book reviews) arranged in 29 categories. In theory all fields of linguistics were addressed; actually, the vast majority of items dealt with Rumanian and Slavic linguistics. There were author and subject indexes as well as a list of about 150 journals canvassed.

0024-3523/7942923   29/551

[505] *Lippische Jahresbibliographie*

Compiled by the Lippische Landesbibliothek, Detmold. The bibliography for 1982 (published in 1983) included more than 1000 items divided into 14 categories and covering all fields of knowledge, with a particular emphasis on history (and with a separate category for Arminius). There is an author index but no list of journals.

0548-3085/4288927   190/457/828

[506] *Literary Criticism Register*

This is a monthly publication in the modified current contents format. Each year perhaps 6000 items are listed, arranged each month by journal title. In addition recent books and dissertations are included, each listing of which is divided into several categories. Although the emphasis is on living authors, coverage extends back to the fifteenth and sixteenth centuries. Listings are extremely current and each issue features a list of journals canvassed (some 300 different titles throughout a year) and subject and author indexes.

0733-2165/8534845

[507] *Literatura Piękna: Adnotowany Rocznik Bibliograficzny*

This indexes Polish belletristic literature. The volume for 1983 carried more than 1300 items published in 1979 arranged into: Polish literature; translations into Polish of foreign literature (minor); and children's literature. Most items are briefly annotated (50 to 150 words). The focus is largely contemporary. There are author, title, and subject indexes but no list of journals.

0459-5505/3252049   608

[508] *Literaturna Istoriia* ("Bulgarska literaturno-istoricheska bibliografiia")

This bibliography of the history of Bulgarian literature appears

annually. That for 1979, which appeared in the 1983 volume, listed
about 1200 to 1400 entries, arranged in several chronological categories, further subdivided within, often by individual authors.
Materials from ancient Bulgaria to the present are included, with
a preponderance of contemporary items. There are no indexes.

---- ----/4344398   205

[509] *Literaturschau zu Fragen der Weltmission*

Literature relating to mission activities by all denominations and
to all parts of the world are listed annually and arranged in 4
geographical and 5 topical categories. Coverage (recently about
600 items each time) is limited to German-language journals, of
which about 40 are listed (though others are canvassed as well).
There is also an author/editor index.

---- ----/4278164   133/242/435/623/858/869

[510] *The Local Historian* ("Recent Publications in Local History")

This appears sporadically and ranges for 25 to 100 items, most often
pamphlets and similar materials, devoted to local and family history
in the British Isles. Much of the material is of a nature to be
overlooked by the standard comprehensive bibliographies in the
field.

0024-5585/2326403   47/568/752/838

[511] *Locke Newsletter* ("Recent Publications")

Appearing irregularly, the most recent had about 30 items arranged
by author. There is not likely to be much not picked up by the
several bibliographies in the field of philosophy.

0307-2606/1642607   398/601/638

[512] *Luther Jahrbuch* ("Lutherbibliographie")

The bibliography in the 1985 volume includes more than 2000 items
divided into four categories, the largest of which is divided into
several theological and historical subdivisions. There is also a
separate section listing book reviews. Reformation Europe as well
as the life and work of Luther is covered. There is an author/
anonymous title index as well as a list of over 100 journals consulted.

0342-0914/1756287   84/232

[513] *MLA International Bibliography*

The *MLA* is a monument as much as a bibliography and testimony that
currency need not necessarily be sacrificed for comprehensiveness.
Coverage for 1983 materials is provided by five volumes (bound together) totalling over 42,000 entries. The first two (over 26,000
entries) are devoted to the various modern national literatures,
being divided chronologically and then by individual author studied.
The third volume, devoted to linguistics (over 10,000 items) is divided into 26 general categories and then into fifteen groups of
language families. The volume on general literary criticism (about
3000 items) includes non-print literature; various kinds of literary criticism and literary theory; literary movements, etc. The
final volume (about 2700 entries) is concerned with folklore, ethnomusicology, folk literature, and related topics. There is an
author index to all five volumes as well as a separate and very extensive subject index particularly designed for data base searching.
There is also a master list of over 3000 journals which are breifly
listed in the *Bibliography* and fully described in the *MLA Directory
of Periodicals*, published every few years. All in all, this is an
indispensable tool for historians, even though such areas as classical antiquity are excluded.

0024-8215/2520540   168/169/222/223/327/474/439/513

[514] Maatschappij voor Geschiedenis en Oudheidkunde te Gent. *Handelingen/*
Société d'histoire et d'archéologie de Gand. *Bulletin* ("Bibliografie
van de Geschiedenis van Gent")

This appears in each annual volume, the latest (covering 1982/83)
including about 140 items on the history of Ghent. These are divided into 11 chronological and topical categories covering the
period from antiquity to the present and are briefly annotated.
There are no indexes or any list of journals.

---- ----/5810158   346/654/676

[515] *Madrider Mitteilungen* ("Veröffentlichungen aus Spanien und Portugal sowie Arbeiten über die Archäologie der iberischen Halbinsel
aus anderen Ländern")

This lists acquisitions by the library of the Deutsches Archäologisches Institut in Madrid. The bibliography for 1983 (covering
most of 1983) included 212 entries on Iberian archeology into the
Middle Ages, arranged by format and country of origin. Since many
entries are for the contents of journals, the actual number of individual items is appreciably larger. There is an author and a
brief subject index.

0418-9744/2349596   73/328/421/667/859

[516] *Magyar Kozgazdasági Irodalom/Hungarian Economic Literature*

Compiled by the Central Library of the Karl Marx University of Economic Studies, Budapest, the volume for 1983 covered materials published in 1980 and earlier. Some 3300 entries were arranged in
seven categories, some of which were in turn subdivided. The emphasis is largely contemporary and two-thirds or more of the entries
refer to Hungary. Titles in Hungarian (the great majority) are
translated into Russian and German, Russian and English, or Russian
and French. There is an author/anonymous title index and subject
indexes in Hungarian, Russian, and English, as well as a list of
about 125 journals canvassed.

0133-0152/4355040   143/783

[517] *Maine Historical Society Quarterly* ("Writings in Maine History")

Each number features a brief listing of from 25 to 40 items arranged
by author and without any indexes.

0163-1152/2263768   25/464/631/837

[518] *Mainfränkische Jahrbuch für Geschichte und Kunst* ("Unterfränkische
Bibliographie")

Prepared by the Universitätsbibliothek Würzburg. In 1983 there
appeared 1679 items relating to the Lower Franconia district of
Bavaria. These were arranged in 12 categories covering all fields
of knowledge, with particular emphasis on local and family history
and culture. There is an author index but no list of journals
covered.

0076-2725/2354604   120/388/846

[519] *Majallat al-Buhuth al-Ta'rikhiyya* ("Libya, Tunisia, Morocco, North
Africa")

When this appears, it usually includes 400 to 450 items in Western
languages dealing with the Maghreb and Libya. These are divided
into about 15 categories, of which history is the largest, within
which items are listed by country. There are no indexes. There
is not likely to be much here that is not also in [41] or [42].

---- ----/6855826   41/42/330/502

[520] *Manitoba History* ("Manitoba Bibliography")

Materials for 1983 appeared in the Autumn 1984 number. Here there
were from 100 to 120 books, articles, and government documents
arranged by author or title and without any indexing.

0226-5036/9137857   235

[521]   *Maryland Historical Magazine* ("A Bibliography of Articles, Books, and Dissertations on Maryland History")

Each year's materials are listed in one number of the following year. Generally these run to between 200 to 250 items arranged into more than 20 categories, the largest of which are on genealogy and family history.   There are no indexes.

0025-4258/1756756   25/464/476/631/837

[522]   *Meander* ("Antyk we Polsce: Bibliografia")

The volume for 1984 carried materials published in Poland on Classical Antiquity (extending into the early Middle Ages). 1569 entries were arranged in 20 categories covering various aspects of the subject.   Many of these are arranged by author studied and these come up as far as Copernicus.   There was an author index and a list of about 200 journal issues analyzed.

0025-6285/1924923   131/607/720

[523]   *Mecklenburgische Bibliographie*

This appears annually, prepared by the Wissenschaftlichen Allgemein-bibliothek des Bezirkes Schwerin and covers the areas of Rostock, Schwerin, and Neubrandenburg in East Germany.   Recently the number of entries has approached 1000 and these are divided into 13 categories covering all fields of knowledge including history, folklore, religion, and genealogy.   Each year there is an author/anonymous title index and every five years a separate subject index is published.

0543-2111/2410239   195/457

[524]   *Medioevo Latino.   Bollettino bibliografico della cultura europea dal secolo VI al XIII*

This has quickly become (along with [434]) the major tool for medieval studies.   Arranged more or less in the fashion of [39], the volume for 1982 (published in 1984) included over 6500 items, many of them briefly annotated (20 to 150 words).   The bibliography is divided into five major sections: authors and texts (nearly one-half the total); survivals; disciplinary studies; reference materials; and miscellany and collective works.   These are in turn extensively subdivided.   Consultation of the "authors and texts" section is not made easier by the fact that Latin is the operative language (e.g., Geoffrey of Monmouth=Gaufridus Monemutensis). There are manuscript (by location), geographical, and author indexes, as well as a list of 850 to 900 journals, plus collective works, consulted.   Not as current as [434] but more useful in many ways; in any case a valuable complement to it.

---- ----/8045004   231/291/434/539

[525] *Memorie storiche forogiuliesi* ("Rassegna delle riviste")

The modified current contents format in the 1983 volume lists 15
issues of 6 journals dealing with northeast Italy, particularly
the Friuli region. In addition there was a "Bibliografia Friuli-
ana," which listed more than 60 books of recent vintage.

---- ----/4363398   66/136/356/619

[526] *Meteorological and Geoastrophysics Abstracts*

This is published monthly by the American Meteorological Society.
Each year about 7000 entries are included, divided each time into
seven large categories, each subdivided variously. Relevant subjects covered include floods, weather records, volcanic activity,
droughts, climatic change, and atmospheric phenomena. Abstracts
run from 25 to 250 words. Each issue has author, geographical,
and subject indexes, which are produced in separate annual cumulations two or three years later. Each issue also includes a selective list of about 100 journals canvassed as well as one of monographic series.

0026-1130/1623665   347

[527] *Mexicon* ("Bibliographie")

This appears in each bi-monthly number and typically lists more
than 25 books and selected contents of some 40 journal titles dealing with pre-Hispanic Mesoamerica. Coverage is very current and
far-reaching. There are no indexes.

0720-5988/5821915   129/368

[528] *Middle East Journal* ("Bibliography of Periodical Literature")

This appears in each quarterly issue and in 1984 aggregated to
nearly 3000 entries. The world from Turkestan to Spain is covered
in twelve subject categories (with no geographical subdivisions),
including a particularly extensive listing of book reviews. Coverage of popular periodicals and Arabic-language journals is good.
There are no indexes but the last number of each year features a
list of about 250 journals regularly covered.

0026-3141/1607025   274/330/529

[529] *Mideast File*

Compiled by the Shiloah Institute and the Dayan Center for Middle
Eastern Studies of Tel Aviv University. Nearly 7000 items appeared
in the four 1984 issues, each of them briefly annotated (50 to 125
words). These are divided into 28 general and regional categories
ranging from (and including) Libya to Iran to Turkey. Not only

books and articles, but documents, reports, reviews, interviews, and broadcasts are included. There are author and subject (key word/phrase) indexes in each issue, but no list of journals surveyed. Coverage is only a few months behind making this a singularly useful source.

0262-818X/8735248   274/330/528

[530]   *Militärgeschichte* ("Zeitschriften aufsätze zur Militärgeschichte")

This bibliography of selected articles usually appears in the fourth number of each year. That for 1983 included some 600 to 700 items divided into five categories covering reference works, historiography, military history, warfare, and individuals, most in turn subdivided geographically or chronologically. There is a list of more than 50 journals consulted but no indexes.

0323-5254/1941186   21/123/165/531/818

[531]   *Military Affairs* ("Recent Articles")

This appears in each quarterly issue and normally runs to between 250 and 300 entries arranged into general and chronological categories. Only English-language materials are included and all aspects of military affairs (largely recent and contemporary) are covered. There are no indexes or list of journals.

0026-3931/1643391   21/123/165/531/818

[532]   *Miscelánea Antropológica Ecuatoriana* ("Bibliografía Antropológica Ecuatoriana")

Compiled by the Museo Antropológico y Pinacoteca del Banco Central del Ecuador in Guayaquil. The first, which appeared in 1981, included in a strictly alphabetical arrangement about 200 items on Ecuadorian anthropology and ethnohistory which appeared between 1973 and 1977. There were no indexes.

---- ----/8854360   264/368/645

[533]   *Mississippi Quarterly* ("A Checklist of Scholarship on Southern Literature")

The Spring 1984 issue carried 856 entries for materials published in 1983 or before. These were divided into four chronological categories (colonial; antebellum; postbellum; 1920 to date), each arranged by the authors studied. Most items were briefly annotated and there is an index for writers without their own entry. Roughly two-thirds of the entries relate to the modern period.

0026-637X/1758368   27/473/476/826

[534] *Missouri Historical Review* ("Missouri History in Magazines")

This appears in each quarterly issue, with up to 100 entries each time, arranged by journal title. There are no indexes.

0026-6582/1758409   25/464/631/837

[535] *Mittelrhein-Mosselland-Bibliographie*

This bibliography, compiled by the Landeshauptarchiv in Koblenz, is concerned with the area in Germany along the middle Rhine, in which the historically important cities of Koblenz and Trier are located. Although not seen, this ran to over 300 pages in 1979 (covering 1978) and so presumably includes several thousand items which are, it is safe to suggest, arranged into numerous categories and equipped with appropriate indexes and a list of journals.

---- ----/10573319   190/457/828

[536] *Mnemon* ("Bibliography of Modern Greek History")

This is published by the Hellenike Palaiographike Hetaireia in Athens, with the materials for 1976 appearing in the 1978/79 volume. There some 1500 items appeared arranged into various geographical, chronological, and topical classifications concerning Greece in the nineteenth and twentieth centuries. In addition to author and subject indexes, there was a list of over 50 Greek-language journals, over 30 non-Greek journals, and a handful of collective works.

---- ----/1796644   3/114/153/208/323/537

[537] *Modern Greek Society* ("Recent Publications")

This newsletter appears twice yearly and the bibliography, which covers Greece from *c.* 1700 to the present, generally totals several hundred items arranged by century (with the twentieth century subdivided topically). There is a separate review section but no indexes or list of journals canvassed.

0147-0779/1449214   3/114/153/208/323/536

[538] *Montfort* ("Vorarlbergische Bibliographie")

Materials from 1978 to 1980 were included in the bibliography in the 1982 volume. There, from 750 to 800 items on the Vorarlberg region of westernmost Austria (capital Bregenz) were listed, probably divided into several categories and appropriately indexed.

0027-0148/9404180   112/585

[539]   *Le Moyen-Age* ("Travaux relatifs à l'histoire du Moyen Age")

Sketchy at best, the bibliography for 1982 appeared in the last
1983 number and included 166 entries arranged in 10 categories,
appearing in journals received on exchange.

0027-2841/2131368   231/291/434/524

[540]   *Music Index*

This appears each month and is cumulated annually. Arranged in
dictionary catalog format, with an integrated author and subject
arrangement, it includes reviews of books and records as well as
books and articles. Entries total many thousand each year, with
of course, a high level of duplication. They are drawn from about
350, mostly English-language, journals, which are listed. *Music
Index* is the only reasonably current music bibliography.

0027-4348/1643737   161/625

[541]   *Musik in Bayern* ("Veröffentlichungen über Themen der bayerischen
Musikgeschichte")

Appearing in each half-yearly number, in 1984 about 50 items were
listed, most of them dating from 1983 and 1984 and devoted in one
way or another to the history of classical and folk Bavarian music.

---- ----/5804086   161/540/625

[542]   *Muslim World* ("Survey of Periodicals")

This appears in every issue, is reasonably current, but decidedly
minor in the field of Islamic bibliography. Fewer than 60 entries
appeared in the first number of 1984, arranged into 10 categories.
About 100 journals are surveyed regularly. There is a discernible
emphasis on doctrinal materials.

0027-4909/2448847   5/330/528/529/621

[543]   *Nan-Pei-Ch'ao Studies*

If this has not ceased (Fall 1981 is the latest issue seen) this
provides a useful if unorganized potpourri of bibliographical information on work on Chinese history from the second to the seventh
centuries A.D., i.e., between the imperial dynasties of Later Han
and T'ang.

---- ----/6062047   177/178/655/718/861

[544] Naples. Università. Istituto Universitario Orientale. *Annali*
("Saggio di bibliografia semitica")

This covers all Semitic languages, including Amharic and extinct
dialects. Materials from 1982/83 were listed in 1983 and totalled
527 items arranged in 29 general and geographical categories, with
emphasis on linguistic issues. There was a list of more than 50
journals and an author index.

---- ----/1758987   555

[545] *Nassauische Annalen* ("Zeitschriftenschau")

Most issues list selectively in a modified current contents format
the contents of from 50 to 100 journals (by journal title) relating
to Nassau and Hessen in West Germany. Although most fields of knowledge are covered, history and related subjects represent well over
one-half the entries.

0077-2887/2531330   190/377/457

[546] *Néprajzi Hirek* ("A magyar néprajztudomány bibliográfiája")

This bibliography appears as a separate number of *Néprajzi Hirek*
and is concerned with Hungarian folklore and folklife generally.
The bibliography for 1981 comprised over 1150 items arranged in 25
categories covering all aspects of the field and largely published
in 1979 and 1980. There was an author index and a list of about
125 journals searched. This bibliography also appears, slightly
later, in *Hungarológiai Ertesitö* (0209-4800/7360695).

0133-8021/8971757   327/439/513

[547] *Nestor* ("Bibliography")

Published by the Program in Classical Archaeology at Indiana University, this appears nine times a year and covers about 1500 items
in 1984. These are arranged alphabetically by author in each issue,
with reviews listed separately. Emphasis is on the Mycanaean and
Minoan civilizations but the larger world of the area is also covered. Coverage is quite current.

0028-2812/1759635   672

[548] *Netherlands Yearbook of International Law* ("Dutch Literature in the
Field of Public International Law and Related Matters")

Compiled by the Interuniversity Institute for International Law,
The Hague, that for 1982 was included in the 1983 volume and totalled 500 to 600 items arranged in 10 categories and with titles
translated into English. There were no indexes nor any list of
journals.

90 247 2916 5/1759647   45/185

[549]   *Neuerwerbungen der Sondersammelgebiete Ägyptologie*

This is published by the Universitätsbibliothek Heidelberg and
ordinarily consists of 5 to 7 issues a year covering Egyptology
(divided into 5 sections); classical archeology; and medieval and
modern art history as received by that library and two American libraries.   There are no indexes.

---- ----/-------   55/81/614

[550]   *Neues Archiv für Niedersächsen* ("Neues Schrifttum über Niedersach-
sen und Bremen")

This appears in each quarterly number and runs to 600 to 700 items
in a typical year.   These cover all aspects of knowledge and are
divided into 10 categories.   There are no indexes or lists of journals.

0342-1511/8181426   196/556/557

[551]   *New Contents Slavistics*

Published by the Bayerische Staatsbibliothek in the classic current
contents format, that is, photocopied contents pages arranged in alphabetical order.   Nearly 400 journals are surveyed each year and
these are listed in each issue together with the particular issues
covered in the current volume of *NCS*.   These are also broken down
into country of origin--all but about 60 emanated from eastern
European countries.   As is normally the case with this format,
coverage is extremely current.

0173-6388/8215856   29/504/687

[552]   *New Guinea Periodicals Index*

Prepared by the Library of the University of Papua New Guinea in
Port Moresby.   This appears quarterly and is about two years behind.   This is not the usual national periodical index; materials
on New Guinea (and Irian Jaya) published anywhere in the world are
included.   Materials (1293 in 1981) are listed in 22 subject categories.   An author index appears in each issue and is cumulated in
the fourth issue, which also includes a cumulated place name index
(which does not appear in each issue).   Coverage of ephemeral literature, particularly that published in Papua New Guinea itself,
is good.

0028-5161/4145349   592/642

[553]   *New Testament Abstracts*

Published 3 times a year with a total of about 1250 abstracts annually, arranged in each number into 5 categories covering the
books of the New Testament and the world of early Christianity.

Each issue also has new book notices. The third issue of each
year has author/reviewer, book review, and Biblical indexes, while
the first issue lists more than 250 journals canvassed.

0028-6877/1759980   308/313/440/466/488/635/636/665/848

[554]   *Newsletter for Targumic and Cognate Studies* (["Bibliography"])

Published by the Department of Near Eastern Studies, University of
Toronto, the 1984/1 issue listed about 150 books and articles on
Targums (Aramaic translations of books of the Old Testament).
These were divided into 4 categories and included titles in Arabic
for which brief annotations were provided. As well, there was a
list of more than 30 journals which were surveyed.

0704-5905/3304682   466/488/578/847

[555]   *Newsletter for Ugaritic Studies* ("Articles")

Published by the Religious Studies Program, University of Calgary,
this appears twice yearly and usually lists 150 to 200 items dealing with Ugaritic studies and studies in northwest Semitic languages
in all languages and including book reviews. There are no indexes
or any list of journals. Materials listed are very current.

0702-8245/11764678   81/308/544/584

[556]   *Niedersächsische Bibliographie*

Compiled by the Niedersächsischen Landesbibliothek, Hannover, the
volume covering 1977/78 was published in 1982 and included about
7500 listings divided into 15 categories and about 375 sub-categories. These cover all fields of knowledge, with history and related fields (especially local and family history) accounting for
the largest portion. In a separate volume are author and keyword
indexes. About 160 journals which were analyzed are also listed.

---- ----/4539476   196/550/557

[557]   *Niedersächsisches Jahrbuch für Landesgeschichte* ("Aus Aufsätzen
        und Beiträgen zur niedersachsischen Landesgeschichte")

Materials published in 1978/80 were listed in the 1982 volume.
These comprised over 100 annotated entries divided into 8 categories
covering the different fields into which history is divided. There
were no indexes or lists of journals. Quicker but much less comprehensive than [556].

0078-0561/2612533   196/550/556

[558]   *Nineteenth Century Theater Research* ("NCTR: A Bibliography")

Materials for 1981 were listed in the 1982 volume, where 176 items on English-speaking theater (excluding Shaw but including Ibsen and Chekhov) were arranged by playwright. There was an author index.

0316-5329/1786242   660

[559]   *Nordfrieslandische Jahrbuch* ("Neues Schrifttum über Nordfriesland")

Compiled by the Nordfriisk Instituut in Braïst. The volume for 1982/83 contained nearly 1000 items divided into 25 categories covering all fields of knowledge, with an unusually heavy emphasis (for such German publications) on the natural sciences. There are no indexes or lists of journals.

0078-1045/1785049   190/457

[560]   *Nordic Archaeological Abstracts*

The volume for 1983 contained 662 annotated entries divided into 11 chronological classifications. These were drawn from about 300 journals and 20 collective works and cover all of Scandinavia (including Finland), Iceland, Greenland, and the Färoes. There is an author index, an extensive subject index, and an index of sites (with 2 maps). Titles of articles not in English are translated.

0105-6492/4563667

[561]   *Nordisk Bibliografi for Folkelivsforskere*

The volume for 1980 was published in 1983 and included 1680 items divided into 17 categories (including urban ethnology; social organization; folklore; religion and mythology; and folklife) covering Scandinavia (including Finland), Greenland, and Iceland. There are author and subject indexes as well as a list of about 225 analyzed journals.

0105-3221/2253707   333/439/513/699

[562]   *Norois* ("Bibliographie de l'Anjou")

This appears every other year, that for 1981/82 appearing in the 1983 volume. Materials on the Angevin region of France (typically from 40 to 60 each time) are arranged in 3 categories: maps; physical geography; human geography. There are no indexes.

0029-182X/1760469   150/563

[563] *Norois* ("Bibliographie du Centre-Ouest")

This appears every other year, alternating with [562] and includes
from 75 to 100 items on the geography of west central France excluding Anjou. These are arranged into several categories, including physical geography, historical geography, rural geography, and
urban geography. There are no indexes.

0029-182X/1760469   150/562/739

[564] *Norsk Litteraer Arbok* ("Bibliografi over Norsk Litteraturforsking")

The volume for 1983 listed about 750 items on Norwegian literature
and literary history published largely in 1982. These were divided
into 8 general categories and one devoted to individual authors
(which comprised three-quarters of the total). Virtually all the
entries refer to literature of the nineteenth and twentieth centuries. There are no indexes but a list of about 40 journals is included.

0078-1266/1792617   567/613

[565] *Norsk Slektshistorisk Tidsskrift* ("Annotert Bibliografi over litteratur i slektshistorie og naerstaende emner")

Dealing with Norwegian family history and related areas, the bibliography for 1983 appeared in 1984. As with previous bibliographies it contained annotated references to about 40 books and articles (largely the former) on the subject, rather unnecessarily
arranged under several headings. It also included a brief regis-
try of genealogical research in Norway. There are no indexes or
a list of relevant journals.

0029-2141/1760485   372/567/581

[566] *Norsk Utenrikspolitisk Arbok* ("Bibliografi")

Each year this consists of separate listings of books and reports,
articles, and official documents relating to Norwegian foreign
policy and its historical background. In 1983 some 125 to 150 of
these were included. There were no indexes.

---- ----/5730583   567

[567] *Norske Tidsskriftartikeler*

Prepared by the library of the University of Oslo, each year several thousand entries are included covering publications in Norwegian journals on all aspects of knowledge. These are organized
into a host of categories in the Dewey Decimal Classification.
There is a subject index as well as an author/institutional index.
Finally, there is a list of the some 400 journals (out of about

3500 Norwegian serial publications) analyzed.

0332-978X/9677346   372/565

[568] *Northern History* ("Review of Periodical Literature and Occasional
Publications")

133 items in 1984 relating to the North of England were listed by
journal title. This is particularly useful for the number of
county and municipal publications canvassed but loses value in that
page numbers are not provided. There are no indexes.

0078-172X/1760664   47/838/842

[569] *Norwegian-American Studies* ("Some Recent Publications")

This is published by the Norwegian American Historical Association
annually. The volume for 1985 listed about 100 books and pamphlets
and 80 articles separately by author. There are no indexes nor is
there a list of journals canvassed.

0078-1983/1760811   402/782

[570] *Novarien* ("Schedario bibliografico novarese")

This bibliography, devoted to the ecclesiastical history of Novara,
Italy, appears annually. The most recent (appearing in 1983), included about 70 items in 8 categories, each subdivided. Entries
are frequently annotated briefly. There are no indexes but a brief
listing of journals canvassed was included.

---- ----/7054533   136/682

[571] *Novodobé dejiny v ceskoslovenské historiografii/Marxisticko-len-
inská. Bibliografie 19--*

The bibliography for 1982 (published in 1984) contained more than
7900 entries arranged in 4 large and many smaller categories dealing principally with Marxist theory and with the recent history of
Communist nations. Of these those devoted to the "social sciences"
and to history (largely arranged chronologically and largely post-
1918) accounted for about 3000 entries each. The other major categories are biography and reference works. There are author, personal name, and geographical indexes as well as lists of over 200
journals and newspapers and about 175 collective works.

0550-239X/2692864   172/498/571

[572] *Novum Testamentum* ("Bibliographia Gnostica")

The bibliography of items published in 1983 (and occasionally earlier) appeared in the last quarterly number of 1984. This comprised about 200 items (with a high proportion of reivews) into four categories dealing with various aspects of early Christian Gnosticism. There are no indexes.

0048-1009/1760885   145/553/670/848

[573] *Nueva Revista de Filología Hispánica* ("Bibliografía")

Compiled by the Centro de Estudios Linguisticos y Literarios of the Colégio de Mexico, Mexico City. The latest (which appeared in 1985) is concerned with materials published in 1981 and earlier. Here 3000 items were listed covering Spain and Spanish-speaking areas of the world (except Latin American literature) and divided into 4 large categories (general; linguistics; literature; folklore) each of which was subdivided many times. A list of about 225 journals was included, but no indexes. This would be of use perhaps to those without access to [513].

0029-5868/1760914   124/207/648/769

[574] *Numismatic Literature*

This is published twice a year by the American Numismatic Society, but appears about a year late. In the September 1984 number there were listed 664 items in numerous categories, mostly by geography and coin type. About 75 reviews were listed separately. Each item is accompanied by a brief abstract. Coverage is worldwide and fairly extensive, although certainly the many numismatic articles appearing in India are not comprehensively included. There are subject and author indexes in each issue but the list of journal abbreviations appears only in the first issue of even-numbered years.

0029-6031/1760920   366/405

[575] *Ny litteratur om kvinnor: en bibliografi*

This is produced by the Göteborgs Universitetsbibliothek four times each year and is based on its acquisitions. For 1984 nearly 4000 items on women were included, divided into 27 categories in each issue. These include history, regional studies, anthropology and ethnology, demography, and biography. Each entry is provided with descriptors in Swedish which in aggregate constitute the subject index in each issue. There is a separate subject index in English as well as an author index but a list of journals is not provided. This is among the most substantial of the bibliographies on women's studies, although there is not unexpectedly a strong emphasis on Scandinavia.

0348-7962/7354719   772/834

[576]   *Ökumenische Rundschau* ("Zeitschriftenschau")

A very brief listing appears in each quarterly issue and includes
such categories as: Luther and the ecumene; and Orthodox-Roman
Catholic relations. Some items are annotated but the bibliography
is very selective and does not seriously compete with [469].

0029-8654/1696668   448/469

[577]   *Old English Newsletter* ("Old English Bibliography")

The bibliography appears in the first of two issues per year. That
for 1983 comprised about 750 items in 8 categories (plus reviews
and research in progress) dealing with Old English language and
literature, ecclesiastical history, archeology and numismatics,
and onomastics from early Anglo-Saxon times into the thirteenth
century. A list of about 45 journals was included.

0030-1973/2428532   32/63/838

[578]   *Old Testament Abstracts*

This appears three times a year and annually comprises about 1250
abstracts of materials relating to the Old Testament and the world
of ancient Israel. These are divided into 10 categories on general
topics and groups of Old Testament books (including the Apocrypha).
Each issue has an author index, an index to scriptural passages,
and an index of Hebrew and other Semitic words. In each issue
there is also a master list of journals canvassed, at present more
than 300.

0364-8591/3789752   308/313/440/466/488/635/636/847

[579]   *Oldenburger Jahrbuch* ("Oldenburgische Bibliographie")

In 1981 over 30 pages were devoted to materials published largely
in 1979 and concerned with the Oldenburg region of Niedersächsen
in West Germany. This would indicate that some 600 entries or more
were included, probably dealing with all aspects of Oldenburg, both
past and present. And, to judge from similar local German bibliographies, these were arranged into several classifications and
well indexed.

0340-4447/6239003   190/457/550/556/557

[580]   *Olifant* ("Bibliographical Note")

Prepared by the American-Canadian branch of the Société Rencesvals.
The most recent appeared in the Spring 1980 number and included
385 items on medieval epic literature divided into general and individual works. There was, in addition, an author index.

0381-9132/2588057   747

[581] *Ons Heem* ("Heemkundige bibliografie"/"Tijdschriftenschau")

This deals with Norwegian folklore and folklife but is several
years behind. Materials for]975 appeared in the 1981 volume,
where several hundred were listed, arranged into several categories
and with author and subject indexes.

---- ----/-------   513/561/565/567

[582] *Ons Geestelijk Erf* ("Literatuuroverzicht")

Materials published in 1983 were listed in the 1984 bibliography,
which contained over 850 items arranged in 10 categories on theology and (largely) church history, almost entirely concerned with
the Low Countries, particularly Belgium. There are no indexes nor
a list of journals canvassed.

---- ----/2671327   77/821

[583] *Oral History Review* ("Selected Bibliography")

Now on an annual basis, this bibliography lists materials in the
burgeoning field of oral history, both in the United States and
throughout the world. In the 1984 volume over 200 items were
listed, divided into such diverse categories as African studies,
gerontology, librarianship/archival management, and women's studies. Largely confined to English-language materials, foreign language titles are translated when they appear. There are no indexes or a list of journals.

0094-0798/1793844   188/864

[584] *Orientalia* ("Keilschriftbibliographie")

This is compiled by the Pontifical Biblical Institute in Rome and
is probably the basic serial bibliography for Ancient Near East
studies along with [82]. The latter suffers by comparison in its
currency but the present bibliography suffers in that it excludes
ancient Egypt from consideration. The latest to appear, in the
last number for 1983, comprised 1930 articles and 618 books, each
arranged in a single listing by author. Although there are personal name, ancient word, text, and broad subject indexes, access
is only moderate under this arrangement. Withal, an indispensable
tool in its field, not least for its excellent currency in a field
where such currency is not at all typical.

0030-5367/2670229   22/81/82/225/308/595/800

[585] *Österreichische historische Bibliographie*

The bibliography for 1982 (published in 1984) comprised about 3400
items arranged into 8 general and geographical categories, of which

that dealing with Austrian history is much the largest. Only materials published in Austria are included (for other materials on Austrian history see [112]). There is no list of journals but there is an author index and an extensive subject index.

---- ----/986645   112

[586]   *Österreichische Volkskundliche Bibliographie*

The volume for 1977/78 (published in 1982) included about 2000 items on the ethnography, folklore, and general history of Austria. These were arranged in over 20 geographical and topical categories, most in turn subdivided. There were author/personal name, geographical, and subject indexes as well as a list of 75 to 100 journals analyzed.

---- ----/6134795   327/439/513/587

[587]   *Österreichische Volksliedwerk* ("Verzeichnis der österreichischen Neuerscheinungen auf den Gebieten Volkslied, Volksmusik, Volkstanz, und Volksdichtung")

This bibliography for 1981 appeared in the 1984 volume where 230 items were listed in 10 categories covering all aspects of Austrian folk music, poetry, and literature, including their historical dimensions. There are no indexes and only a partial list of journals canvassed.

0473-8624/1761052   540/586/625

[588]   *Østjysk hjemstavn* ("Litteratur om Østjylland")

One of several Danish local bibliographies, this deals with the Østjylland (or eastern Jutland) region (main city Aarhus). Each year 50 to 60 relevant items are listed arranged in various categories but without indexes.

---- ----/-------   336

[589]   *Ostkirchliche Studien* ("Bibliographie")

This is the major bibliography on the Eastern churches but suffers from the way it is organized. Each quarterly issue includes from 100 to several hundred items in a rotating fashion among theology (much the largest and subdivided into 10 sections), philosophy and literature, and history. These are covered in different issues or even range over several issues. As a result, it can be several years before a particular category is repeated. Arrangement in all cases is alphabetical by author and all languages are covered. Each year there is an author index in the last number. In addition there is a separate "Zeitschriftenschau," which lists, in modified current contents format, articles by journal title. Despite these organizational problems, this is by far the most important serial bibliography on eastern Christendom.

0030-6487/1761572   374/448/576

[590] *Otto/Novecento* ("Bibliografia Manzoniana")

Appearing in most numbers, this is dedicated to materials on the nationalist poet and novelist Alessandro Manzoni, who was prominent in the Risorgimento. Usually about 100 items (including reviews) are included, arranged by author and drawn largely from newspapers and literary journals, though historical material is included to the extent available. Items are occasionally annotated.

0391-2639/4756458   684/763

[591] *Overijsselse Historische Bijdragen* ("Lijst van historische publikaties over Overijssel")

Each year this devotes 15 or so pages (and so perhaps 300 items) to literature on the history of Overijssel province of the Netherlands (capital Zwolle).

---- ----/9459693   13/187/396/640/797

[592] *Pacific History Bibliography and Comment*

Published as an annual supplement to the *Journal of Pacific History* (where it previously appeared), that for 1984 included 250 to 300 books and about 500 articles, plus a list of theses and a few reviews. Arrangement is largely geographical and includes all of Oceania except New Zealand. There are no indexes or any list of journals. Coverage is quite current and this very usefully fills a gap in the work of [631].

0729-1000/8225240   552/642

[593] *Paedagogica Historica* ("Index Bibliographicus")

The bibliography in the 1984 volume covered 1981 and preceding years and included over 1600 items drawn from about 200 journals. These are divided into: general; history by epoch; and comparative, national, and local history, each in turn subdivided. There is extensive cross-referencing. Focus is largely European, with some materials on North America, and few on the Third World. There is an author index but no list of journals.

0030-9230/1641215   171/219/277/724

[594]   *Paleopathology Newsletter* ("Annotated Bibliography")

This is published quarterly and usually contains 20 to 40 annotated
entries on recent publications on the study of human and animal
skeletal remains throughout the world and therefore of interest to
medical historians, archeologists, ethnohistorians, and epidemiolo-
gists.

0148-4737/3303159   98

[595]   *Paléorient* ("Bibliographie")

These are concerned with materials on the prehistory and protohistory of ancient southwest Asia, from Turkestan to Egypt, and thus
are largely archeological in nature. The latest to appear, that
for 1982, lists from 200 to 250 items by author, with a list of
more than 20 journals consulted but no indexes.

0153-9345/2552402   81/82/225/352/584

[596]   *Passauer Jahrbuch für Geschichte, Kunst und Volkskunde* ("Neuerscheinungen zur Geschichte und Landeskunde von Niederbayern")

This covers the area around Passau in southern Bavaria. The 1983
volume included over 1200 items, largely from 1981, divided into
10 chronological and thematic categories covering various aspects
of history and folk life, with particular emphasis on local history. There are author and onomastic indexes as well as a list of
some 70 journals canvassed.

0078-6845/2682585   120/600/846

[597]   *Pays Haut* ("Bibliographie du Pays-Haut")

This deals with the Meurthe-et-Moselle *département* in northeastern
France. Each year from 100 to 200 items on various aspects of the
area, largely historical, are included.

---- ----/-------   34/150

[598]   *Pensamiento* ("Bibliografía Filosófica Hispánica")

This bibliography is devoted to the history of philosophy (and,
less, to philosophy generally) as it was published in Spain and
other Spanish-speaking areas. The listing in the 1984 volume
(largely 1983 and preceding years) included over 1300 items, 800
on the history of philosophy and the balance on various aspects of
philosophical thought. Each of these categories is in turn divided, with the first classified largely by philosopher. There are
no indexes but a list of more than 60 journals is included.

0031-4749/1585663   601/602/760/638

[599]   *Pensamiento Iberoamericana* ("Revista de revistas iberoamericanas")

Prepared by the Instituto de Cooperación Iberoamericana in Madrid,
the most recent (published in 1983 and covering 1982/83) listed
the contents (by journal title) of one or more issues of 131 journals published in Latin America, Spain, and Portugal which deal
with Latin American political economy. Page numbers are not included nor are there any indexes. About 150 articles are singled
out and provided with abstracts in a section called "Resúmenes de
Artículos." Coverage is current and comprehensive and a fair
amount of historical material is included but it is not always easy
to find.

0212-0208/8790796   776/865

[600]   *Pfälzer Heimat* ("Bucher- und Zeitschriftenschau")

Each issue lists from 75 to 100 items on the history, geography,
and culture of the German Palatinate. These are arranged in a
single author alphabet and there are no indexes or a list of journals covered.

0031-6679/2723096   120/846

[601]   *The Philosopher's Index*

This is published quarterly and cumulated annually and attempts
to cover all aspects of philosophy as expounded in books and articles in English, French, German, Spanish, and Italian. Materials (several thousand each year) are first arranged in a very refined subject index which leads users to a succeeding author index
in which full bibliographical details and abstracts are provided.
Finally there is a book review index. Publication details on more
than 350 journals are included in each issue. History is well
covered, though it is probably easier to find materials on an individual philosopher than on a philosophical movement.

0331-7993/4187784   602/638/661

[602]   *Philosophie: Bibliographie*

This appears four times a year and in 1984 totals nearly 3000 items
divided in more than a dozen categories, most in turn subdivided.
The emphasis is on historical materialism, which, along with the
history of philosophy, constitutes two-thirds of the entries. There
are author and subject/personal name indexes in each issue as well
as a brief list of about 30 journals (most German and east European)
canvassed.

0034-2262/2258308   601/638/661

[603]   *Pietismus und Neuzeit* ("Pietismus-Bibliographie")

The bibliography for 1983 was published in the 1984 volume. It included about 300 items concerning the Pietist movement in modern
Protestantism, especially in Germany as a result of the influence
of Zinzendorf. These are divided into 19 topical, geographical,
and biographical categories. There are no indexes but there is a
list of about 30 journals which were consulted.

0172-6943/4801883

[604]   Pisa. Domus Mazziniana. *Bollettino* ("Appunti per una bibliografia
mazziniana")

This varies in size but the most recent (in the 1984/2 volume) included 125 items, most annotated, sometimes extensively, on the
life of Giuseppe Mazzini and nineteenth-century Italian nationalism.
There were no indexes.

0480-5542/5503864   590/628

[605]   *Point de repère. Index analytique d'articles de périodiques qué-
becois et étrangers*

Published six times a year this replaces *Radar* and *Périodex*. In
1984 265 Francophone journals were canvassed, two-thirds from Quebec, the rest from France, the rest of Canada, Belgium, and Switzerland. Any material in these is included but of course most of the
citations relate somehow to Quebec. The arrangement is alphabetical by a host of narrowly-defined subjects and brief annotations
are provided in most instances. There are no indexes but a list of
journal issues canvassed is included in each number.

0822-8833/11591907   235/657

[606]   *Polish-American Studies* ("A Bibliography on Polish Americans")

Designed to update recent retrospective bibliographies on a recurring basis, the listing for 1975/1980 included about 550 items drawn
from Polish and U.S. publications. These are arranged by author
under bibliographies; books and pamphlets; and articles. There are
no indexes but a list of more than 100 journals surveyed is included.

0032-2806/1762549   402

[607]   *Polish Archaeological Abstracts*

This covers Polish archeology from the Paleolithic era to the fifteenth century. The volume for 1980 (published in 1983) included
184 abstracts in English arranged chronologically, as well as an
author index and a list of more than 50 journals canvassed.

---- ----/1781255   720

[608]   *Polska Bibliografia Literacka*

The two volumes for 1978 were published only in 1985. The first
included more than 7600 entries (some with more than a single item)
on Polish literature through the ages while the second volume in
cluded another 4500 or so on non-Polish literature which, except
for the more than 1000 items on Russian literature and another
1000+ on mass media, is unlikely to be of particular interest.
The arrangement is largely by author studied. Volume 2 includes
author and subject indexes for the whole while in volume 1 is a
list of more than 700 journals canvassed.

0079-3590/2826406   507

[609]   *Pomorania Antiqua* ("Bibliography of Prehistoric and Early Medieval
        Archeology in Eastern Pomerania")

214 items were included in the volume for 1979 divided into general
and chronological classifications. There are author and onomastic
indexes but no list of journals.

0556-0691/2781312   453/844

[610]   *Population Index* ("Bibliography")

Prepared by the Office of Population Research, Princeton University,
this constitutes a major portion of each issue of *Population Index*
and is based on acquisitions of the library of the Office of Population Research and several others. About 3000 items are included
in 1984, arranged in about 20 categories, many further subdivided,
and featuring brief abstracts. Biological, medical, and geographical literature are excluded, being covered by their own bibliographies. Coverage is largely on contemporary demographic issues but
a fair amount of historical literature is nonetheless included.
Each issue has author and geographical indexes, which are cumulated
annually. In the cumulative annual index there is also a list of
about 500 journals and other serial publications.

0032-4701/1762666   160/166

[611]   *Portuguese Studies Newsletter*

Published by the International Conference Group on Portugal, each
semi-annual issue includes separate listings of recent books, articles, and chapters on Portugal, as well as on Portuguese-speaking
Africa and Asia, and the Portuguese in America. There are no indexes.

0738-9841/4386702   199/214/331/421

[612]   *Post-Medieval Archaeology* ("Post-Medieval Britain in Periodic Literature")

The bibliography for 1983 appeared in 1983, arranged by journal title in a modified current contents format. From 40 to 45 journals concerned with historic and industrial archeology in the United Kingdom were canvassed and were arranged geographically. This was preceded by a list of sites.

0079-4236/2834163   63/179/198/296

[613]   *Prazský Sborník Historický* ("Přehled Pragensií za Léta")

The most recent bibliography appeared in the 1981 volume and covered publications of 1976 to 1978. 767 of these were grouped into 20 categories dealing with the history of Prague, some broken down further. There were no indexes but a useful list of over 500 Czech journals was included.

0555-0238/1762783   253/759/852

[614]   *Preliminary Egyptological Bibliography*

Sponsored by the International Association of Egyptologists in Berlin, this appears irregularly but several times yearly and is intended to anticipate coverage provided by [55] which lags several years behind, although it lacks the annotations of [55]. In each issue items are arranged into several categories consistent with [55] and there is an author index. Moreover, recent acquisitions of several major Egyptological libraries are included.

---- ----/-------   15/55/549

[615]   *Przeglad Antropologiczny* ("Bibliografia Antropologii Polskiej")

Materials published from 1976 to 1980 were listed in a supplement to the 1981 volume. Comprising works by Polish anthropologists, over 1800 items were listed (many cross-referenced, however) and arranged in a single author sequence. In addition there were nearly 200 supplemental items. There was a subject index and a list of more than 70 journals.

0033-2003/2266559

[616]   *Public Affairs Information Service Bulletin*

The standard tool covering English-language public affairs and public policy literature, this appears twice a month and is cumulated quarterly and then annually. The main arrangement is by subject, of which thousands are included each year. This is followed by an author arrangement in which most bibliographical details are repeated. More than 1400 journals are surveyed annually and a list

of these is provided with publication details. There is also a
list of publishers and organizations. In addition to articles,
books, official documents, and reports are included selectively.

0033-3409/4227283   1/209/298/431/617

[617] *Public Affairs Information Service: Foreign Language Index*

This, the foreign language analog of [616], is similarly arranged--
an extremely refined subject listing followed by an author listing
repeating the essential information. This, however, appears only
quarterly but is also cumulated annually. It covers economics and
public affairs literature in French, German, Italian, Spanish, and
Portuguese, and its citations are occasionally very briefly annotated. It is to some extent based on the same sources as [616] and
for these materials is probably somewhat slower to appear. More
than 500 journals are analyzed, for which full publication details
are provided, a valuable source in itself. Moreover, there is a
list of publishers and organizations.

0033-3409/4227283   1/209/298/431/616

[618] *Quaderni di archeologia della Libia* ("Bibliografia archeologica
della Libia")

Materials for 1978/79 appeared in the 1980 volume. These were divided into materials on Cyrenaica (105) and those on Tripolitania
and Fezzan (100), each preceded by a brief introduction. There
were no indexes.

0079-8258/2807400   149/503

[619] *Quaderni Giuliani di Storia* ("Bollettino Bibliografico")

This covers materials dealing with Istria, Friuli, and other areas
of the Julian March of northeast Italy and northwest Yugoslavia.
Although cast in the form of book reviews, all materials, whether
in book or article form, are covered and are heavily annotated.
In the most recent listing (1984/1) 100 to 125 items are included,
arranged in chronological order. As well, there is a list of over
40 journals from which they are drawn.

---- ----/9835263   66/136/356/525

[620] *Quaker History* ("Articles in Quaker Periodicals")

A minor compilation, from 15 to 30 items appear in most issues
(only 15 in the latest--1984/1).

0033-5053/1776671

[621]   *Quarterly Index Islamicus*

Now the major tool on Islamic studies, this comprised more than
4500 in 1984 divided into nearly 40 regional and topical categories covering Islam from Spain to Southeast Asia, with historical
aspects well covered. There is a subject index in each issue (cumulated annually) and an annual author index, but no list of journals canvassed.

0308-7395/3415908   5/330/528/529/542

[622]   *Quondam et futurus: Newsletter for Arthurian Studies* ("Current
Publications")

A listing of 50 to 75 items on the Arthurian cycle appears in each
quarterly issue. All languages are included, materials are arranged
in a single author sequence, and there are no indexes.

8755-3627/7618478   427

[623]   *RIC. Répertoire bibliographique des institutions chrétiennes*

Published by the Centre de Recherche et de Documentation des Institutions Chrétiennes in Strasbourg, this appears twice yearly and in
1984 more than 3200 items were included. These are arranged geographically by country and each entry carries a code indicating
religious denomination and importance. There is a subject index
in English, fairly unrefined and not very helpful, as well as even
smaller subject indexes in French, German, Spanish, and Italian.
About 1400 journals are analyzed but these are not listed (a basic
list appeared in 1972). An interesting mixture of benefits (good
currency and wide coverage) and disadvantages (poor typography and
indifferent indexing) of a computer-produced bibliography. Special
supplements (3 to 4 a year) abstract materials on specific subjects
over a number of years (e.g., ecumenism; Christian communities;
evangelization and missions).

0079-9300/6466966   226/362/635/636/637/707/858

[624]   *RILA. Répertoire internationale de la littérature de l'art*

Published twice yearly, the 1984 volumes comprise about 8500 briefly
annotated entries (books, articles, reviews, exhibition catalogs,
and dissertations). These are arranged into reference works; general works; medieval art; Renaissance, Baroque, and Rococo art;
Neo-Classicism and modern art to 1945; modern art since 1945; collections and exhibits. There is extensive cross-referencing and
multiple issues of more than 200 journals are typically listed in
each issue. Finally, there is an author index and an extremely
detailed subject index.

0145-5982/2408596   57/98/99/100/639/851

[625] *RILM Abstracts of Music Literature*

Materials for 1979 were published only in 1984. There were over
6000 of these, dealing with music history and performance and divided into 11 categories. The abstracts are brief, seldom exceed-
ing 50 words. Coverage is global and includes reviews, dissertations, and catalogs in addition to books and articles. There is an
author index in each issue and annual cumulative author, composer,
and subject indexes appear in the fourth number of each year.

0033-6955/1853507   117/161/540

[626] *Railroad History* ("Recent Articles and Dissertations")

A brief listing of 25 or so articles, arranged by author, appears
in each semi-annual number.

0090-7847/1785797   479

[627] *Rassegna di letteratura tomistica* ("Bibliografia Tomistica
Critica")

Materials for 1981 were published in the 1984 volume, where 1381
items were listed. These were divided into 7 categories dealing
with St. Thomas, his writings, his philosophy and theology, and
his influence on later authors (the largest section). Most items
are annotated (in various languages), some extensively. There are
author and subject indexes as well as a list of about 250 journals
canvassed.

0557-6857/1776676   127/601/602/638/661

[628] *Rassegna storica del Risorgimento* ("Spoglio di periodici")

Materials published in 1983 and earlier were listed in the first
and third numbers of 1984. Over 600 items dealing with Italian
history and culture in the nineteenth century were classified in
numerous topical, biographical, and geographical categories. There
are no indexes but cross-referencing is extensive. A list of more
than 150 journals, very largely Italian, is included.

0033-9873/1608137   590/604

[629] *Raydan* ("Bibliographie sudarabique")

Published by the Yemeni Centre for Cultural and Archaeological Research in Aden, the volume for 1981 included 125 to 150 items arranged into several categories and incorporating material in all
languages except Arabic. South Arabia from the earliest times to
the seventh century A.D. is covered (included ancient South Arabia
in later Islamic literature). There are no indexes and no list of
journals (or even a list of abbreviations in every volume). Even

so, a useful complement to the irregular bibliography in [82].

---- ----/6860724   82

[630] *Recent Polar and Glaciological Literature*

This is published triannually by the Scott Polar Research Institute, Cambridge, U.K. Each issue of 1000 or more entries is arranged into a host of categories by the Universal Decimal Classification ranging from "frost action on rocks" and "hail" and "soft
hail" to the more relevant "native peoples" and regional history.
There are no indexes or lists of journals.

---- ----/7302930   59/321

[631] *Recently Published Articles*

Published by the American Historical Association, *RPA* is growing
in size and coverage year by year and at least 15,000 items appear
in the three 1984 numbers. These are arranged in 20 (1 general;
19 geographical or chronological) classifications (most of which
are further subdivided), each prepared by a specialist in the field.
Coverage varies from excellent (the ancient world, Africa) to good
(most sections) to poor (South and Southeast Asia) to non-existent
(the Ancient Near East and Oceania) but on balance it is the superior tool in the field as measured by comprehensiveness and currency.
However, as regards access there remain problems. Items are not
numbered, there are no indexes and no lists of journals, and the
system of abbreviations devised for journal titles permits far too
many permutations and sometimes defies decoding. Nonetheless, any
libraries on proverbial desert islands or with (now almost proverbial) shrinking budgets should certainly own this bibliography before all others in the field of history.

0145-5311/2280829

[632] *Records of Early English Drama* ("Annotated Bibliography of Printed
Records of Early British Drama and Minstrelsy")

This is published biennially, with the latest (covering 1982 and
1983) appearing in the second issue of 1984. This includes over
300 briefly annotated entries on pre-eighteenth-century British
drama, excluding the Shakespeare claimants (other than Shakespeare
himself), and preceded by a short introduction. Books, articles,
and records series are included in a straight alphabetical sequence, without indexes.

0700-9283/3350219   311/558/660

[633] *Recusant History* ("Newsletter")

This annual listing (around 100 items in 1985) is devoted to the

history of Catholicism in the British Isles from the sixteenth
century to the mid-eighteenth century (specifically, from 1558 to
1870). Citations are divided into history, literary, and theses.
There are no indexes or lists of journals and materials published
by local recusant societies are not included.

0034-1932/1894865   244/245

[634] *Referativnyi Zhurnal: Geografiia*

One of a series of Russain bibliographies in the natural and physical sciences, each monthly issue is composed of a series of separately numbered, paged, and indexed parts, dealing with theoretical and general issues; cartography; oceanography; geomorphology;
biogeography; meteorology and climatology; and several geographical areas arranged regionally. Each entry is annotated (100 to
250 words) and each section also carries its own list of journals
canvassed, aggregating to several thousand annually. Finally there
are separate subject, author, and geographical indexes.

0034-2378/1763609   164/276

[635] *Religion Index One: Periodicals*

Published twice yearly (with the second number cumulative) by the
American Theological Library Association and intended to incorporate
the entire field of religion in all languages (though English pre-
dominates). In 1984 about 11,000 articles were indexed in a dictionary catalog subject arrangement, with nearly 40,000 subject entries in the two volumes. In addition more than 12,000 book reviews
are cited separately. About 370 journals are analyzed and these
are listed in each number together with publication details (including ISSN numbers). Besides the subject arrangement there is an
author index in which bibliographical details are repeated and annotations (20 to 200 words) provided for over one-third of the citations. Beginning in 1985 the subject classification and the author listing/book reviews will be published in separate volumes.
In addition to this slightly monumental approach to the literature,
RIO is the most current of the many religious bibliographies, though
not nearly so thorough in its coverage of European publications as
some of the others.

0149-8428/3568980   226/362/623/636/637/707/858

[636] *Religion Index Two: Multi-Author Works*

This counterpart of [635] is published annually and attempts to
canvass materials published in varous kinds of collective works,
which are more frequent in the field of religion than in any other.
The volume for 1983 (published in 1985) included over 4700 items
from over 300 collective works, which are arrayed alphabetically
in some 23,000 subject headings. A list of the collective works
is included but publication details are given under editor's name

in the second listing. As with [635] there is in addition to the
subject listing, a separate author/editor index with bibliographical details and annotations for one-quarter to one-half the entries.

0149-8436/3569016   226/232/623/635/637/707/858

[637]   *Religious and Theological Abstracts*

This is published 4 times a year and for 1984 nearly 3500 abstracts
were included, divided into biblical, theological, historical, and
practical, each in turn subdivided, with the sections on the Bible
and history accounting for about one-half the total. Generally,
materials appear less than a year after being published. Each year
the last number includes subject, author, and scriptural indexes
as well as publication details of the 200 or more journals currently
being canvassed.

0034-4044/1607912   226/362/623/635/636/707/858

[638]   *Répertoire bibliographique de la philosophie*

Published as a quarterly supplement to *Revue philosophique de Louvain* by the Institut Supérieur de Philosophie of the Université
Catholique de Louvain. Along with [601] this is the major bibliographical tool in the field of philosophy and in 1983 comprised
more than 12,000 citations to works in western European languages.
These are arranged in several general and chronological categories.
A list of reviews (more than 2000 in 1983) and an author/reviewer
index comprise the last number of each year, while in the first
number is a list of journals consulted (about 500 presently).

0034-4567/1713864   601/602/661

[639]   *Répertoire d'art et d'archéologie*

Published four times a year by the Centre de Documentation Sciences
Humaines of the Centre National de la Recherche Scientifque, Paris,
this is very similar in format to the series of Bulletins Signalétiques ([164], [219-227]) also published by CNRS. All and all it
is probably the most useful serial bibliography in its field, although it is well to bear in mind that it only covers western art
from early Christian times to 1939, leaving ancient art to the
archeological bibliographies and non-western art to no tool in particular. In 1983 it included more than 10,000 items arranged in
several general and chronological categories, most of which are in
turn subidivded geographically. Each item is briefly (30 to 150
words) annotated, while each number includes the journals and collective works analyzed (more than 300 in 1983), many of which are
not directly related to the history of art. As well, each issue
features artist, subject, and author indexes which are cumulated
annually in a fifth number. For a detailed comparison of *RAA* with
[624], to the general advantage of *RAA*, see *Simiolus*, 15 (1985),
61-64.

0080-0953/1641055   57/99/624/851

[640] *Repertorium van Boeken en Tijdschriftartikelen betreffende de Ges-chiedenis van Nederland*

The volume for 1982 (published in 1984) included over 4900 items on Dutch history from prehistory to the present divided into 10 classifications, each further subdivided in various ways. The Dutch experience overseas is included. There is extensive cross-referencing; author, personal name, and geographical indexes; and a listing of more than 750 journals and about 150 collective works which were analyzed.

---- ----/1763718   13/582/797

[641] *Research and Publications in New York State History*

The volume for 1982 (covering materials which appeared in 1980) included over 800 items (usually briefly annotated) in about 30 topical, chronological, and regional categories covering all aspects of New York history. There was an author/subject index and a list of some 40 journals.

0080-1488/3798154   25/464/631/837

[642] *Research in Melanesia* ("Publications, Reports, Theses, and Papers on Melanesia")

The number for June 1983 included 300 to 350 items, mostly published in 1982, some earlier. These were arranged in a strict author sequence and there were no indexes or list of journals.

0254-0665/2464815   552/592

[643] *Restoration* ("Studies in English Literary Culture, 1660-1700: Some Current Publications")

This is included in each semi-annual issue and usually comprises about 100 briefly annotated entries, largely arranged by seventeenth-century author. Materials seem very current but there are no indexes.

0162-9905/4095276   49/513/632

[644] *Review of African Political Economy* ("Current Africana")

This appears in most issues (though less regularly lately) and generally encompasses all of Africa. The most recent, however (in the September 1984 issue) was devoted entirely to Francophone west Africa, Lusophone west Africa, and Kenya and comprised 178 items dealing largely with "political economy," "underdevelopment," and the like. Good for ephemeral publications, particularly those published in Africa.

0305-6244/2243506   19/270

[645]   *Revista Andina* ("Revista de las Revistas")

Published by the Centro de Estudios Rurales Andinos Bartolomé de
las Casas in Cusco.   In the most recent number (July 1984) the
contents of about 45 journals were arranged by journal title.
Reasonably current and especially good for local Peruvian, Ecuadorian, and Bolivian publications, this is probably the best source
nowadays for Andean materials.

---- ----/10142753   264/368/532

[646]   *Revista Camoniana* ("Bibliografia")

Published in São Paulo, the latest (seen), that for 1980 and published in 1982, included more than 60 items published in 1979 and
1980 on Luis de Camões and his times.   These were arranged alphabetically by author and there were no indexes.

0486-6460/3602313

[647]   *Revista de dialectología y tradiciones populares* ("Bibliografía")

The bibliography in the 1983 volume included about 1000 items devoted to dialects, linguistics, ethnology, and folklore, with the
last two comprising four-fifths of the total and including the entire world (whereas dialects and linguistics include only Spain,
Portugal, and Latin America).   Materials are grouped into many categories, largely regional.   There is a list of about 40 journals
but no indexes.

0034-7981/9244636   573/631

[648]   *Revista de filología española* ("Bibliografía")

The latest, which appeared in the 1983 volume, included more than
600 items devoted largely to the Spanish languages and literatures
and most published in 1980 or 1981.   A list of about 100 journals
is included but there are no indexes.

---- ----/4275088   573/631

[649]   *Revista Española de Teología* ("Boletín bibliográfico de historia
de la teología en España")

The bibliography in 1983 included over 1200 items divided into 15
topical and denominational categories covering all aspects of Spanish ecclesiastical history (Islamic, Jewish, and Protestant as well
as Catholic) from the beginning of the Christian era to the present,
making it a major source for its field.   Currency is good, there is
an onomastic index and a list of about 125 journals canvassed.

0210-7112/1884217   90/661

[650]   *Revista Internacional de Estudos Africanos* ("Bibliografia das
publicacões sobre Africa de lingua portuguesa")

The first listing, appearing in the maiden issue of 1984, listed
over 1000 items published on Portuguese Africa between 1975 and
1983, although coverage will proceed on an annual basis. These
were divided into 6, mainly geographical, categories, each subdivided in turn and with numerous cross-references. There were no
indexes.

---- ----/11665361   17/18/154/270/271/297/426

[651]   *Revue Archéologique de l'Est et du Centre-Est* ("Bibliographie
régionale")

This appears every two years. The latest, published in 1984, included over 200 items dealing with the archeology of east and east-
central France. These are arranged in five categories ranging from
the Stone Age into the Middle Ages (the last very slightly) and em-
phasizes material that appears in the many local French historical
and archeological journals. There are no indexes or list of journals canvassed.

0035-0745/1713683   125/328/666

[652]   *Revue belge d'archéologie et d'histoire de l'art* ("Bibliographie
de l'art nationale")

This bibliography totalled 501 items in 1984 (down from 1220 in
1982) and is divided into: Préhistoire et Antiquité; Moyen Age et
Temps Modernes; Epoque Contemporaine, each further subdivided,
usually by art form. The history of art (and much archeology as
well) of what is now modern Belgium (and some of the neighboring
areas) is covered. There are no indexes or a list of journals.

0035-077X/1607886   654/676

[653]   *Revue belge de musicologie/Belgisch Tijdschrift voor Musiekweten-
schap* ("Bibliographie de l'histoire de l'art national: musique")

This is a spinoff of the bibliography in [652] which no longer includes music. The first, covering the years 1979 to 1983, appeared
in the 1982/84 volume, but it is hoped to put bibliographies on an
annual basis. In any event this first listing totalled more than
500 items arranged year by year in 3 categories (general; places;
persons). Books and articles on Belgian musical history, but not
sound recordings, are included. There is an author index and a
brief list of journals canvassed.

0771-6788/1681218   161/540/625

[654]   *Revue belge de philologie et d'histoire* ("Bibliographie de l'histoire de Belgique")

More than 1800 items, mostly published in 1982, were listed in the
bibliography in the 1983 volume. These were arranged in three
large categories (bibliography and auxiliary sciences; general
works; and history by epochs). The last was very much the largest
and included local history. Each of these was in turn subdivided
into several categories. Although unfortunately there are no indexes nor is there a list of journals, this must be considered the
major Belgian historical bibliography.

0035-0818/1641459   652/676

[655]   *Revue Bibliographique de Sinologie*

Until 1982 (when the volume covering the years 1968/70 was published) the bibliography lagged a dozen years behind. However, it
began anew in 1983, when the first of a new series was published.
For 1984 this included nearly 400 abstracts (50 to 100 words) for
materials published largely in 1983. Abstracts are in French and
English, whatever the language of the original (and all languages
are covered) and are classified into 7 categories covering all
fields of knowledge, but more than one-half relate to history and
archeology from legendary times to the present. There are author
and subject/personal name indexes and a list of about 100 journals
(largely Chinese-language) which were analyzed. Fewer items are
included than in the past but this bibliography is now a usable
tool instead of a relic (coverage for 1971 to 1982 is to be continued separately).

0080-2484/1764013   177/178/299/543/655/718/784/785/861

[656]   *Revue d'Alsace* ("Publications des sociétés d'histoire d'Alsace")

Most numbers feature a listing of the contents of various local
Alsatian historical journals, arranged by journal title, but not
including page numbers. Many of the items included are obscure
and not included in other, more general, bibliographies.

---- ----/6827362   34/148/150/742

[657]   *Revue d'histoire de l'Amérique française* ("Bibliographie")

This appears in each quarterly number of the *Revue* and for the four
numbers of the 1984/85 volume totalled no fewer than 2600 items,
covering French Canada, past and present, as well as the French
Antilles. In each issue items are arranged by author in 8 chronological and geographical categories and are drawn from more than
400 journals (which are not listed). Although there are no indexes
this remains an extremely useful tool, not least because of its
admirable currency.

0035-2357/1764125   11/25/235/605/736

[658] *Revue d'histoire de l'eglise de la France* ("Périodiques généraux"/
"Périodiques régionaux")

These appear in alternate issues and are arranged slightly differ-
ently. In 1983 nearly 70 general journals were listed, followed
by 200 to 300 very briefly annotated citations. The local journals
on the other hand are arranged by journal title into a number of
regional categories and perhaps 500 or more entries were included
in 1983. Coverage is very extensive, especially for the publications of the very numerous local French historical and archeological societies. There are no indexes.

0300-9505/1774092   661

[659] *Revue d'histoire de la deuxième guerre mondiale* ("Bibliographie")

Prepared by the Bibliothèque de Documentation Internationale Contemporaine in Paris, this appears regularly though not in every
issue. This makes it difficult to estimate annual production but
certainly several hundred entries are listed in a typical year.
These are arranged in about a dozen categories and include several
aspects of warfare, diplomacy, and "the Jewish question." There
are no indexes or lists of journals. Occasionally, special bibliographies are published, including a recurring one on World War I.

0035-2314/1605395   367/500/774/831

[660] *Revue d'histoire du théâtre* ("Bibliographie d'histoire du théâtre")

This is ordinarily in (and sometimes is) the last number of each
year. That in 1982 included over 5000 items in 15 categories dealing with all aspects of theatrical and dramatic history. The historical section (over 1900 entries) is arranged by country and then
by playwright. There was a list of about 200 journals but no indexes.

0035-2373/1589751   295/558

[661] *Revue d'histoire écclésiastique* ("Bibliographie")

This constitutes one-half or more of each thrice-yearly number.
In 1984 a total of nearly 10,000 items were included and were divided into 3 large categories and a host of smaller ones, as well
as a separate list of reviews of books which had been listed in
the previous year. Church history is defined rather broadly and
much philosophy and political history (for example) is included.
An author index and a list of 750 to 800 journals are published
annually.

0035-2381/1644972   28/58/93/145/244/313/661/682/850

[662] *Revue d'histoire littéraire de la France* ("Bibliographie")

This appears in each issue (that is, six times a year) and each
time about 1000 items are listed in several chronological categories, some of which are subdivided. Until 1980 this was cumulated
annually into *Bibliographie de la littérature française du Moyen-
Age à nos jours* but now each bi-monthly compilation seems to stand
alone. There are no indexes and a short list of journals consulted. Materials listed are quite current.

0035-2411/1238324   158/342/343/531

[663] *Revue de Géographie de Lyon* ("Bibliographie rhodanienne")

The most recent of these bibliographies (that for 1983) included
over 100 items on geographical (and to some extent historical)
characteristics of Lyon and the Rhône valley. These were arranged
into 9 classifications. There were no indexes and a list only of
journals newly cited, together with publication details.

0035-113X/1764045   562/563

[664] *Revue de Pau et de Béarn* ("Bibliographie béarnaise")

This appears annually; that for 1983 (covering 1982) included 168
entries classified into: reference works; environment; archaeology
and prehistory; history and biography; language and literature;
folklore; tourism and sports. The area of the French central Py-
renees is included. There are author and subject indexes and a
list of about 40 journals canvassed.

---- ----/6446086   150

[665] *Revue de Qumran* ("Bibliographie")

This appears in each semi-annual issue and is devoted to the Essene
sect and the Dead Sea Scrolls. The most recent (June 1984) included over 150 citations, first of books, then dissertations, and
finally articles arranged by journal title. There are no indexes.

0035-1725/1764081   466/553/848

[666] *Revue des études anciennes* ("Chronique Gallo-Romaine")

Appearing annually, the most recent of these (in the 1981 volume,
which was published only in 1984) included several hundred items
arranged in 41 categories covering all aspects of Roman Gaul.
Each section is in the form of a brief bibliographical essay.
There are no indexes or any list of journals.

0035-2004/1196181   73/125/328/651

[667]   *Revue des études anciennes* ("Histoire et archéologie de la péninsule
ibérique ancienne")

This appears every several years; the latest (covering 1973/77) was
in the volume for 1979 (published in 1982). In it were 1240 items
arranged as a series of bibliographical essays arranged in four
broad categories and covering ancient Spain and Portugal from prehistoric through Visigothic times. There was a geographical index
covering over 300 sites, together with a map, as well as a list of
30 journals not canvassed by [39].

0035-2004/1196181   73/328/515

[668]   *Revue des études augustiniennes* ("Bulletin Augustinien")

Materials published in 1983 appeared in the listing in 1984. Here
451 items were divided into 6 categories covering Augustine's life
and times; his philosophical and theological writings; and his sub-
sequent influence. Entries are annotated, sometimes quite extensively. There are no indexes nor any list of journals.

0035-2012/1764098

[669]   *Revue des études augustiniennes* ("Bulletin canoniale")

That which appeared in 1985, the second of the series, covered the
years 1982 and 1983. Over 200 briefly annotated items were arranged
in 7 categories covering various aspects of canon law from the
seventh century to the present. There are no indexes and no list
of journals.

0035-2012/1764098   79/216/238

[670]   *Revues des études augustiniennes* ("Chronica Tertulliana")

The most recent was included in the 1984 volume and listed 32 items
(usually annotated, sometimes at length) including editions and
translations of Tertullian's work as well as critical studies on
Tertullian and his milieu.

0035-2012/1764098   145/553/572/848

[671]   *Revue des études grecques* ("Bulletin archéologique: céramique")

This appears every year or so. Most recently (1984/1) 231 items
were listed, broken down variously geographically and by subject,
and subdivided thereunder into many smaller categories. Nearly
all entries are annotated, some quite extensively. The entire
Greek world is covered. There are no indexes but a brief list of
journals is included.

0035-2039/1764100   73/103/328

[672]   *Revue des études grecques* ("Bulletin des études égéo-anatoliennes")

Compiled by the Institut d'archéologie orientale of the Université
de Lyon, this appears about every three years. The latest listing
(in the 1984/1 volume) includes 297 items published on Minoan Crete,
Mycenaean Greece, the Aegean and western Anatolia in the second
millennium B.C. These are annotated, sometimes at length and deal
largely with linguistic, historical, and epigraphic matters. There
are no indexes, but a list of more than 40 journals canvassed is
provided.

0035-2039/1764100

[673]   *Revue des études grecques* ("Bulletin épigraphique")

Appearing annually, the most recent (published in 1983, covering
1982 and earlier) included 495 items on Greek epigraphy, both Classic Greece and overseas Greece. These are arranged geographically
and are usually annotated, sometimes very extensively. There are
no indexes.

0035-2039/1764100   73/328/354

[674]   *Revue des études slaves* ([various bibliographies])

Bibliographies are a standard feature of *RES* but they often take
the form of self-contained unannotated listings of specific subjects that may be repeated at some unspecified interval, or might
not. Some recent examples of apparently recurring bibliographies
are: "Ukraine: histoire" (83 entries); Tchécoslovaquie: histoire"
(94 entries); "Bulgarie: histoire" (121 entries); "Hongrie: histoire" (67 entries); "Albanie: histoire" (71 entries); "Littérature
russe" (341 items); "Domaine sorabe ou serbe de Lusace" (264 items).
In every case materials in all languages are covered and the listings are divided into various categories. There are no indexes.

0080-2557/1764107   3/118/119/323/692

[675]   *Revue des sciences philosophiques et théologiques* ("Recension des
revues")

This appears in each quarterly number in a modified current contents format, arranged by journal title. Just about anything on
theology and philosophy might be included and most items are briefly
annotated. From 25 to 50 journals might be analyzed in any given
issue. Largely for the browser.

0035-2209/1764115   601/602/661

[676]   *Revue du Nord* ("Bulletin d'histoire de Belgique")

Over 430 items which appeared in 1982 or 1983 were included in the

bibliography in the 1984/4 number. These were divided into 2 general and 3 chronological categories covering the period from the
Middle Ages to the present. Each item was annotated, sometimes
extensively, and there was an author index but no list of journals
consulted.

0035-2624/1764146   654

[677] *Revue roumaine d'histoire* ("Bibliographie historique")

This appears in most quarterly numbers on a kind of rotational
basis. The bibliography for 1979 began appearing in 1982 and still
continues in 1984, having in the meantime aggregated to 1103 items
arranged into a number of topical and chronological categories.
Titles in Rumanian are translated into French. It appears likely
then that this bibliography will become even less timely in the
future, unfortunate since this is the most thorough bibliography
in its field. At the beginning of the 1979 bibliography a list of
about 75 Rumanian journals was provided.

0556-8072/1764247   3/114/134/153/323/857

[678] *Revue savoisienne* ("Bibliographie savoisienne")

The most recent, published in 1982, includes about 100 items devoted to the Savoy area of southeastern France/northwestern Italy,
with most of them concerned with its history. These are arranged
by author, with no indexes or list of journals.

---- ----/1764248   136/150/744

[679] *Rhetorik* ("Bibliographie zur deutschsprachigen Rhetorikforschung")

Materials for 1979/80 were listed in the 1983 volume. About 100
of these were listed in a single alphabetical sequence with materials on the Middle Ages to the present included. Most of these
probably appeared more quickly in one of the several bibliographies
dealing with German language and literature. There were no indexes.

0720-5775/7663756   570/682

[680] *Richerche storiche sulla Chiesa Ambrosiana* ("Rassegna bibliografica
       Milanese")

The latest (seen) covered 1978/79 and included over 1100 items on
the history (particularly the church history) of Milan. These were
listed in a single author sequence and there were no indexes. There
was, however, a list of over 60 journals canvassed.

---- ----/1786825

[681] *Rivista d'arte/Studi documentari sulla storia delle arti in Toscana*
        ("Notiziario bibliografico")

        A new series of this journal began in 1984 and is to be published
        annually. Its bibliography deals with publications related to doc-
        umentary studies of the arts in Tuscany.

        ---- ----/1680960   57/65/624/639

[682] *Rivista di storia della chiesa in Italia* ("Bibliografia")

        In the first number of 1984 were listed 626 items, dating mostly
        from 1981 and 1982. These were divided into general history (30%
        of the total and arranged chronologically) and local history (ar-
        ranged by region). Most items were very briefly annotated. An
        author index appears in the second (and last) number of each year
        and there is a brief and incomplete list of about 20 journals.

        0035-6557/1589073   150/570/680

[683] *Rivista di studi fenici* ("Bibliografia")

        The most recent (which appeared in 1983) included citations to 22
        books, 131 articles, and 24 reviews dealing with the Phoenician
        world, arranged in three separate author sequences. There is (for
        some reason) an author index but no list of journals.

        ---- ----/2438951   544/555

[684] *Rivista di studi Italiani* ("Rassegna bibliografica")

        Materials for 1983 and 1984 were included in the bibliography in
        the June 1984 number. 747 citations were divided into 13 chronolog-
        ical and genre categories, under each of which books, articles, and
        reviews of materials on Italian language and literature were listed
        separately. There were no indexes, but a list of 108 journals con-
        sulted.

        0821-3216/10051568   23/286/450

[685] *Rivista di studi liguri* ("Bibliografia critica")

        This bibliography covers the history and archeology of Liguria from
        Paleolithic times through the Middle Ages. The bibliography for
        1973 appeared in the 1975 volume and listed 431 items grouped in
        several chronological divisions and with brief annotations. There
        were no indexes.

        0035-6603/2450256   136/728/730

[686] *Rivista Liturgica* ("Bollettino bibliografico")

This consituted the sixth issue of each year but the latest to appear was that for 1982, where 230 books and journal issues (with relevant contents listed) were included. Divided into 8 categories, items were frequently annotated very extensively but tended to be from 3 to 5 years in arrears. There were author/reviewer and subject indexes.

0035-6956/1774101   80/454

[687] *Rocznik Slawistyczny/Revue Slavistique* ("Przeglad bibliograpficzny"/ "Bibliographie raisonnée")

Behind times but with good coverage, the most recent (covering 1977) was published as the second number of the 1983 volume. There 5178 entries were divided into 10 categories--one general, the rest by Slavic language groups. Of these Russian and its dialects consituted over one-half. There were author/reviewer and personal name indexes as well as a list of about 250 relevant journals.

0080-3588/1910013   29/504/551

[688] *Roczniki Dziejów Spolecznych i Gospodarczych* ("Recenzje, sprawozdania, bibliografia")

Materials for 1982 were published in the 1984 bibliography. Several hundred items on Polish economic and social history were divided into 12 categories dealing with such aspects of history as urban and rural history, mining and manufacturing, demography, and class and social movements. There are no indexes nor any lists of journals.

0080-3634/1904732   131/139/766

[689] *Romania* ("Périodiques")

Each quarterly issue includes the contents of 10 to 15 journals dealing with early medieval literature, particularly in Latin. These are arranged by journal title and, as it is not particularly current, is of use only in the absence of several other relevant serial bibliographies.

0035-8029/1606691

[690] *Romanische Bibliographie/Bibliographie romane/Romance Bibliography*

A major bibliography but not particularly current since the three volumes for 1977/78 were published only in 1983. The first of these listed details on 400 journals as well as a basic list of journals totaling about 1000 titles. In addition this volume contained author and reviewer indexes for the three volumes. The second vol-

ume covered linguistics and comprised more than 4600 items divided
into 10 categories by language (general; Latin; Romansch; Rumanian;
Italian; French; Occitan; Catalan; Spanish; Portuguese) with each
of these subdivided into numerous sub-classifications. The third
volume listed another 8500+ items divided into 10 (somewhat different) categories, largely by language, with again each of these
further subdivided in a number of ways. If only this were more
current. . .

---- ----/2381586

[691] *The Romantic Movement: A Selective and Critical Bibliography*

The volume covering 1982 was published in 1983 and included perhaps
1400 to 1600 items dealing with the arts and literature associated
with the Romantic Movement (defined as extending from 1789 to 1837
in England and slightly different years elsewhere). Most items are
annotated, frequently extensively and critically. Works in English,
French, German, Italian, and Spanish are covered and the bibliography is arranged by these languages, within which items are generally listed by author studied. There is a list of about 800 journals searched but no indexes.

---- ----/9292276   355/485/613

[692] *Russia Medievalis* ("Bibliography")

This journal, which suspended publication in 1979, has now reap-
peared and a complete bibliography through 1977 is promised for
the second number of 1984, which has not yet appeared. The previous bibliography, which was published in 1979, included more than
1500 items on medieval Russia divided into 17 categories, including
political history; art/archeology; and travelers' accounts. Many
items (the majority of which were in Russian) were briefly annotated. There were no indexes but a list of about 70 journals was included.

0721-9431/2925747   3/323

[693] *Saarländische Bibliographie*

The volume for 1979/80 was published in 1982 and included 3242
items on the Saar region divided into about a dozen categories,
most of them relating to history either directly or indirectly and
each subdivided in turn. There was an author index.

0563-1513/1586504

[694] *Sachsen-Anhalt: Regionalbibliographie für die Bezirke Halle und
       Magdeburg*

Compiled by the Universitäts- und Landesbibliothek Sachsen-Anhalt in Halle, the volume covering 1977/78 was published in 1981 and included about 4000 items in nearly 20 categories, most of them well subdivided. All fields of knowledge were covered, but by far the largest dealt with the history of Saxe-Anhalt and its major cities. There was an author/anonymous title index and a list of about 200 journals canvassed.

---- ----/7259615   695

[695] *Sächsische Bibliographie*

Compiled by the Regionalbibliothek für die Sächsische Landesbibliothek, Leipzig. The volume for 1982 (published in 1983) listed 1564 items on Saxony divided into 14 general and 3 geographical categories, each in turn subdivided, as well as a separate family history/biographical section. There are author/anonymous title and subject indexes but no list of journals.

0419-7305/1914696   694

[696] *Sage Race Relations Abstracts*

Published four times a year. In 1984 about 650 abstracts (50 to 200 words) were published divided into over 40 categories, comprising only a fairly slight historical component. Author and subject indexes appear in the fourth number each year.

0307-9201/2163916

[697] *Sahel Bibliographic Bulletin*

Published by the Sahel Documentation Center, Michigan State University, this largely includes reports and other ephemeral publications of governments and parastatal institutions both in and outside the Sahel. Over 1000 such items were listed in 1984. All entries are in both French and English. Periodically a list of dissertations on the Sahel countries is also included. In addition to a much-needed list of acronyms, an author/institutional index for each year appears in the first number of the following year.

0145-9481/2809978   17/162/426

[698] *Salmanticensis* ("Bibliografía Patristica Hispano-Luso-Americana")

This is published biennially and consists of material contributed to [145] and gathered from Spain, Portugal, and Latin America. The 1984 volume carried 323 items related to patristic studies organized in 8 large and many smaller categories in much the same fashion as [145]. Of these the largest deals with works devoted to individual Church Fathers. There are no indexes but a list of some 60 journals is included.

0036-3537/5931290   145/553/572/670/848

[699]   *Samlaren* ("Svenska litteraturhistorisk Bibliografi")

The bibliography in the 1981 volume covers 1979 and lists 600 to
700 items in seven categories of religious literature and folklore
as well as (and the largest section) a listing by individual Swedish authors. There are no indexes or any list of journals.

0348-6133/1623854   780/781

[700]   *Sankt Eriks Arsbok* ("Stockholmianakrönika")

This bibliography deals with Stockholm and vicinity and appears to
run to about 10 pages annually, suggesting in the neighborhood of
100 to 150 entries.

0348-2081/8003824   780

[701]   *Saothar* ("A Bibliography of Irish Labour History")

Published by the Irish Labour History Society, materials published
in 1982/83 were listed in the 1984 volume. Some 250 to 300 of
these were arranged into: bibliography and reference; economy, society, and culture; crafts, trade, and industry; land and agricultural labor; labor organizations; politics and the labor movement;
Irish labor abroad; biography and autobiography; and general. There
were no indexes or list of journals.

0332-1169/6470111   47/443/839

[702]   *Scandinavian Economic History Review* ("Select Bibliography")

The most recent, appearing in the 1983/3 number, covered 1982 and
listed 174 items, drawn largely from Scandinavian publications,
dealing with all aspects of the economic--and to a lesser extent
social--history of the Scandinavian countries. There were no indexes or a list of journals.

0358-5522/1765081   160/284/303/430

[703]   *Scando-Slavica* ("List of Books and Articles Published by Scandinavian Slavists and Baltologists")

Items published in 1983 were included in the bibliography in the
volume for 1984. There were about 200 of these (books, articles,
and reviews) arranged by author. Narrow in focus, this does man-
age to be current for what it attempts.

0080-6765/1765094

[704] *Der Schlern* ("Literatur Rundschau")

A listing of 20 to 40 items on south Tyrol district of Italy and (to a lesser extent) Austria appears in each monthly number arranged by books and then by journal title for articles. There appears to be no effort to cumulate these materials which, obviously, are listed quite currently.

---- ----/5634548   112/136/585

[705] *Schrifttum zur deutschen Kunst*

Prepared by the Deutscher Verein für Kunstwissenschaft, Berlin, the 1983 volume included 2342 items, largely from 1982. These were divided into four classes, the largest dealing with art history and artistic genre. Emphasis is on material published in and dealing with German-speaking areas. There are author, geographical, and artist indexes but no list of journals.

0080-7176/1566490   57/99/102/624/639/851

[706] *Science Citation Index*

Elder sibling of [102] and [724] and with much the same features, organization, strengths, and weaknesses (particularly the impossibly small print). *SCI* appears bi-monthly with annual and quinquennial cumulations and covers science, medicine, agriculture, technology, and the behavioral sciences, and the historiography of these, so that such fields of interest as psychohistory, historical epidemiology, and the history of technology are included. Recently there have been some 600,000 citations to articles drawn from more than 3,000 journals and other serials each year. Access is through author and key-word in context.

0036-827X/1604320   446

[707] *Science of Religion. Abstracts and Index of Recent Articles*

Sponsored by the International Association for the History of Religions, this quarterly included about 700 abstracts (75 to 200 words) in 1984. These were divided into 11 categories, largely devoted to specific religions throughout the world. A list of about 200 journals appears in the first number of each year and there are subject and author indexes as well. There is not likely to be much here that would not appear elsewhere (if not abstracted) sooner.

0166-0519/7473926   226/362/635/636

[708]   *Scottish Economic and Social History* ("Bibliography of Scottish
Economic and Social History")

Prepared by the Department of Economic History of the University of
Glasgow, this appears in each number, with materials published in
1982 being listed in 1984. 275 to 300 items were arranged in 15
categories covering agriculture, domestic and overseas trade, industry, finance, labor, urbanism, religion, demography, education,
and social conditions. There are no indexes or list of journals.

---- ----/9296306   47/52/710/838

[709]   *Scottish Geographical Magazine* ("Recent Geographical Literature
Relating to Scotland")

That covering 1980 appeared in the 1982/2 number and listed about
150 items arranged in 8 categories covering physical and human
geography. There were no indexes or a list of journals canvassed.

0036-9225/1604208   164/276

[710]   *Scottish Historical Review* ("A List of Articles on Scottish History")

About 180 items published in 1983 appeared in the October 1984 number arranged in several chronological categories from the Dark Ages
to the present. "History" is defined narrowly in deference to the
several other serial bibliographies devoted to various aspects of
Scotland's past. There are no indexes.

0036-9241/1585736   47/52/708/858

[711]   *The Scriblerian and the Kit-Cats* ("Recent Articles")

This comprises the greater part of each semi-annual issue and consists of extensively annotated citations from American and English
publications devoted to certain English authors of the eighteenth
century. Major figures such as Defoe, Dryden, Pope, and Swift are
included in each issue while the others are dealt with less frequently. Material is not particularly current but the annotations
are of value. See [872].

0190-731X/2759643   49/513/872

[712]   *Scripta Ethnológica* ("Aportes para un indice bibliográfico de antropología argentina")

That which appeared in the 1983 volume, covering 1980/81, encompassed over 700 entries arranged in over 60 categories keyed to
the Dewey Decimal Classification. In fact both more than Argentina
and more than anthropology are included, with forays into geography,
demography, and the like. A list of 59 relevant Argentine journals

complete with publication details is included and there are onomastic and (very brief) subject indexes.

0325-6669/1925800   60/61/126/368/429

[713] *Scriptorium* ("Bulletin codicologique")

The most recent, which appeared in the first number of 1985, included about 600 extensive (as long as 1000 words) annotated items arranged in a single author index and relating in large part to medieval and early modern philology, paleography, and allied subjects. The bibliography appears in each semi-annual issue but there are no indexes or any list of journals.

0036-9772/1714630   397/524/761

[714] *Sefarad* ("Elenco de artículos de revistas")

The most recent (which appeared in the 1982 volume) listed by journal title the contents of nearly 100 journals dealing in some way with Spanish and Sephardic Judaism and their Near East relationships (actually the coverage is much broader). Annotations are frequently accompanied by very brief annotations in Spanish. However, the citations are not particularly current and in most cases can be found elsewhere sooner.

0037-0894/1640500

[715] *Seventh-Day Adventist Periodical Index*

This annual bibliography (1982 published in 1983) is arranged in separate subject (in dictionary catalog form) and author arrangements and includes a book and media review index as well. Of late about 1000 items have been listed each year dealing with Seventh-Day Adventism in general, with some materials on its history since it was founded in the 1840s.

0270-3599/5977061

[716] *Shakespeare-Jahrbuch* ("Shakespeare-Bibliographie")

Published by the Deutsch Shakespeare-Gesellschaft in Weimer, the volume for 1982 (published in 1984) included 1476 items in 5 categories, the largest arranged by particular play. Coverage is global but emphasis is on materials emanating from Germany. There is an author index and a list of 75 journals canvassed, mostly German.

0080-9128/1765433   513/717

[717]   *Shakespeare Quarterly* ("Shakespeare: Annotated World Bibliography")

Prepared by the Folger Shakespeare Library in Washington, this is
the major Shakespeare bibliography, both in number of citations
and currency. Materials from 1983 were included in the 1984 volume, in which over 3200 books, articles, book and production reviews were listed, arranged into 11 categories plus a classification (nearly two-thirds of the whole) on particular works arranged
by play or other writing. Most of these 12 categories in turn are
subdivided. There are author/editor, actor/director/producer,
personal name, and subject indexes as well as a list of more than
500 journals canvassed. In all, a model of the genre.

0037-3222/1644507   513/716

[718]   *Shixue qingbao (Shih hsüeh ch'ing pao)*

This is a quarterly update of [861]. Each number abstracts a selected group of articles on Chinese history, discusses archival
materials and the results of recent archeological work, and lists
recent books and articles, the last feature totals several thousand each year and is divided into general; ancient and modern
Chinese history; art and archeology; and world history. Finally,
most issues feature a bibliographical/historiographical essay on a
particular subject.

---- ----/8868383   177/178/543/655/799

[719]   *Singapore Periodicals Index*

The volume for 1982 (published in 1985) included over 2400 articles
drawn from 96 Singapore and Brunei journals (which are listed) in
either English, Malay, or Chinese and arranged by many subjects in
dictionary catalog format. Access to broader topics is facilitated
by a subject index and there are also two author indexes, one each
for Roman and non-Roman scripts. All fields of knowledge are covered.

0377-7928/5705342   177/417

[720]   *Slavia Antiqua* ("Przeglad polskich prac dotyczacych Slowiánszczyzny
starozytnej i wczesnośredniowiecznej na podstawie")

This appears in each volume, with the latest, covering 1979, appearing in 1981/82. This comprised a bibliography essay followed by a
listing of 225 to 250 items published in Poland on the history and
archeology of the Slavic peoples from prehistory to the end of the
Middle Ages. There are no indexes or any list of journals. Less
frequently similar but shorter recapitulations of work done in
Czechoslovakia, East Germany, and the Soviet Union also appear.

0080-9993/1775072   607

[721] *Slovenska Bibliografija*

This annual publication is published by the university library in
Ljubljana and serves as a regional bibliography for Slovenia, the
northernmost constituent republic of Yugoslavia (cap. Ljubljana).
All fields are covered and in the latest volume (1977, published
1984) several thousand books and collective works and more than
10,000 articles are listed, all of which were published in Slovenia.
The former were arranged by author, the latter in a modified Dewey
Decimal Classification. More than 900 journals, with publishing
details, are listed alphabetically as well as arranged in the modified DDC. Finally, there was an author/editor/personal name index.

0350-3585/1765635   114/153/460/860

[722] *Slovenský Národopis* ("Bibliografia slovenskej ethnografie a folk-
loristiky")

The most recent seen, that covering 1976 which appeared in the 1980
volume, included over 750 items on Slovene ethnography, folklife,
and related matters. These were arranged into 11 categories, the
largest and most relevant of which is folklore. There were author
and geographical indexes as well as a list of nearly 100 journals
canvassed.

0037-7023/1588888   288/513/721

[723] *Social Compass* ("Bibliographie internationale de sociologie des
religions")

The most recent, which appeared in 1983/2-3, included about 300
articles published in 1982 divided into many categories, some of
the more important of which are: methodology of the sociology of
religion; fundamental theoretical approaches; the distribution of
religions worldwide; and religious change. There is a list of
about 125 journals but no indexes. The subject matter is extremely
amorphous and it seems that almost anything relating to religion
might appear.

0037-7686/1765673

[724] *Social Sciences Citation Index*

On a somewhat larger scale, this performs functions similar to
[102] in the fields of sociology/anthropology/linguistics; social
issues and philosophy; psychology; psychiatry; public health and
social medicine; rehabilitation and special education; education;
library and information science; geography/planning/development;
law/economics/business; and management. 1400 journals are analyzed
fully and another 3100 selectively.

0091-3707/1784460   275/418/725

[725]   *Social Sciences in the USSR: Annotated Bibliography for 19--*

Published annually by the Institute of Scientific Information on
Social Sciences of the Academy of Sciences of the USSR, the 1984
volume included over 400 abstracts in English divided into more
than 20 categories covering the various social sciences (among
which are 4 categories on history).   Items are selected to show
"the main trends" in these fields in the Soviet Union and abstracts
run from 25 to 100 words and both articles and books are canvassed.
There are no indexes.

---- ----/10719269   275/724

[726]   Sociedad Bascongada de los Amigos del Pais. *Boletín* ("Revista de
revistas")

Arranged in a modified current contents format, in 1983 the contents
of some 35 journals, largely published in 1982 and 1983, were listed, but without page numbers.   Such materials dealt with northern
Spain, southwestern France, and the Basques, with some attention
to the Basques in diaspora.   There were no indexes.

---- ----/6803343   265/421

[727]   Società di Studi Valdesi. *Bollettino* ("Schede bibliografiche")

The most recent bibliography (in the July 1984 number) listed by
author about 70 brief annotated items on the history, culture, and
doctrine of the Waldensians, inside and outside Italy.

0037-8739/2994153

[728]   Società ligure di storia patria. *Atti* ("Notiziario bibliografico")

About 600 items were listed in the 1982 bibliography, divided into
five chronological and two general categories, which together encompass all aspects of the history of Genoa and of Liguria generally from prehistory to the present.   There was an author index.

---- ----/8833920   136/685/730

[729]   Società Romana di storia patria. *Archivio* ("Periodici pervenuti
alla Società")

Includes materials from journals and books acquired by the Società.
In the 1981 bibliography (published in 1983) 53 books and 164 articles (arranged by journal title) dealing with the history of Rome
and Latium were listed, obviously far short of the total number of
such items.

---- ----/7185550   93/136

[730] Società savonese di storia patria. *Atti e Memorie* ("Bibliografia del Savonese")

About 200 entries on the history of Savona in particular and central Liguria in general were included in the bibliography in the 1983 volume. These were divided into 5 chronological categories, with no indexes or any list of journals consulted.

---- ----/2729432   136/685/728

[731] Société académique du Nivernais. *Mémoires* ("Bibliographie nivernaise")

Covering the city of Nevers and its region, the 1982 bibliography (appearing in 1983) included slightly over 100 items arranged into 7 categories, nearly all dealing in some fashion with history. There are no indexes but there is a list of some 20 local journals which were canvassed.

---- ----/1772454   150

[732] Société archéologique du Finistère. *Bulletin* ("Bibliographie annuelle de l'histoire du Finistère")

The 1982 bibliography, covering materials published largely in 1981 and 1982, included nearly 500 items on historical aspects of Brittany, particularly western Brittany. These were divided into: general; archeology; political history; institutional history; military history; religious history; economic history; social history; cultural history; local history (by localities). There were personal name and author indexes but no list of journals analyzed.

---- ----/2996690   150/733/745

[733] *Société archéologique du Finistère* ("Bibliographie des publications consacrées à la langue et à la littérature bretonnes")

The bibliography for 1981/83 included over 800 items, preceded by a bibliographical essay and divided into 36 categories dealing with Breton language, literature, history, and several related fields. There was an author index.

---- ----/2996690   513/732

[734] Société archéologique et historique du Limousin. *Bulletin* ("Notes bibliographiques")

Compiled by the Bibliothèque municipale in Limoges, the 1984 bibliography included 316 items on the history of Limousin arranged into: general; archeology and the history of art; history (the largest); language and literature; auxiliary sciences; biography; geography; sciences. The arrangement in each is a single author listing and there are no indexes.

0184-7651/1772457   150

[735]   Société Châteaubriand. *Bulletin* ("Bibliographie générale")

In 1984 about 100 items were listed covering Châteaubriand's work, his life, times, and influence. These are listed by author and in some cases annotated. There are no indexes or a list of journals consulted.

0081-0754/1941200

[736]   Société d'histoire de la Guadeloupe. *Bulletin* ("Chronique biblio-graphique de l'histoire des Antilles françaises")

The most recent is that which appeared in the 1984/1 number and included materials published from 1979 to 1982. More than 1000 items were listed, briefly annotated, and classified into 15 categories including Guadeloupe, Guyane, Martinique, slavery, trade, religion, plantations, and refugees. There were no indexes.

0583-8266/5745643   657

[737]   Société d'histoire et d'archéologie de Dambach-la-Ville, Barr, Obernai. *Annuaire* ("Publications récentes")

About 100 items, arranged by the three towns in the *département* of Bas-Rhin in northeastern France appeared in the 1983 volume. There were no indexes and no list of journals canvassed.

---- ----/2998045   148/150/656

[738]   Société d'histoire et d'archéologie de Genève. *Bulletin* ("Chronique bibliographique")

The listing in the 1983 volume, mainly for materials published in 1981 and 1982, includes 75 to 100 miniature bibliographical essays on the history of Geneva and vicinity which are arranged in chronological order. There are no indexes.

0081-0959/1946430   159/232

[739]   Société des Antiquaries de l'Ouest. *Bulletin* ("Bibliographie")

That in 1984 included nearly 1000 items concerned with the history of Poitiers, Poitou, and west central France. These were divided into: general; archeology and art history; history; and literature and covered from prehistory to the present. There are no indexes.

0037-9190/5856055   150/562/734

[740]   Société des sciences historiques et naturelles de l'Yonne. *Bulletin* ("Bibliographie")

Confessedly less complete than [33], this bibliography included 60

to 70 items in 1982 devoted in whole or part to the history of the
département of Yonne from prehistory to the present. Most are
books and all are briefly annotated but there are no indexes.

---- ----/1643940   150

[741] Société des sciences naturelles et archéologiques de la Creuse.
Mémoires ("Bibliographie creusoise")

The 1982 volume included about 175 items listed by author and de-
voted to the history of the *département* of Creuse in central France.
These were divided into 10 chronological and topical categories.
There were no indexes and no list of journals consulted.

---- ----/1777543   150

[742] Société historique et archéologique de Corbeil, d'Etampes et du
Hurepoix. *Bulletin* ("Bibliographie")

This is largely concerned with the history of the *département* of
Essonne, just southeast of Paris. The 1982 bibliography included
over 100 items listed by books and by articles with no indexes and
no list of journals.

---- ----/3012695   148/150/656

[743] Société Jean-Jacques Rousseau. *Annales* ("Chronique")

A bibliography for 1972/77 appeared in the 1981 volume and included
about 1250 items on Rousseau, his life, work, times, and influence.
These were arranged in several categories but, given its lateness,
it is likely that most items had already appeared in one or more
other serial bibliographies. There were no indexes nor any list
of journals.

---- ----/1227540   306

[744] Société jurassienne d'emulation. *Actes* ("Bibliographie jurassienne")

The bibliography for 1981 appeared in the 1982 volume and dealt
with the Jura region of east central France. It ran to over 50
pages, suggesting 1000 or more entries, probably covering all aspects of the region and organized accordingly and with appropriate
indexing. It appears that it is also published separately as *Bibliographie jurassienne*.

---- ----/-------   150

[745] Société polymathique du Morbihan. *Bulletin* ("Bibliographie annuelle
de l'histoire du Morbihan")

The 1983 bibliography listed more than ·450 items covering the his-

tory of the Breton *département* of Morbihan. These were arranged
in 13 chronological and topical categories and included a personal
name index but no list of journals canvassed.

---- ----/3012535   150/732

[746] Société préhistorique francaise. *Bulletin* ("Bibliographie")

This appears in each monthly number and is based on materials received as gifts or on exchange by the Société's library. Each
issue lists these, with the articles grouped under journal by
title. Items are almost entirely of European provenance and deal
largely with France.

---- ----/5309466   125

[747] Société Rencesvals. *Bulletin bibliographique*

The volume for 1982/83 included 355 items, many of them annotated
(and two-thirds of them book reviews), dealing with the medieval
epic. These were drawn from about 85 journals and were arranged
by country of publication. There are no indexes and thus no way
to narrow a search.

---- ----/1788994   580

[748] Society for the Study of Labour History. *Bulletin* ("Bibliography")

The bibliography for 1983 is in the Spring 1984 issue and includes
over 1000 items divided into 12 categories, some further subdivided,
and encompassing all aspects of British labor history from the
eighteenth century to the present. There are no indexes and but a
partial list (fewer than 40) of journals consulted. The listings
for local labor history are particularly extensive.

0049-1179/2267840   202

[749] *Sønderjyske Årbøger* ("Oversigt over årsskrifter og periodica")

This normally lists by journal title (but without page numbers) the
contents of about a dozen journals relating to the Sønderjylland
region of Denmark.

0106-4452/-------   336

[750] *Sörmlandsbygden* ("Sörmland i nyutkommen litteratur")

Presents in bibliographical essay form in over 20 categories 100
to 150 items relating to all aspects of the Sodermansland region
of southeastern Sweden (capital Nykøbing). There are no indexes;
none is needed.

---- ----/7198410   780

[751] *Southern Baptist Periodical Index*

This indexes more than 40 Southern Baptist periodicals, arranging
materials in an integrated author/subject dictionary catalog format.
The bibliography for 1983, published in 1984, included several thousand entries, few of which deal with historical matters (these were
once included in *Baptist History and Heritage*, but this no longer
seems to be the case).

0081-3028/1696794   420

[752] *Southern History* ("Annual Review of Periodical Literature")

The volume for 1984 carried a listing of more than 70 very briefly
annotated references to materials on the history of Southern England arranged in 3 chronological categories. Page numbers are not
included, nor were there any indexes. There was, however, a list
of about 20 journals.

0142-4688/6001787   47/838

[753] *Spenser Newsletter* ("Articles, Abstracts, and Notices")

This appears in each number, that is, three times a year. For 1984
over 100 abstracts of articles, conference papers, and dissertations
dealing with Edmund Spenser, his work and times, were included.

0038-7347/1981052   513

[754] *Sport Bibliography/Bibliographie du Sport: Update 19--*

Compiled by the Sport Information Resource Center in Ottawa and
designed as periodic updates of an eight-volume *Sport Bibliography*
published in 1981/82. The first of these updates, for 1983, included in two volumes over 28,000 items published from 1979 on.
The first volume includes "sport specific" topics, the second
"sports science" matter.The titles of articles not in French or
English were translated, while scholarly materials were provided
with abstracts. The first volume was divided into 27 categories,
most subdivided; the second into more than 100 categories. Historical materials were common to all. There is a brief subject index,
rather less impressive than the work as a whole, and there was no
list of journals, a vast number of which must have been consulted.

0 920678 20 3/9503518   477/755/873

[755] *Sport Dokumentation. Literatur der Sportwissenschaft*

This is published six times a year by the Bundesinstitut für Sportwissenschaft in Cologne, in a fiche format and totalling in 1984
nearly 2400 entries in three major categories: sport science; the
domain of sports; and individual sports. Each of these is broken

down into several sections, of which that dealing with sports medicine habitually constitutes more than one-third of the whole.
Each entry is annotated, usually in German or English and running
to 100 to 150 words. In each issue the contents of a few journals
are listed by journal title. Each issue also contains key word
and author indexes (cumulated annually), but no list of journals.

0170-2890/6118720   477/754/873

[756] *Die Sprache* ("Indogermanische Chronik")

This appears twice yearly; the listings in the 1983 volume totaled
1800 items arranged in 13 categories, 11 of them individual Indo-
European languages or language groups. Entries are occasionally
briefly annotated and there is extensive cross-referencing among
categories.

0038-8467/1716759   168/169/513

[757] *Sprog i Norden* ("Nyere litteratur av interesse for språkrøktsar-
beidet")

Published annually, this lists books and articles (largely the
former) on various aspects of Scandinavian linguistics. Some 125
items in the 1982 volume were arranged by general topic and then
by country and most are annotated, some quite extensively. There
are no indexes nor is there a list of journals consulted.

87 00 56732 9/6655444   168/169/513

[758] *Starinar* ("Répertoire d'archéologie, d'art et d'histoire cultur-
elle")

Published by the Archaeological Institute, Belgrade, the bibliography in the 1980 volume (published in 1983) included 1000 to 1200
items published in 1977 and 1978 dealing with Yugoslav history and
archeology through the Middle Ages. Materials were subdivided into
4 chronological categories, each subdivided many times. Titles
were occasionally translated into French or German. There was an
author index.

0350-0241/1586392   3/323/449

[759] *Středočeský Sborník Historický* ("Historicko-Vlastivědna Bibliografia Středočeskeho kraje")

The volume for 1980 included 620 items published in 1977 on Czech
(particularly Bohemian) history. These were divided into regional
history; auxiliary sciences; archives and museums; archeology; general history; and topography (divided by place). There was an
author index as well as a list of more than 50 journals canvassed.

---- ----/1680893   3/323/613/852

[760] *Stromata* ("Fichero de Revistas Latinoamericanas")

This includes material from more than 350 Latin American journals
on theology and philosophy. In 1982 282 items relating to the
former and 52 on the latter were listed, covering any and all areas
of the two fields, and canvassing journals probably not thoroughly
and regularly covered by any other serial bibliography.

0049-2353/4530692   137/598/760

[761] *Studi e problemi di critica testuale* ("Spogli dalle riviste")

This appears in each semi-annual number and is devoted to textual
studies, mainly of works from the medieval and early modern period.
The most recent bibliography (October 1984) included more than 200
annotated citations arranged by country of origin. Though nominally international, in fact Italian journals consistently comprise
about 90% of the total, although of course these often deal with
non-Italian literature. There are no indexes and, although materials are loosely organized chronologically, access is difficult,
but the results can also be interesting.

0049-2361/2000256   267/397/713

[762] *Studi Etruschi* ("Rassegna bibliografica")

The bibliography for 1981 appeared in the 1984 volume and encompassed about 400 items dealing with the Etruscan civilization as
it preceded, co-existed with, and was part of the Roman civiliza
tion. These are arranged into 5 categories covering all fields,
but those dealing with archeology and history constitute about
three-quarters of the whole. Most items are briefly annotated and
there is an author index.

0391-7762/1766651   39/73/328

[763] *Studi Novecenteschi* ("Contributo monografici")

This is concerned with nineteenth- and twentieth-cnetury Italian
literature. The bibliography for 1982 (in the 1983 volume) included
300 to 350 items largely arranged by author studied. Although selective, it seems to cover ephemeral literature well. There are
no indexes.

0303-4615/1005525   450/590/684

[764] *Studi sul Boccaccio* ("Bollettino bibliografico")

73 items arranged in a single author sequence and largely published
in 1980 appeared in the 1981/82 volume. These dealt with Boccaccio's life, work, times, and contemporary and subsequence influence.

0585-4997/1987254   23/286

[765]   *Studia Fennica* ("Ethnological Bibliography")

This appears every two years as a separate issue. The most recent
was published in 1984 and included nearly 1400 items on Finnish
folklore and folklife which appeared from 1980 to 1982. These
were arranged in a single author sequence. This was supplemented
by a subject index (in Finnish but with a glossary to English), as
well as personal name and geographical indexes. There was no list
of journals canvassed.

0085-6835/2002593   327/439/513/561

[766]   *Studia Historiae Oeconomicae* ("A Bibliography of Publications in
Economic and Social History Printed in Poland")

The most recent, which appeared in the 1983 volume, covered 1980
publications. There, 319 items divided into 16 categories covered
all aspects of economic and social history, with a natural emphasis
on Poland. Titles were translated into English. There were no indexes but there was a list of about 150 journals consulted.

0081-6485/1645756   303/688

[767]   *Studia Historica Slavo-Germanica* ("Bibliographia")

The latest available appeared in the 1980 volume (there were none
in the 1981 to 1983 volumes) and covered materials published in
1976/78 which dealt with German-Slavic relations throughout time.
901 of these were classified into 9 mostly chronological categories.
There were no indexes.

---- ----/3566266   3/323/457

[768]   *Studia Philonica* ("Abstracts of Recent Articles on Philo")

This deals with Philo of Alexandria or Philo Judaeus (first century
A.D.) in particular and, more generally, with Hellenistic Judaism.
"A Bibliography of Philo Studies" usually accompanies it, in which
many of the same materials are listed but without annotation. Ordinarily some 50 to 75 abstracts are included, running from 100 to
400 words and arranged by author.

0093-5808/1792591   463

[769]   *Studier i modern Språkvetenskap* ("Bibliography of Swedish Works on
Romance, English, and German Philology")

The latest of these, which appeared in the 1980 volume, included
from 1000 to 1200 items mostly published from 1975 to 1978 by Swedish authors but not necessarily in Swedish journals. These were
divided into Romance, English, and Germanic philology, with an alphabetical author sequence within each category. There are no in-

dexes but a list of about 150 journals is included.

0585-3583/3100504   122/168/169/223/513/757

[770] *Studies in the Age of Chaucer* ("An Annotated Chaucer Bibliography")

That published in 1985 covers 1983 publications and is in fact based on [513], with additions and annotations. In total there are 262 citations to books and articles as well as 53 reviews. These are divided into general categories and by work. There is an author index as well as a list of more than 40 journals canvassed.

0190-2407/4676149   248/513

[771] *Studies in Zionism* ("A Selected and Annotated Bibliography for 19--")

This covers various philosophical and political aspects of Zionism from 1882 as well as the history of the modern state of Israel until 1967. The bibliography for 1981 (published in 1982) included nearly 300 items in 8 categories, with Hebrew titles translated into English. There are no indexes but there is a list of about 60 journals (including a few Israeli newspapers).

---- ----/7937788

[772] *Studies on Women Abstracts*

Published six times yearly, this totals about 900 items each year, devoted to various aspects of the literature on women, largely contemporary but including historical studies as well. Abstracts run from 100 to 250 words and are arranged adventitiously in each number, although there are author and subject indexes (which are cumulated annually). Each issue also includes a listing of some 250 journals with publication details.

0262-5644/9447685   341/575/834

[773] *Studime filologjike* ("Bibliografi për gjuhësinë dhe onomastikën shqiptare/Bibliography of Albanian Linguistics and Onomastics")

In the 1982 volume were listed 491 items, largely published in 1980. These were arranged by author, largely Albanian of course, and titles were frequently translated into French. There were author, geographical, and lexical indexes as well as a list of more than 120 journals which were canvassed.

---- ----/2268583

[774]   Stuttgart. Bibliothek für Zeitgeschichte. *Jahresbibliographie*

This is divided into several sections, including "Neuerwerbungen." In this were listed in the 1983 volume some 4000 to 5000 items on recent times divided into 12 categories, mostly subdivided extensively. The largest of these deal with World War II and with a country by country global survey. Of the latter, about two-thirds deals with Europe and probably well over half the items in the whole listing are German publications.

---- ----/11485737   367/500/659/831

[775]   *Style* ("Annual Bibliography Number")

That published in 1983 (as a separate number of *Style*) covered 1981 materials and included 758 items classified as: bibliographical resources; general theory; culture, history, and style; habitual usage: the author; individual choice: the text; individual response: the reader. Authors covered range from Plato to the present. There are indexes of terms and of author/stylisticians, as well as a list of 176 relevant journals.

0039-4238/1154245   259/506/513

[776]   *Sumario actual de revistas*

Published by the library of the Instituto de Cooperación Iberoamericana in Madrid, this is a "current contents" publication dealing with Latin America journals. Not quite current, the April 1983 number was published only in late 1984. It included the table of contents pages of about 300 journal issues arrayed alphabetically in 13 categories covering all fields, including history. Unlike most such compilations there is an author index, as well as the publication details for each of the journals represented. In all, useful depsite its only modest currency.

0210-0592/1667264   199/211/230/262/368/378/865

[777]   *Suomen Aikakauslehti-indeksi/Index to Finnish Periodicals*

The volume covering 1979 was published by the Turku University Library in 1982 and included about 8000 entries arranged by the Dewey Decimal Classification, rendering it fairly easy to locate specific historical materials (although they are not numerous, and most of them relate to Finland). There was an author index.

0081-9395/2002627   392/765

[778]   *Surrey Archaeological Collections* ("Surrey in Periodical Literaature")

An annual listing of the contents of a dozen or so journals arranged by title. Journals specifically devoted to Surrey are excluded. . .

---- ----/1641502   47/269/752/838

[779] *Svensk Geografisk Arsbok/Swedish Geographical Yearbook* ("Svensk geografisk bibliografi/Swedish Geographical Bibliography")

Materials for 1982 appeared in the 1983 volume. There were about 60 of these, mostly reports and largely on Sweden. Narrow but useful in that many of these items would not be canvassed elsewhere.

0081-9808/1609051   780

[780] *Svenska tidskriftsartiklar*

Each month this canvasses about 450 Swedish journals within a few months of their appearance. Materials are divided into 22 categories including literary history, archeology, history, and geography. Each issue has an author index, a subject index (in Swedish), and a list of the journal issues canvassed.

0039-6915/1643385

[781] *Svensklärarföreningens Arsskrift* ("Bibliografi over litteratur rörande svenskundervisningen")

Materials from 1978 were listed in the 1980 volume. These are divided into 7 categories dealing with textual studies, teaching languages (i.e, Swedish), dictionaries, linguistic and literary studies. There are no indexes or a list of journals.

---- ----/-------   699

[782] *Swedish-American Historical Quarterly* ("Swedish-American Bibliography")

The last number of 1984 carried 117 items published largely in 1983 and dealing with the experience of Swedish immigrants in the United States (and to some extent Canada) and arranged in a single author/ anonymous title listing, with no indexes. Coverage is international in terms of language and place of publication.

0730-028X/7941673   402/569

[783] *Századok* ("A Magyarországon megjelent történelmi munkák")

This extensive bibliography usually appears in the sixth number of each year. That in 1982 covered books, articles, and dissertations on history published in Hungary in 1981 and preceding years. The some 2000 to 2500 items were divided into: general works; Hungarian history (nearly two-thirds of the whole); and general history (largely eastern Europe), each in turn subdivided in various ways. A list of about 100 journals used is included but there are no indexes.

0039-8098/2007784   3/14/300/323

[784]   *T'ang Studies* ("Recent Archaeological Discoveries on the Sui and T'ang: Articles from Chinese Journals")

The first of these appeared in the 1985 number (and presumably will continue). Some 60 articles are classified in 6 general (materials from tombs, etc.) and specific (e.g., studies on the Longmen caves) categories. Each entry is briefly annotated in English. The six major PRC archeological journals are included in the survey. There are no indexes.

0737-5034/9151673   177/178/543/655/719/785/799/861

[785]   *T'ang Studies* ("Western-Language Works on T'ang Studies")

The first of these, covering 1981/1984 appears in the 1985 number. In it are listed from 125 to 150 items, listed separately by author into books, articles and notes, and dissertations which deal in part or whole with Chinese history from the late sixth to the early tenth centuries. There are no indexes.

0737-5034/9151673   177/178/543/655/719/784/799/861

[786]   *Tanzania Notes and Records* ("Tanzania Bibliography")

The most recent of these appeared in the 1980 volume and covered 1976. It listed 566 items on all fields, divided into the various disciplines and global in its sources. The natural sciences fared particularly well but materials on history, geography, and anthropology were all extensive. There were no indexes.

0039-9485/1767133   18

[787]   *Technikgeschichte* ("Zeitschriftenschau")

This appears in each quarterly issue and usually consists of 40 to 60 items classified in 6 chronological categories, and largely German-language materials. There are no indexes. A list of more than 50 journals appeared in the first number of 1979 and has not been repeated.

0040-117X/7471031   221/446/706/789

[788]   *Technologia* ("Notes bibliographiques")

The most recent, in the fourth number of 1984 included 318 items on the history of science by Belgian authors or relating to Belgium. These were arranged by author, with a personal name index and subject indexes in French and Flemish.

0771-6826/-------   221/446/706/789

[789] *Technology and Culture* ("Current Bibliography in the History of Technology")

Compiled by the libraries of the Smithsonian Institution, this, the basic bibliography in its field, covers publications in a given year in the April number of the second year following. That for April 1985 listed some 1500 items divided into: Twentieth Century and General (two-thirds of the total); Prehistory, Antiquity, and Primitive Societies; Middle Ages; From the Renaissance Through the Seventeenth Century; and the Eighteenth and Nineteenth Centuries. Each of these is in turn subdivided into 17 standardized sections, some of which are even further divided. Author and subject indexes are included in each bibliography but there is no list of journals canvassed.

0040-165X/1640126   221/446/706

[790] *Teiresius* ("Bibliography [of Boiotian Studies]")

The most recent included about 175 books, articles, and reviews in history and another 167 dealing with literature, arranged in these two major categories, with no indexes.

0381-9361/2227823   39/673

[791] *Temenos* ("Nordic Research in Comparative Religion: A Bibliography")

This is published every two years, with that covering 1980/81 being published in 1982. In it over 600 entries were listed in a single author sequence, with titles in Scandinavian languages (probably the majority) translated into English. Both "comparative" and "religion" are notably elusive concepts and this is betrayed in the rather unfocused coverage. There was a subject index.

0497-1817/1767248

[792] *Teología y Vida* ("Noticias de Revistas Latinoamericanas")

In a modified current contents format, this lists from 30 to 50 articles in each quarterly issue on the church in Latin America, with much of it drawn from popular journals. Items are briefly annotated.

0049-3449/1715270   137/760

[793]   *Terrae Incognitae* ("Recent Literature in Discovery History")

Once classified, this is now a straight author sequence of writings
on the age of discovery. The most recent, that in 1982, listed
about 175 items in all languages, but without any indexing.

0082-2884/968369   378/386/637

[794]   Tetuan. Biblioteca Española. *Cuadernos* ("Bibliografía de historia
de Marruecos en lengua castellana")

That in the 1980 volume included over 100 items, most published in
1979. These were all in Spanish and were arranged in one general
and four chronological sections, dealing with Morocco from Roman
to contemporary times. There were no indexes.

0563-2129/3157530   41/42/502/519

[795]   *Theologische Revue* ("Theologische Bibliographie")

This bibliography appears in each bi-monthly issue, where some 400
to 500 items are usually listed. These are arranged in 15 classifications covering all aspects of the field including those that
are directly or indirectly historical. Coverage is very current
but there are no indexes. A listing of over 600 journals used was
published in 1971 and none has appeared since.

0040-568X/1696877   213/313/675/858

[796]   *Thüringen-Bibliographie*

The bibliography for 1981/82 was published in 1983. It included 3476
items divided into 13 categories, most in turn subdivided. General
history *per se* totalled fewer than 100 entries, but closely related
fields, particularly personal and family history (the largest single
category) were well represented, as were nature, economics, and
culture. There was a combined author/subject index but no list of
canvassed journals.

---- ----/4588212   457

[797]   *Tijdschrift voor Geschiedenis* ("Bibliografisch overzicht van boeken
en tijdschriftartikelen")

This appears in each quarterly issue and totals 1200 to 1500 items
a year. Worldwide in scope and therefore extremely selective, its
major interest is its coverage of Dutch history. Materials are
arranged in 5 chronological categories and then geographically within these. There are no indexes.

0040-7518/2096663   13/582/640

[798] *Tijdschrift voor Rechtgeschiedenis* ("Article concernant l'histoire du droit")

This appears in each quarterly issue, is arranged by journal titles, and runs to 15 to 50 titles each time. Coverage is global and secular, canon, and traditional law are all included. There are no indexes.

0040-7585/1585956

[799] *Toyogaku konkyu bunken ruimoku/Bibliography of Oriental Studies*

Published annually by the Research Institute for Humanistic Studies of Kyoto University. That for 1980 was published in 1983 and included over 10,000 articles and nearly 1,000 books in Oriental languages and over 900 articles and 1000 books in Western languages, with each classification being divided into 18 categories, each in turn subdivided (materials on Japan proper are not included). These were drawn from over 900 journals in Oriental languages and about 100 in Western languages. There are indexes to authors in Japanese characters and Chinese characters, as well as in the Roman and Cyrillic alphabets.

---- ----/5121740   177/178/543/655/719/861

[800] Turk Tarih Kurumu. *Bulleten* ("Tilinin Ikinci Yarisinda Kitapligimiza Gelen Kitap ve Dergiler")

Each year this lists books and articles received by the Society's library in Ankara. That for 1982, which appeared in 1983, included about 650 books and more than 200 articles arranged by journal title and drawn from a listing of over 300 journals canvassed. Geographically, listings are largely confined to modern-day Turkey, but Anatolia is covered from the period of the Ancient Near East, thereby supplementing [830] in this respect. There are no indexes.

0041-4255/1767827   22/83/528/529/584/672/801/830

[801] *Türkiye Makaleler Bibliyografyasi*

This index to Turkish periodicals and other serial publications is published quarterly by the National Library in Ankara. In 1982 there were nearly 12,000 and that number will increase for 1983 (most coverage of which will be published in 1985). In each issue entries are arranged by the Dewey Decimal Classification as all fields of knowledge are included, of which the social sciences (i.e., DDC 300s) by far the largest category. Each number has an author index (cumulated in the last number of the year) as well as a list of issues canvassed (about 200 journals each quarter).

0041-4344/1481194   528/529/800/830

[802]   Universitetet i Oslo.   Slavisk-Baltisk Institutt. *Meddelelser*

Each year one of the volumes of this series is entitled *Norsk litteratur om de slaviske og baltiske folks kultur*. That covering
1980 was published in 1984 as *Meddelelser* no. 42. It includes
more than 400 items on Slavic and Baltic culture published in Norway and arranged in a single author sequence. There is an author/
personal name index.

---- ----/4533532   551/687

[803]   *Urban History Review/Revue d'histoire urbaine* ("Recent Publications
Relating to Canada's Urban Past")

The listing in the October 1984 issue included nearly 1200 items
arranged in 5 subject categories, each subdivided in its turn, and
a large (70% of the whole) geographical classification arranged by
region, province, and urban center. There were no indexes nor any
list of journals.

0703-0428/1787360   160/804/805

[804]   *Urban History Yearbook* ("Current Bibliography of Urban History")

The bibliography for 1982/83 is in the 1984 volumes and lists about
1400 items in 10 classifications, each subdivided in a number of
ways. Only British books are included but the scope of articles
included is a bit wider. Even so, the great majority of entries
relate to the British Isles. All aspects of urbanism and urban history are covered. There is an index of towns as well as a list of
about 225 journals consulted.

0306-0845/1798625   160/803/805

[805]   *Urbanism Past and Present* ("Bibliography")

Each issue includes several hundred items in a general (about one-
half the total) category and several geographical ones covering
the entire world. There are no indexes. Strongest on North American coverage.

0160-2780/2140253   160/803/804

[806]   *Vendsyssel Arbog* ("Vendsyssel-litteratur")

The bibliography for 1983, published in the 1984 volume, included
about 200 items on the history of the Vendsyssel region of northern
Jutland, Denmark. These were divided into several topics, most notably local and personal history. There were no indexes or list of
journals.

0085-7645/6012976   281/282/336

[807]   Verein für Geschichte der Stadt Nürnberg. *Mitteilungen* ("Neue
Arbeiten zur Nürnberger Geschichte")

That appearing in 1984 included over 40 items of recent vintage on
the history of Nürnberg. These are arranged largely by author and
with no indexes.

---- ----/2159141   120/388/846

[808]   Verein fur lübeckische Geschichte und Altertumskunde. *Mitteilungen*
("Besprechungen und Hinweise")

Materials are listed by journal title in quasi-bibliographical
essay form. The most recent, that for 1980/81, appeared in the
1982 volume. There are no indexes.

---- ----/1773217   369/457/550

[809]   *Vergilius* ("Vergilian Bibliography")

The most recent appeared in the 1984 volume and included 203 items
published in 1983/84. These were listed according to several categories, covering modern editions and translations, critical studies
of individual works, Vergil's sources, Vergil's influence, extant
manuscripts, etc. There are summing annotations but no indexes
nor any key to the abbreviations used.

0506-7294/1605232   39

[810]   *Victorian Periodicals Review* ("Victorian Periodicals: A Checklist
of Scholarship and Criticism")

The Fall/Winter 1983 number included a listing of 182 items, arranged by author and dealing with various aspects of British journals (largely literary journals) from 1800 to 1914. These were
occasionally very briefly annotated and there were personal name,
subject, and periodical title indexes.

0049-6189/5359718   54/811

[811]   *Victorian Studies* ("Victorian Bibliography")

That for 1983 appeared in the Summer 1984 number and included 1200
to 1500 items classified in several categories by format or topic.
Much the largest of these is devoted to authors of the Victorian
period and their works. Book reviews are noted in the appropriate
sections. There are no indexes, though there is an incomplete list
of about 80 journals canvassed.

0042-5222/1769095   54/810

[812]   *Viertelsjahrhefte für Zeitgeschichte* ("Bibliographie zur Zeitgeschichte")

Compiled by the Institut für Zeitgeschichte in Munich, this appears
as a supplement to each quarterly issue and in 1984 totaled over
3000 entries.   The bibliography covers world history (largely European, in turn largely German) since 1945 thereby supplementing
[457] in bringing coverage of German history to the present.   Arrangement is rotational so that not every area is covered in each
issue.   There are no indexes.

0042-5702/1717063   457

[813]   *Virginia Historical Abstracts: A Guide to the Periodical Literature*

Begun in 1982 this adheres closely to the format of [383].   For
1982 some 750 abstracts appeared, arranged into 32 categories covering all aspects of the history of Virginia from protohistoric
times to the present.   Each semi-annual issue includes a combined
author/subject index, which is cumulated in the second issue.   As
well, a list of about 150 journals that are regularly canvassed is
included.

0734-5089/8755536   25/464/476/631/837

[814]   *Vjesnik za Arheologiju i Historiju Dalmatinsku* ("Bibliografski
Vjesnik")

Materials published from 1976 to 1979 on the history, archeology,
and art history of Dalmatia until the fifteenth century were listed
in the bibliography in the 1983 volume, where 600 to 700 entries
appeared under these three categories under which they were listed
by author.   There was a separate list of reviews and a list of
about 125 journals, nearly all Yugoslav, but no indexes.

0350-8447/5246717   66/114/153/356/449

[815]   *Vlastivadný Vestnik Moravský* ("Vlastivedná literatura")

That for 1981, which appeared in the 1983 volume, comprised 230
items devoted to Moravian history and culture.   These were arranged
in a single author sequence with each entry coded to one of 27
topics.   In addition the contents of more than 40 journals were
listed by journal title, followed by a list of 75 reviews and a
personal name index.

---- ----/5247511   3/253/323/461

[816]   *Voprosy Istorii KPSS* ("[Documents and Articles on the History of
the CPSU and the International Communist Movement]")

Virtually every monthly issue includes this bibliography on the

history of the Communist Party in the Soviet Union and elsewhere.
Materials are divided into 10 categories and typically total more
than 200 entries each time. There are no indexes, transliterations,
translations, or lists of journals.

0320-8907/1607171   172/498/571

[817] *Vox Romanica* ("Bibliographie der schweizer Romanistik")

The bibliography for 1982 (published in the 1983 volume) listed 225
to 250 items dealing with Romance language study in or about Switzerland and other German-speaking areas. This is arranged in a
single author sequence and, as expected, has little coherence, with
almost anything likely to appear and even more likely not to.

0042-899X/1714382

[818] *War and Society Newsletter*

This appears as a separately published annual supplement to *Mili-
tärgeschichtliche Mitteilungen* and is the best single bibliography
on military history. The latest, published in 1984 and covering
1983, included about 1000 items, drawn from 461 journals and 33
collective works (both listed) and divided in 7 chronological categories plus general, international law, and military law. There
are no indexes.

---- ----/2380825   21/123/165/530/531

[819] *Warwickshire History* ("List of Publications on the History of Warwickshire")

Materials published in 1983 appeared in the Winter 1983/84 number.
Some 75 to 85 were listed, arranged by author, some with very brief
annotations.

---- ----/2183988   47/838

[820] *Welsh History Review* ("Articles Relating to the History of Wales")

The most recent of these, covering 1982 and appearing in the December 1984 issue, includes about 100 citations arranged in chronological order, from the fourth century to the present. Unfortunately,
entries are in the form of brief annotations and exact titles are
not provided, although other bibliographical data are. There are
no indexes.

0083-792X/1769587   47/71/186/191/838

[821] *Wereld en Zending* ("Bibliografie van in Nederland en nederlandsta-
lig Belgie verschenen missiologische literatuur")

Includes materials emanating from the Netherlands or Flemish-speak-
ing Belgium dealing with Christian missions. In the 1984 bibliography are listed 354 items published largely in 1983. These are
arranged in a general category (one-half the total) and then by
continent (within which by country). Emphasis is on contemporary
missiological issues but many entries are of a historical or anthropological nature. 42 journals are listed but there are no indexes.

---- ----/2181003   133/242/435/509/623/858/869

[822] Werkgroep Historie en Archeologie van het Koninklijk Zeeuwsch Genootschap der Wetenschappen. *Bulletin* ("Regionaal-historische Bibliografie van Zeeland")

This appears to be concerned with the history of Zeeland, one of
the provinces of the Netherlands and (to judge from its length) to
include up to 200 items each time it appears.

---- ----/-------   187/396

[823] *Wesley Historical Society Proceedings* ("Bibliography of Methodist
Historical Literature")

Materials published in 1981 appeared in the 1983 volume. There
were fewer than 100 of these, arranged in 14 countries, including
regional and local history, biography, and theology. Cross-referencing is extensive (if hardly necessary) and there are no indexes.

0043-2873/1633161

[824] *West-Frieslands Oud en Nieuw* ("Bibliografie van West-Friesland")

This is published by the Historisch Genootschap Oud West-Friesland
in Hoorn and each year includes up to 100 items on the history of
that region of the Netherlands. There are no indexes or any list
of journals.

---- ----/-------   187/396

[825] *West Virginia History* ("State History Featured in Periodical Literature")

From 50 to 75 items, largely drawn from local West Virginia publications, were included in the 1984 bibliography, arranged by journal title.

0043-325X/1769679   25/464/476/631/813/837

[826] *Western American Literature* ("Annual Bibliography")

The most recent appeared in the 1983/84 volume. This included some 250 to 300 items arranged by author studied, including among them several historians of the West. In addition there is a listing of M.A. theses and doctoral dissertations on various aspects of Western U.S. literature. There are no indexes or lists of journals.

0043-3462/1586008   27

[827] *Western Historical Quarterly* ("Recent Articles")

Recently these annual bibliographies have included from 175 to 225 items arranged in about 20 categories dealing with numerous aspects of the history of the western United States. There are no indexes.

0043-3810/1769730   25/464/631/837

[828] *Westfälische Bibliographie*

Compiled by the Stadt- und Landesbibliothek Dortmund, the 1982 bibliography (published in 1983) included nearly 2400 items on various aspects of Westphalia. These were arranged in 13 categories, by far the largest being an alphabetical arrangement by locality. There was an author index but no list of journals.

---- ----/1769777   190/457

[829] *Wiener Geschichtsblätter* ("Neue Viennensia")

This covers materials relating to Vienna and, to judge from the number of pages it runs, totals between 100 and 200 items, not all necessarily concerned with history.

0043-5317/1769862   112/492/585

[830] *Wiener Zeitschrift für die Kunde des Morgenlandes* ("Türkologischer Anzeiger")

This bibliography, published as an annual supplement, is an interesting example of a major bibliography appearing in an unlikely place. At any rate, the bibliography for 1984 (covering 1983 and previous years) comprised more than 2500 items classifield in 13 categories (each further divided) dealing with all aspects of Ottoman Turkish history, with a smattering of materials (largely in the sections on language and literature) dealing with the Turks in central Asia. Titles in Turkish or other non-western languages are translated, usually into German. There is an author index and a list of about 250 journals canvassed.

0084-0076/1589789   528/529/800/801

[831]   *Wojskowy Przeglad Historiczny* ("Materialy do bibliografi 2 wojny
światowejz zgromadzone")

The bibliography on World War II usually appears in each quarterly
issue and runs to 1200 to 1500 items each year. It is divided into
such categories as: bibliography; methodology; biography; the in-
terwar period; and World War II proper (much the largest). International in coverage, though most items are from Poland and the
Germanies. There are no indexes.

0043-7182/3219176   367/500/659/774

[832]   *Wolfenbütteler Barock-Nachrichten* ("Beiträge zur Barockliteratur")

Compiled by the Herzog August Bibliothek, Wolfenbüttel, this appears
three times a year, each listing running to 200 to 550 entries divided into textual studies, critical studies generally, and studies
of individual authors (listed by authors studied). Emphasis is on
the literature and culture of the German Baroque, mid-seventeenth
to mid-eighteenth centuries.

0340-6318/3220012   12/157/436/437

[833]   *Wolfenbütteler Notizien zur Buchgeschichte* ("Bibliographie")

This bibliography dealing with all aspects of the history of the
book in the German-speaking world, comprises about 3000 items annually, appearing in each quarterly number. It is broken down into
several chronological and topical categories, as well as listing
reviews separately. There are no indexes nor a list of journals.

0341-2253/3679878   2/156

[834]   *Women Studies Abstracts*

Published quarterly, this aggregates to 2000 to 2500 entries yearly.
Citations in each issue are divided into about 25 categories, each
of which begins with a series of cross-references to items in other
categories. Emphasis is on contemporary women's issues but historical material does appear. Perhaps one in 8 to 10 items is provided
with an abstract. There is a subject index but no list of journals.

0049-7835/1770074   772

[835]   *World Agricultural Economics and Rural Sociology Abstracts*

This is published monthly by the Commonwealth Bureau of Agricultural
Economics in Oxford. Each issue contains about 500 brief (75-200
words) abstracts arranged in 10 categories, of which the economics
of production, cooperatives and collectives, and international
trade are most likely to interest historians. Titles in foreign
languages are translated into English. In each number there are

author and subject/geographical indexes which are cumulated annually. A list of about 50 journals which are fully canvassed is
featured in each issue and a list of more than 10,000 relevant journals, *CAB Serials Checklist*, is available separately.

0043-8219/1770119   10/143/348/706

[836] *World Textile Abstracts*

Published by the Shirley Institute in Manchester, this appears
twice a month and in 1984 totalled over 7800 English-language abstracts (50 to 100 words) for scientific, technical, and technico-
economic literature. In each issue these are arranged in 10 categories, including fibers, yarn, fabrics, and generalities. In the
year's first issue some 400 journals from around the world are
listed and yearly author, subject, and patent indexes are issued
(there are no indexes in individual issues). Historical coverage
is slight but what there is is unduplicated in any other source.

0043-9118/1770193

[837] *Writings on American History: A Subject Bibliography of Articles*

Published by the American Historical Association, this consists
largely of a consolidation of relevant entries already published
in [631], with some updating and the inclusion of completed dissertations. The volume covering August 1983 to July 1984 comprised
over 8800 entries divided into 12 chronological, 7 geographical,
and about 40 subject classifications. Those interested in immedi-
acy will be satisfied with [631] but the present bibliography has
the advantage of being consolidated, fairly current, and boasting
an author index. In addition it includes a list of over 500 journals canvassed.

0364-2887/1770230   25/464/478/631

[838] *Writings on British History*

Prepared by the Institute of Historical Research of the University
of London, this covers all aspects of British history from *ca.* 450
to 1939. It is unconscionably out of date, however, for the 1969/70
volume was published only in 1984. In it were about 4300 items in
12 general/geographical and 7 chronological categories, all with
little emphasis on the history of science, literature, and the
arts. There is an extensive author/subject index and a list of
about 400 journals consulted. Despite its impressive apparatus,
it is hard to imagine that it usefully serves more than a historical role, given the great number of relevant and much more current
serial bibliographies in the field.

0084-2753/3115346   32/47/52/568/710/752/839

[839]   *Writings on Irish History*

This appeared in *Irish Historical Studies* until 1980; now it is
published in fiche form every two years by the Irish Committee of
Historical Sciences. That covering 1981 and 1982 was published in
1983 and included about 1500 items on Irish history, arranged
largely chronologically. Coverage is especially useful for the
numerous local history publications. A list of about 200 journals
and 50 collective works preceded the bibliography.

---- ----/11632231   47/179/443/701/838

[840]   *Yearbook of German-American Studies* ("Bibliography of German-
Americana")

The volume for 1984 included about 750 items published in 1982 and
1983 and dealing with various aspects of the German-American experience including immigration itself. These are arranged alphabetically by a series of topics and there is a list of more than 25
journals consulted but no indexes.

0741-2827/8802101   402

[841]   *Year's Work in Modern Language Studies*

The volume for 1983, published in 1984, is the most recent and
covers work done on general linguistics, Latin, the Romance languages, Celtic languages, Germanic languages, and the Slavonic languages. These are arranged in a series of extended bibliographical
essays under each of these categories and hence there is (and can
be) no attempt to be comprehensive. Even so, coverage is extensive
and the annotations in English of foreign language materials useful.
There is a list of about 900 journals plus more than 50 additional
Cyrillic journals, as well as about 120 collective works canvassed.
There are also subject and author indexes.
                                     •
0084-4152/1770339   513

[842]   *Yorkshire Archaeological Journal* ("Yorkshire Bibliography")

That published in the 1983 volume (there is none in 1984) largely
covered 1982 and included more than 300 items divided into 17 categories, including all aspects of history. There are no indexes
but each bibliography contains that part of a master list of over
80 journals, mostly local, from which entries have been drawn.

0084-4276/1770350   47/63/198/568/838

[843]   *Yukon Bibliography*

Prepared by the Boreal Institute for Northern Studies, University
of Alberta, the bibliography for 1980/81 was published in 1983.

It included over 300 annotated entries arranged in 22 categories, including history, archeology, and geography. There were author, corporate author/publisher, and subject indexes.

0068-0303/2320088   25/235/321

[844] *Zapiski Historyczne* ("Bibliografia Historii Pomorza Wschodniego i Zachodniego")

That which appeared in the 1984 volume covers 1982 and lists over 900 items on southern Baltic history divided into 4 categories: General; East Pomerania; West Pomerania; and the Baltic countries. There is an author index but no list of journals canvassed.

0044-1791/2098337   115/369/453/609/854/855

[845] *Zeitschrift für allgemeine Wissenschaftstheorie* ("Zeitschriften-schau")

Most semi-annual issues carry a listing of the contents of from 25 to 75 recent issues of journals in the fields of the philosophy and the history of science, arranged alphabetically by journal title. Coverage is particularly good for central and eastern Europe and is quite current. There are no indexes.

0044-2216/1800152   221/446/706

[846] *Zeitschrift für bayerische Landesgeschichte* ("Bayerische landes-geschichtliche Zeitschriftenschau")

The most recent, that which was included in the 1983 volume, largely covers 1982 and was arranged by journal title, organized on a re-gional basis. These journals are largely Bavarian, with a few from other areas of Germany and some 90 of these are analyzed. There are no indexes.

0044-2364/1770428   120/457

[847] *Zeitschrift für die alttestamentliche Wissenschaft* ("Zeitschriften- und Bücherschau")

This fairly extensive listing appears in each quarterly issue and is in a modified current contents format alphabetically by journal title. Perhaps 150 to 200 journal issues are analyzed each time and entries are usually briefly annotated. There are no indexes.

0044-2526/1607310   308/313/440/466/488/578/635/636

[848]   *Zeitschrift für die neuttestamentliche Wissenschaft und die Kunde
der älteren Kirche* ("Zeitschriftenschau")

Arranged by journal title, this is a modest effort covering the
contents of 15 to 30 journal issues in each quarterly number.
There are no indexes.

0044-2615/1773087   308/313/440/466/488/553/635/636/665

[849]   *Zeitschrift für Geschichtswissenschaft* ("Zeitschriftenaufsätze zur
deutschen und zur allgemeinen Geschichte")

This appears 3 to 5 times a year in this monthly journal and typically comprises from 150 to 300 entries with emphasis on materials
published in Germany (especially the DDR), with a historical mater-
ialist point of view, and dealing with the twentieth century.
There are no indexes or any lists of journals.

0044-2828/1770474   172/498/571

[850]   *Zeitschrift für Kirchengeschichte* ("Zeitschriftenschau")

This appears sporadically, the latest appearing in the 1984/1 number, where the contents of 8 journals on various aspects of church
history were listed, together with annotations for most articles.
There are no indexes and this must be regarded as both idiosyncratic and minor.

0044-2925/949350

[851]   *Zeitschrift für Kunstgeschichte* ("Bibliographie zur Kunstgeschichte")

This appears annually as a supplement to *ZfK*. That covering 1982
publications, which was published in 1983, included about 3300
items arranged into several categories, the most important of which
were: general; iconographic; architecture; plastic arts; painting
and graphics; and crafts. There was an author index but no list
of journals.

0044-2992/930029   57/99/102/624/639/705

[852]   *Zeitschrift für Ostforschung* ("Auswählbibliographie zur Geschichte
und Landeskunde der böhmische Länder")

One of several recurring bibliographies in *ZfO*, the most recent
(covering 1981) appeared in the 1983 volume and consisted of nearly
300 entries classified in 11 categories covering all aspects of
the history of Bohemia. There are no indexes.

0044-3239/1624049   253/613/759

[853] *Zeitschrift für Ostforschung* ("Auswählbibliographie zur Geschichte von Ost- und Westpreussen")

This appears intermittently, the latest being published in 1980 and covering 1978 publication. In it were listed over 250 items on Prussian history divided into 10 fields representing all aspects of the past. There were no indexes.

0044-3239/1624049   195/523

[854] *Zeitschrift für Ostforschung* ("Baltische Bibliographie")

Materials for 1982 were published in the 1983/4 number and included about 350 items divided into 10 categories which cover various aspects of the history of Estonia and Latvia (for Lithuania see [855]). There are no indexes.

0044-3239/1624049   115/305/369/844/855

[855] *Zeitschrift für Ostforschung* ("Litauische Bibliographie")

Nearly 300 entries for materials published in 1981 and 1982 comprised the bibliography which appeared in the 1983/2 issue. These were arranged in 12 categories covering Lithuanian history from the earliest times to the present. There were no indexes.

0044-3239/1624049   115/369/844

[856] *Zeitschrift für Ostforschung* ("Schrifttum über Schlesien")

This intermittent listing last appeared in the 1980/4 number and included about 600 items on Silesian history published in 1977 and 1978, which were divided into 11 categories. There were no indexes.

0044-3239/1624049   132/135/452/453

[857] *Zeitschrift für Siebenbürgische Landeskunde* ("Bibliographie zur siebenburgischen Geschichte und Landeskunde")

This appears in each semi-annual issue. The most recent included from 175 to 200 entries dealing with the history of Transylvania and surrounding areas from the earliest times to the present. These are arranged in a single alphabet by author and there are no indexes or any list of journals.

0344-3418/5064183   3/114/134/153/323/677

[858] *Zeitschrifteninhaltdienst Theologie*

This monthly publication appears in a current contents format and totals 12,000 or more articles annually. Contents pages are ar-

ranged in 12 categories including church history and missions, and
including extensive coverage of materials appearing in collective
works. Each issue also carries author, personal name, and Biblical
citation indexes. In a typical year about 450 journals are analyzed
and, as is usual with this format, coverage is very current.

0340-8361/3082085   90/213/313/627/635/636/675/795

[859] *Zephyrus* ("Crónica de linguistica y epigrafía prerromana de la
       Península Ibérica")

This first appeared in 1980 and in the 1982 listing (covering 1981)
there were 65 annotated items arranged in several categories and
dealing with linguistic and epigraphic aspects of the earliest in-
scriptional material from the Iberian peninsula. There was an author index and a list of about a dozen journals.

0514-7336/5062765   73/354/515/667

[860] *Zgodovinski Casopis* ("Zgodovinske publickacije v letu 19--")

The most recent, covering 1980, was published in the 1981/4 number
(which, however, appeared only in 1983) and included 275 to 300 entries dealing with Slovenian history, largely in the twentieth century. These were arranged in about 25 categories but there were
no indexes nor any list of journals.

0350-5774/2226054   3/114/323/460/721

[861] *Zhongguo linshixue nianjian* (*Chung-kuo li shih hsüeh nien chien*)

This *Chinese Historical Studies Yearbook* lists historical work in
the People's Republic of China. In the 1983 volume (covering 1982)
there were first about 30 bibliographical and historiographical
essays covering Chinese history in 16 chronological and 12 thematic
divisions. This was followed by a listing of about 450 books and
then by over 7000 entries to articles, also arranged chronologically and then thematically. There are no indexes nor any list of
journals canvassed.

---- ----/7480125   177/178/543/655/718/799

[862] *Zwingliana* ("Literatur zur schweizerischen Reformationsgeschichte")

The most recent (in the 1984/4 number) includes 175 to 200 items
on Huldrych Zwingli and the Swiss Reformation. These are divided
into four categories, much the largest listing relevant critical
studies.

---- ----/2287528   84/159/232/512

[863] *Årbok for Telemark* ("Bibliografi over Telemarkslitteraturen")

This deals with the Telemark region of southern Norway (capital Skien). The bibliography for 1984, published in the 1984 yearbook, contains only three pages and therefore probably fewer than 50 items, doubtless of various aspects of the area, including history.

---- ----/------- 372/567

[864] *Bibliographie des études en langue française sur la littérature personnelle et les récits de vie*

Published as a *Cahiers de Sémiotique Textuelle* of the Université de Paris X, the first biennial number appeared in 1984 and covered 1982 and 1983. In it were two separate listings: first nearly 300 biographical items arranged by author. This was followed by nearly 450 autobiographical and oral history items. In the former articles predominated; in the latter books. The first list is preceded by a subject index divided into six classifications: general problems; repertoires; genres, themes, and particular subjects; foreign domains; epochs; and personal names. All but the first two are subdivided.

---- ----/12045740 188/583

[865] *Dokumentationsdienst Lateinamerika. Ausgewählte neuere Literatur*

One of a series of fichier bibliographies produced by the Deutsches Ubersee-Institut in Hamburg. It appears quarterly and for 1985 is is likely to run to 2000 or more items (all articles) largely concerned with Latin American economic and social development. These are arranged into South America and Middle America and then country by country but within these classifications there seems to be no order whatever. To some extent this is mitigated by an extensive subject index keyed to descriptors (in German) included with each entry. In addition there are geographical and author indexes, a list of German libraries holding the canvassed journals, nearly 150 of which are listed.

0342-037X/5424151 599/776

[866] *Europäische Integration. Auswählbibliographie*

Published three times a year, this totals nearly 1000 items annually on the European Economic Community and other European multilateral organizations. These are arranged into 7 categories, of which the largest are: the structure of the EEC; its foreign relations; and its constituent organisms. There are no indexes.

---- ----/-------

[867]   *Från bergslag och bondebygd* ("Örebro län i litteraturen")

The bibliography for 1982 appeared in the 1984 volume and was concerned with various aspects of the past and present of Örebro county
in east central Sweden. It probably runs to from 100 to 150 items
each year.

---- ----/8775652   780

[868]   *Hudební veda* ("Muzikologická produkce v Ceských zemích")

This annual bibliography concerns musicology and the history of
music in Czechoslovakia. Materials for 1982 appeared in the first
number of the 1985 volume. Nearly 300 of these were arranged in
several general categories; a chronological category (the largest)
devoted largely to classical music; one on jazz and popular music;
and one on the teaching of music. Each is arranged by author and
there are no indexes nor a list of journals canvassed.

0018-7003/2407897   117/161/540/625

[869]   *Missionalia* ("Missiological Abstracts")

These appear in each of the three issues per year as a separately-
paged supplement and in 1984 totaled about 950 abstracts. Each
time the abstracts (50 to 150 words) are divided into a general
and 5 geographical categories. The first constitutes two-thirds
of the whole and is in turn divided into 6 categories including
history and theology of mission; religion, religions, and dialogue;
and environment, society, and development. In the third issue each
year appears an author index, a subject index organized along the
lines of the 6 categories, and a list of journals canvassed, currently over 150. Although worldwide in its coverage, emphasis is
on South African publications.

---- ----/2250882   133/242/435/509/623/858

[870]   *Revue International d'Histoire de la Banque* ("Revue des revues")

Recently this journal has tended to appear annually in a double
number and about two years late. The bibliography, included in
each issue, typically runs to from 250 to 300 items divided into:
généralités; banques, bourses et histoire de la banque; problèmes
monétaires and covers the year the journal is dated. There are no
indexes or a list of journals canvassed.

0080-2611/1764206

[871]   *Schweizer Afrika-Bibliographie/Bibliographie Africaine Suisse*

This appears yearly, published by the Schweizerischen Afrika-Gesell-
schaft in Bern, and consists of a listing of Africa-related mater-

ials published in Swiss journals. The volume for 1983, published
in 1984, listed bewteen 400 and 500 such items, many of them reviews. These were divided into 15 topical categories and then
country by country. There were no indexes but a list of more than
30 Swiss journals and 5 Swiss newspapers was provided.

---- ----/5217090   17/426

[872] *The Scriblerian and the Kit-Cats Bibliography and Index*

This quinquennial compilation brings together all citations in
[711] plus all other references to the Scriblerians, Kit-Cats,
Dryden, and Rochester, as well as novelists and other writers who
published between 1700 and 1740. For the years 1978 to 1983 over
1300 such items were listed, first in 16 topical categories and
then alphabetically by 98 individual authors. There is an author
index as well as an author/work studied index and a list of over
200 journals canvassed. Unlike [711] there are no annotations.

0190-731X/2759643   49/513/711

[873] *Sports Periodicals Index*

Beginning publication in 1985, this is to appear monthly and draws
its data from 130 American popular sports publications (which are
listed in each issue with publication details). Materials are arranged in dictionary catalog format by over 80 different sports,
within which they are arranged by subjects including "history" and
"records." Each main entry is provided with a brief (10 to 50 word)
abstract. Coverage is confined almost entirely to events in the
U.S. (e.g., cricket is not one of the 80 sports listed). The lack
of indexing is mitigated by extensive cross-referencing, particularly for individual athletes.

0883-1580/12074596   477/754/755

[874] *Västmanlands fornminnesföreningen årsskrift* ("Västmanlands län i
       litteraturen")

Materials on the Västmanland region of east central Sweden (capital Västerås) published in 1983 were listed in the 1984 volume.
The ten pages of bibliography probably aggregated to 150 or so
items, probably covering all fields of knowledge.

---- ----/-------   780

INDEX

Numbers in this index refer to entry numbers in the body of the text. Users should also consult cross references at the end of each entry.

ABOUT THE COMPILER

DAVID HENIGE is African Studies Bibliographer at the Memorial Library of the University of Wisconsin. He is the Founding Editor and a frequent contributor to *History in Africa* and was coeditor of *African Economic History* from 1981 to 1984. He is the author of *Work in African History: An Index to Reviews, 1978-1982; Oral Historiography: The Art of the Partly Possible; Catholic Missionary Journals Relating to Africa: A Provisional Checklist and Union List for North America;* and numerous articles appearing in such diverse journals as *Tarikh, Behavioral and Social Science Librarian, Journal of Egyptian Archaeology,* and *International Journal of Oral History.*